Splendors of the East

SPLENDORS

OF THE EAST

Temples, Tombs, Palaces and Fortresses of Asia

Edited by Mortimer Wheeler

Photographs by Ian Graham

G. P. Putnam's Sons 200 Madison Avenue New York

© 1965 by George Weidenfeld and Nicolson Ltd
Designed by John Wallis for George Weidenfeld and Nicolson Ltd, London
Library of Congress Catalog Card No. 65–19762
Printed in Italy by Arnoldo Mondadori Editore Officine Grafiche, **Verona**

CONTENTS

CONTENTS

6

CONTENTS

8

CONTENTS

INTRODUCTION

Splendours of the East: a scrap-book of course, but has it a theme? Is there an entity that can in fact be called the East? – or is this merely a literary and sentimental hangover from Fitzgerald and Flecker? Only half a century ago the answer was not in doubt; then the mechanized West had yet scarcely penetrated the fiery portals of the East. In the bazaars of Istanbul turbans waved in unceasing gesture; in Cairo it could be said by the admirable Baedeker in 1908 that 'the Street Scenes presented by the city of the Caliphs afford an inexhaustible fund of amusement and delight, admirably illustrating the whole world of Oriental fiction, and producing an indelible impression on the uninitiated denizen of the West'. For a visit to Palmyra from Damascus a 'guard of soldiers' was 'indispensable' as late as 1912. Today a sombre Westernized crowd darkens the Istanbul market; the streets of Cairo are as perilous and uniform as those of any other modern metropolis, and tall glass cubes of the international sort are ill-redeemed by the two excluded pyramids which shyly peep through them from the peripheral sands of Gizeh; from Damascus an hour or less in a little aeroplane takes us to the City of the Desert, on the principle that it is better to arrive hopefully than to travel. The East is not what it was, and would proudly boast of the fact.

Yet there is still an East, a definable East, which begins with the Arab world and ends, no doubt, in the China Sea (my own wanderings cease at the Brahmaputra). And if it were demanded of me to define this 'East' more nearly, I should do so not in terms of turbans or Taj Mahals but in terms of *smells*. It is regrettable that, in spite of some trivial endeavour, we have as yet no working connotation for the recording of smells. Why not a symphony of smells? For even in dissolving Cairo, the East first strikes us fairly and squarely in the overpoweringly nostalgic scents of the spice-shops in the tiny lanes off the Muski. And thence right across Asia it is the *smell* of the land that reveals, varying subtly from region to region but at any given moment proclaiming Asia, or even a particular part of Asia. I could wish that by some miracle it were possible to accompany the pictures here assembled with the odours that are a part of the personality of each one of them!

But all this is generality. What of the chosen buildings themselves, ranging as they do from the deserts of Iraq to the jungles of India and the further east, from the mosque of Samarra to the Forbidden City? Here is every kind of shape and colour, and it were difficult enough to find any common basic factor. Unless this: the recurrent interrelationship of function, environment and genius. On these matters I shall say a little in one or two of the regional introductions. Here let it be emphasized that the most constantly neglected of the three agents is *environment*.

Often enough this is no longer self-evident; the historian has to reconstruct it from the man-made wreckage of our ancient landscapes. And without such reconstruction our understanding is invariably the poorer. Look at the traditional Western misunderstanding of Indian sculpture and architecture. 'There is no temptation to dwell at length on the sculpture of Hindustan,' observed the Professor of Sculpture at the Royal Academy (Westmacott) in 1864. 'It affords no assistance in tracing the history of art, and its debased quality deprives it of all interest as a phase of fine art.' And that view was typical enough before and long after Westmacott. It merely meant, of course, that Indian art and architecture were less at home in the Strand or Piccadilly than in the tangled and even sinister luxuriance of the Indian jungle which was their home. The true question is not, primarily, the Olympian one of 'good' or 'bad'; it is one of aptness, of the intelligent and imaginative interpretation of an environment by minds already shaped within it.

And so, in alliance with many other qualities, the buildings here selected must be judged. They are mostly, though not wholly, monuments of religion or death, for the accidental reason that such monuments tend more readily to survive. There is consolation in the fact; they tend to present the best workmanship of their age, as though born for immortality. But there are also secular works of high distinction: the palace of Persepolis, the palace-fortresses of Lahore and Delhi, the palace-city of Fatehpur Sikri, the Forbidden City of Peking, and others. The descriptions are contributed by those who know the buildings well; and as for the photographs, Mr Ian Graham, after much arduous journeying not always devoid of incident, would be one of the first to agree with Bacon that 'That is the best part of beauty, which a picture cannot express.'

MORTIMER WHEELER

THE MIDDLE EAST

Introduction by Mortimer Wheeler

What is meant by the phrase 'the Middle East'? It is mainly, I believe, a heritage from the Second World War, and represents western Asia in a transatlantic perspective. Previously much of it had been more familiar as 'the Near East', implying a myopic outlook which can no longer be sustained. In the present context, at any rate, let the Middle East include Iraq and Iran, with an arbitrary salient to Samarkand for convenience' sake.

The inclusion of Iran – let us say Persia – in this considerable slice of Asia gives that slice a measure of unity which it might not otherwise claim. Persia, though described by untravelled geographers as a plateau, is in fact a jagged highland, core of the mountain-zone which stretches from the fringe of the Indian subcontinent to Anatolia and the Caucasus. Its valleys and ranges tend to run northwest to south-east, separating the steppes of Turkestan from the sands of Iraq and Arabia. Its miscellaneous inhabitants have thus been inclined to experience a sense of remoteness alike from the desert Arabs and from the mid-Asian mongoloids. Nevertheless, in prehistoric times its sturdy hill-men seem to have helped to fertilize the cultures which became the city-states of Mesopotamia, and on the other side no doubt played a comparable part, as yet undefined, in the genesis of the Indus civilization.

Between the sixth and fourth centuries BC its Achaemenid rulers controlled for a moment the whole of this vast upland from the Aegean to the Punjab. Apart from their positive achievements, which were far from negligible, their destruction of eastern Greece kindled the genius of Periclean Athens, and their own political destruction by Alexander the Great one-and-a-half centuries later provided, however accidentally, much of the inspiration of Mauryan India. Later again, in the cultures, and particularly the arts, of the Parthians, the Kushans and the Sassanids, the contribution of Persia was of primary though not yet fully comprehended meaning in the make-up of the schools of Constantinople in the west and Gandhara in the east. *Per contra*, in the tenth century AD Persia was itself overrun by the Seljuk Turks, who evolved a lively civilization there, with an architecture which may be described as a sort of Eastern counterpart of the Romanesque of the West. In one way and another, Persia was recurrently the focus or workshop of creative phases of Asian thought and artistry.

In these pages our time-table begins with the Persian Achaemenids in the fullness of their power at Persepolis where Darius I, the Great (521–486 BC) built – or began to build – his great fortress-palace. But historically this was not of course the beginning of the story of the Persian Empire. Fifty miles further north, at Pasargadae, Darius's elder cousin Cyrus, first as a resistant vassal and later as King of Kings, had planned, towards the middle of the sixth century BC, a massive citadel with a fortified annexe of about seventy-five acres and with widely scattered suburbs upon the broad plain below. Here still stands the small but strangely impressive tomb-house of the Great King, slain far away on the steppe to the east of the Caspian but brought here to lie amidst his golden tomb-furniture beneath the inscription (now gone) 'O man, I am Cyrus, the son of Cambyses, who founded the Empire of the Persians and was king of Asia. Grudge me not therefore this monument'. Alas, Alexander the Great found the tomb already violated; but with political piety and, no doubt, genuine respect, he had it set in order, the doorway walled up and the inscription faithfully renewed in Greek.

In recent years Pasargadae has been explored afresh. Its crowning structure is a great platform, built of fine ashlar and approached by monumental stairs. This is known locally as the Throne of Solomon; in fact or intention it was the basis of the palace of Cyrus, though whether it was ever completed is more doubtful. Certainly after the death of its founder in 530 BC its function changed. It was now covered with buildings of mud-brick – storehouses and a residence or barracks, with a large courtyard or parade-ground – set within a fortification of the same material. The son and successor of Cyrus, Cambyses II, had turned his eyes towards Egypt and no doubt gave little thought to his

OPPOSITE: A view of Qum, one of the sacred places of Persia, from Dr Olfert Dapper's *Description of the Kingdom of Persia* (1672)

15

father's unfinished dream. And when in 521 Darius succeeded to the throne, new and more grandiose ideas were in the air.

Away to the south, on a terrace carved out snugly at the foot of an impending cliff, were now laid the first stones of the vast palace which is the material expression of Achaemenid majesty. Tablets of gold and silver found encased in the masonry bear the names of Darius and of his son Xerxes. The palace of Persepolis was in fact still under construction when Xerxes marched his armed hosts against Greece and sacked the Athenian acropolis in 480 BC, and the subsequent Grecian victory did not end the work. The motive of its ultimate ending, whether an act of exuberance or of unmitigated diplomacy, is disputed, but charred timbers bear witness to the powerful conflagration which destroyed the palace shortly after Alexander had taken it in the year 330.

It may be that the act of destruction was one of cold-blooded revenge: 'retribution for the destruction of Athens, the burning of the temples, and all the other crimes which they [the Persians] had committed against the Greeks'. So Arrian, drawing briefly on earlier sources On the other hand the fuller and more vivid picture left by Diodorus Siculus, Curtius and Plutarch, all writing in the first centuries BC–AD, and no doubt with the same records of Alexander's staff-historians before them, carries conviction. The story is one of the more dramatic interludes of history. The exultant young conqueror, in his mid-twenties but already well accustomed to interchange hardship with indulgence on a heroic scale, was celebrating in the palace of the King of Kings, and the riper moments of a good party had arrived. Thaïs, the Attic courtesan, had an idea: 'King Alexander, it would be the most splendid of your deeds in Asia if we all formed a triumphal procession and set fire to the palace, letting the hands of mere women destroy in a moment the most renowned achievements of the Persians.' The guests, like their leader, were 'young and excited by wine beyond reason'; the procession was formed with blazing torches, song, and an orchestra of pipes and flutes. The king cast his torch, and Thaïs followed him with the others of the rout. The whole palace and the buildings about it went up in flames. 'The impious act of Xerxes, king of the Persians, against the Acropolis of the Athenians was repaid, like by like, many years afterwards by one woman of that same city, as a jest' (Diodorus).

Enough is left, however, to enable us to say that in all architecture there is of its kind nothing comparable with Persepolis. Its great staircases, its platforms and promenades, its myriad columns of stone and (formerly) of timber, its majestic doorways, above all the superb carving of its reliefs, bespeak a fathomless treasury, undaunted assurance, and a matchless skill that was heir to the mastery of Babylon and Assyria. There was perhaps little in it that pointed forward to new worlds, but it was a superb finale to an old one. This verdict is not falsified by the fact that some of the elements of the Persepolitan mode were sub-sequently adapted to the alien context of Buddhist India and found a new life there.

After the fall of the Achaemenid Empire there is nothing of consequence in the present context until the middle of the third century BC. After the death of Alexander in 323, one of his successors, Seleucus I, had seized the Asian sector of his unshaped 'empire', and after adjustment ruled in more or less nominal fashion as far as the Hindu Kush. His capital had for a time been the city of Seleucia, which he founded on the west bank of the Tigris below the later Baghdad. The new metropolis was well sited as a centre for the east–west commerce which was now developing between the growing cities of the eastern Mediterranean and the lands of India and China, rich in spices, gems and silks. When Antioch replaced Seleucia politically, as it soon did, the latter retained its commercial primacy; and in or about 144 BC it was the natural objective of new invaders from the north-east.

These were the Parthians, a semi-nomadic tribe of the Sakas or Scythians who had been on the move since the middle of the third century to the east of the Caspian, some of them in the direction of India, others eventually drifting through Persia towards Mesopotamia and Syria; the latter picking up their tribal name from Partheva (modern Khurasan) which they overran en route. As these Parthians now approached the Tigris and saw the widespread Graeco-Asian city on the further bank, they paused and pitched their tents. The reason for their hesitation can only be guessed; it may be that the unsettled folk of the desert were simply awestruck by the prospect of so much experienced wealth, and had sense enough not to pour it into the sand. Be that as it may, where they pitched their tents they eventually built a kingly city, and called it Ctesiphon. For several centuries the two foundations looked upon one another across the width of the river and, with such neighbourly disputation as was inevitable, established a sufficiently symbiotic way of life.

With these Parthians we are not concerned, save to remark that, in constant contact and conflict with the Romans of Syria, they produced as early as the first century BC a Romano-Asian art with a hard, brittle, decorative, inhuman quality of an astonishingly individual kind, an art which indirectly but significantly contributed to the making of the Byzantine art of a later age. This Parthian art is best known from Palmyra, Hatra and Dura-Europos, all in Syria and Iraq. Its achievement on Persian soil, much of which was under Parthian control, is at present scarcely known.

In AD 224 the Arsacid dynasty of Parthia was overthrown by the Sassanids, who claimed descent from the Achaemenids and so, if their claim be sustained, picked up again the main thread of Persian history. The conflict is represented in vivid if symbolical fashion by a spirited relief carved upon a rock near Firuzabad in southern Persia. The scene is pure medieval tilt-yard; the Sassanid Ardashir in chain-mail rides at his Arsacid opponent with long and lowered lance, and the warriors are crested with more than a hint of feudal heraldry. Nor is this mere isolated accident. There is in the whole Sassanid age, which endured thence until the arrival of the Arabs in the seventh century, a recurrent anticipation of the aristocratic mind and habit of the Middle Ages, at the same time with a touch of archaism that links it remotely with the heroic age of Alexander and his successors. Architecturally it reaches its climax in the great vaulted throne-room of Ctesiphon. True, an eminent but hostile critic (Ernst Herzfeld) refers to this astonishing vault and its flanking screens as 'the aberration of Ctesiphon'; but that is for later argument.

And now the Arabs and Islam have come upon the scene. Devoid of artistic traditions of their own, they were impetuously ready to adopt and adapt the magnificence of established civilizations, just as their faith was itself a selective synthesis of established religions. We shall here travel with them to three great cities where their handiwork is proudly manifest: Samarra, Isfahan and Samarkand. The names alone are poems, and one of them, Isfahan (I have not seen Samarkand), is an almost unspoilt oriental scene. The heart of it is still metropolitan Persia, much of it as it was in the famous days of Shah Abbas, contemporary of Queen Elizabeth I and Akbar the Great. (What a world it was in the year 1600!) Here in a relatively small space is some of the best that Persian Islam can show: the pavilioned bridges, the long central *place* or *maidan* where the Shah's court played royal polo between stone goal-posts; the palace on one side of it, the superb blue-enamelled Royal Mosque on another, on the third a smaller golden-brown

mosque to which the guide-book word *délicieuse* is for once apt, and on the fourth the great vaulted market which is probably the finest in Asia. Here, amongst inevitable junkery, the traditional crafts still flourish after a fashion; above all, the colour-stamping of cloth with patterned blocks swiftly and faultlessly applied by trained hands. In one way and another, the heart of Isfahan is still in the right place. May it remain so a little longer.

Unhappily on the other hand, Samarra of the Khalifs has long been wreckage. Even in its brief prime, eleven centuries ago, it can never as a spectacle have rivalled the jewelled architecture of Persia. At the same time, comparison between the mosques of Persia and those of the Mesopotamian desert is not of a helpful kind. They are responses to different environments. To the mountainous, stony upland of Persia the compact plan and emphatic dome were fitting; to the broad plains, the native brick-work and spreading courts with shaded, white-washed arcades were no less appropriate. It is a pity that with the plaster so much of their decorative detail has vanished. Even so, the strong functional lines of the Samarra minaret demand inclusion in any list of great buildings of the East.

As to far-off Samarkand which, like the Rome of Kipling's centurion, I have seen only in a picture, the handiwork of Tamerlane is rightly included here as a sort of culmination of its kind. Jacquetta Hawkes will tell us how it expresses the accumulated talent of Persia and India in the full tide of the Middle Ages, accented by the fierce genius of a prince of darkness who on occasion turned for a moment to the light.

The ruins of Persepolis, from Carsten Niebuhr's
Voyages en Arabie (1780)

17

CTESIPHON

*The mighty vault which still looms over the Tigris
plain, memorial of the Eastern city which here confronted
its Western rival across the great river*

At the point where the land of the Twin Rivers narrows north
of Babylon, a ship-canal, the Nahr al-Malik, in ancient times
linked the Tigris with the Euphrates. At this strategic point two
great cities confronted each other across the Tigris. The earlier
foundation, Seleucia, lay upon the west or right bank; there it
was established by Seleucus I about 301, when as a victorious
successor of Alexander the Great his kingdom stretched from
Asia Minor to the Hindu Kush. For a moment indeed it had
reached out into India, but this ultimate salient was not held.
Without it, the immense, loosely knit realm was more than one
man's competence.

And so it proved. A century and a half later occurred one of
those upsurges from central Asia which have, from time to time
through the ages, upset and perhaps in a measure renewed
Western civilization. Scythians, Yueh-chi, Huns of one kind or
another, Turks, Mongols are merely examples of a formidable
list. On this occasion it was the Parthians, led with determina-
tion by their Arsacid dynasty, who swept across Seleucid Persia
and Media and in 144 BC confronted Seleucia itself on the
Tigris. There, for reasons which can only be guessed, they halted
and camped on the eastern or left bank. The camp became
the palace and garrison-town of Parthian Ctesiphon.

At its inception, Seleucia had been the metropolis of the
Seleucid kingdom, as it were the new Babylon of western Asia.
Before long, however, the capital had been moved to Antioch in
Syria, better placed for contact with the Mediterranean world
where lay the major markets and the major rival powers.
Seleucia remained what geography had destined it to be; a
centre of East–West trade, supplied by arterial traffic-routes
from the Persian Gulf and inner Asia. The advancing Parthians
may for this reason have abstained from the destruction of so
much accumulated commercial wisdom without compensating
political advantage.

At any rate, the two cities long co-existed in tolerant rivalry,
the one basically Greek, the other basically oriental. Rivalry

'View of Ctesiphon' from *On a Raft and through the
Desert* .(1881) by Tristram Ellis

OPPOSITE: The summit of the great Sassanid vault, showing the holes
for ropes to suspend the cradles used for building and repairs

19

showed its teeth in the earlier part of the first century AD, when Seleucia seems to have come somewhat the worse out of the conflict. This may have been little more than a momentary set-back; but in the following century three Roman emperors – Trajan, Lucius Verus and Septimius Severus – led hungry and destructive armies against Ctesiphon with momentary success, and neither city can have benefited from these incursions. Indeed in 165 the legate Avidius Cassius, commander of the troops of Verus, is said to have razed Seleucia to the ground, presumably for some act of real or imagined treachery; it was already in large measure under Parthian control.

Ctesiphon suffered similarly but now survived to assume the lead. When the Persian Sassanids took over from the Arsacids in 226, Seleucia was an insignificant remnant of a city whilst Ctesiphon was once more a prosperous capital. The latter's last major conflict with the Roman power came in 363, when it was vigorously attacked by Julian the Apostate and was saved from capture only by a timely javelin in the ribs of that redoubtable emperor. Henceforth Ctesiphon spread far beyond its original boundaries and became rather a congeries of towns than a single coherent city. When the Arabs conquered the region in 636 they gave the whole group the portmanteau name of *al Mada'in* or 'The Cities'; but the great days of Ctesiphon were now over, and the vast site rapidly became the untidy miscellany of mounds and cultivation which we see today. Its place was taken first by Basra and Wasit and, after 762, by Baghdad, twenty-five miles to the north. The village of Salman Pak which overlies a small part of it contains the mosque-tomb of the Barber of the Prophet but can scarcely claim continuity with its metropolitan predecessor.

The topography of Seleucia and Ctesiphon is complicated by the fact that the Tigris, which formerly divided them, has changed its course so that it now cuts through the site of Ctesiphon, leaving the greater part of this city on the 'wrong' or Seleucid bank. Neither city has been adequately explored, but it would appear that Seleucia was laid out on an oblong plan while Ctesiphon was roughly a circle, as was the later Baghdad. Both cities had extensive suburbs which have only in part been identified.

Of the vast potentiality of this immense dual site, let it be said at once that, whatever future excavation may reveal, the outstanding feature will remain the massive brick structure which looms over the plain long before the visitor arrives. It is a truly astonishing spectacle. It consists, briefly, of a mighty eliptical vault rising to a height of 123 feet above the floor and 83 feet wide at its base. This vaulted salon is – or was – flanked by two wings enriched by six or more arcades of which only the lowest was in part functional. (The north wing fell in 1909 as a result of flooding.) Each of these three features deserves a separate note.

First the arch. It has been described, no doubt correctly, as 'the widest single-span vault of unreinforced brickwork in the

Aerial view of the brick vault from the east, with the surviving south wing. Behind, the river Tigris

world'. But its overwhelming magnitude is not its only quality. The subtlety with which its curves change centre and ultimately produce what is inadequately called an oval shape gives the whole structure a lightness and intelligence which lift it out of the rut of purely mechanical engineering. We are told that it was built without temporary centring, somewhat in the fashion of a corbel-vault, 'on a principle common in later Persian buildings, which involves constructing the first triangular panels obliquely, supported at their base by the side and at their head by the end walls. After this it was merely a matter of each vertical ring of bricks leaning back and being supported on the previous one.' It might almost be described as a hand-made vault, in contradistinction to a machine-made one. It has *personality*.

It has been observed with puzzlement that the vault is perforated by pairs of small openings lined with terracotta piping, which passes through the fabric. The function of these holes is in fact readily explicable; it was to pass through the ropes for pulling up wooden 'cradles' when the underside of the vault was plastered or repaired. Professor Seton Lloyd records that the apertures were spontaneously used for this purpose by workmen repairing the vault in 1947!

If the vault may properly be described as a masterpiece, the wings which flank and 'support' it are a more controversial matter. They have been criticized for the lack of consistent axes in their arcaded decoration; for the unstructural fashion in which the panels are superimposed one upon another, with no great regard for the verticality which we expect and find, for example, on the exterior of the Colosseum at Rome. Is this to say more than that the Ctesiphon building was not designed by a classical architect? Medieval buildings of repute are not always pedantic in this matter. And at Ctesiphon it has been counter-claimed that the extreme shallowness of columns and arcading – their projection is 1–2 feet only – reduces the whole design to free pattern rather than to scholastic structure, the intention being to emphasize horizontal lines which carry the eye to the great central vault, rather than vertical lines to carry the eye up into the air. It is indeed a characteristic example of the oriental disregard of mathematical law in favour of impressionistic design, and may be held to give the Ctesiphon façade something of the quality of an oriental rug.

We have to remember, too, that the brickwork was originally plastered and coloured, no doubt with a vividness and gaiety that would itself distract the mind of the viewer from architectural deviation. So when a modern critic of repute remarks that the flanking façade is 'in some ways a masterpiece of bad taste, a surprising example of the unimaginative application of the bare principles of copy-book Roman architecture, and suggests imperfectly assimilated classical culture', it may be urged that he is applying the wrong canons. The Ctesiphon façade, with its towering central feature, is neither copy-book Roman architecture nor indeed any other kind of copy. Naturally it has

Brick arcading on the eastern face of the south wing

absorbed tradition as is the habit of evolving thought, but it has transmuted that tradition into something that we may best describe as new and Sassanian.

What was the function of this masterpiece, and when was it built? First the date. The Arab tradition is expressed in the name *Taq-i-Kisra.* 'Arch of Chosroes', with reference to one or other of the Persian rulers of that name. If the tradition has any substance – and this is not impossible – the choice lies between Chosroes I, 531–579, and Chosroes II, 590–628. If there is substance in the story that the building contained a wall-painting of the capture of Antioch, Chosroes I is probably to be preferred, since he destroyed that city in 540 and is more likely than his later namesake to have commemorated the event. But is there anything at all in the tradition? One knows how readily famous names recur in legendary 'history'. No inscription enlightens us, and no stratigraphical excavation on modern standards has been attempted. In the absence, likewise, of any detailed understanding of the stylistic development of Sassanian architecture, the field is wide open to conjecture. Nor has conjecture been lacking. Herzfeld prefers to put the date back to Sapor I, 241–272. Seton Lloyd guesses 'about the fourth century A.D.' Reuter and Wachtsmuth choose Chosroes I, and if commitment be necessary I am with them. Certainly Herzfeld's dating would appear to be much too early; it scarcely leaves time, with full allowance for oriental idiosyncrasy, for so transmuted an adaptation of Roman motifs to spring up in the environs of the classical world. But that is merely another guess.

The function of the building is less in doubt. Arab tradition has it that the vast vaulted hall was the *Iwan-i-Khosrau*, the throne-room where the royal Sassanid conducted business and ceremony in the Persian fashion, which demanded regular contact between monarch and people. The hall or *iwan*, with its

The eastern front of the vault, with the arcaded south wing

adjoining rooms, was a central feature of a large palatial complex, preceded by a considerable space for assembly and parade. Many, perhaps all, the apartments behind the main vault and its lateral wings were vaulted. To the south and the east, separated from the main block, incomplete excavation has revealed expansive buildings, of which that facing the main hall at a distance of 110 yards was apparently a second *iwan* of comparable width but unascertained depth. To the south of the principal block traces were found of a large oblong building or enclosure, some 110 yards from north to south and 76 yards from east to west, built of mud-brick with a baked-brick skin and with internal pedestals or buttresses. The building is known locally as ad-Dhabai ('Hyena Hill'), or as the Harim al-Kisra. No more factual name has yet been suggested.

Of the stucco and other veneers which formerly graced these buildings nothing can now be said save that they once existed. Fragments show that there were coloured marble wall-facings and glass-mosaic on some of the ceilings. Floors were of marble or of brick coated with gypsum. Other Sassanid buildings in the neighbourhood have been a little more productive; enough to indicate a great variety and some considerable liveliness of design, including medallions and friezes enclosing animals and birds and a conventionalized flora, together with occasional human figures of a crude but not inexpressive kind. Unhappily these fragments have mostly perished beyond recall in the saline sand and cannot be reassembled into any sort of over-all picture. In particular they have lost practically all the polychromy which was of their essence: yellow, red, brown ochre, ultramarine, black. In some instances there appears to have been an inlay of precious or semi-precious stones. The result must have been one of splendour, if of a somewhat ostentatious kind.

This may bring us to the final scene, the last days of Ctesiphon. In the year 637 the warriors of Islam passed the Tigris and burst into the city. Let Edward Gibbon write the epitaph. 'The naked robbers of the desert were suddenly enriched beyond the measure of their hope or knowledge. Each chamber revealed a new treasure, secreted by art and ostentatiously displayed; the gold and silver, the various wardrobes and precious furniture surpassed the estimate of fancy or numbers . . . One of the apartments of the palace was decorated with a carpet of silk, 60 cubits in length and as many in breadth; a paradise or garden was depictured on the ground; the flowers, fruits, and shrubs were imitated by the figures of the gold embroidery and the colours of the precious stones; and the ample square was encircled by a variegated and verdant border . . . Regardless of the merit of art and the pomp of royalty, the rigid Omar divided the prize among his brethren of Medina; the picture was destroyed; but such was the intrinsic value of the materials that the share of Ali alone was sold for twenty thousand drachms . . .

'The sack of Ctesiphon was followed by its desertion and gradual decay.' MORTIMER WHEELER

View from the south, showing remains of the south wing, with the top of the great vault beyond. (The buttress on the right is modern)

SAMARRA

*The short-lived capital of Islam with
its immense mosque and towering minaret, one of
the great 'functional' buildings of antiquity*

Samarra, on the left bank of the Tigris eighty-five miles north of Baghdad, is today a town of modest distinction. It possesses a circuit of mid-nineteenth-century fortifications and is dominated by a Persianizing Shi'a mosque with an emphatic dome of gilded copper. Within the mosque are the remains of two of the holy men of Islam, the tenth and eleventh imams; and nearby is the spot where the twelfth imam, the Mahdi, vanished to await the final resurrection. The infidel treads warily hereabouts.

The locality was already in human occupation far back in the fifth millennium, and much later the Sassanians of Persia, between the third and seventh centuries AD, built a little town here which, at the time of the Arab conquest in 637, included a Christian monastery. But the crowning episode in its history began two centuries later, in circumstances of some remark.

From the year 762 the city of Baghdad had been the capital of the Abbasid khalifate. It was there, for example, that about the year 800 the romantic Harun ar-Rashid lived in fabulous splendour and played (or did not play) the pranks that are associated with his name. Thereafter there occurred one of those seemingly arbitrary acts which are not unfamiliar in oriental annals. In 836 the khalif al-Mu'tasim, supported by his redoubtable Turkish mercenaries, vacated Baghdad and established a new capital several days' journey away, at Samarra.

First, those Turkish mercenaries, whose presence no doubt helped in the transaction of what cannot have been a universally popular operation. During the preceding khalifate, al-Mu'tasim had made it his business, as we are told by Ya'qubi, the contemporary Arab historian, to send each year to Samarkand to purchase young Turks as reinforcements in the khalif's campaigns against the Byzantine Empire. When he succeeded to the khalifate he continued this recruitment until he had at his command some thousands of these wild foreigners who, when they went out riding, 'would gallop and collide with people right and left'. In such fashion he established a rough and unquestionable control over his less martial subjects.

The brick minaret of the Great Mosque, the largest mosque in the world, built about AD 850. The ramp rises more steeply as it ascends in order to preserve an equal height for each diminishing circuit

OPPOSITE: The wall of the Great Mosque, with its remarkable brick towers or buttresses

The cinquefoiled inner face of a window in the Great Mosque. The outer face is a simple arrow-slit, but the opening was intended to admit light, not for defence

Secondly, while I have described the drastic move to Samarra as arbitrary, it is possible on analogy to invent contributory reasons. Examples are known of the removal of a capital under the stress of changing civic or military standards, as when the famous Taxila in the Punjab was at least twice rebuilt on new sites to facilitate the imposition of new types of planning and civic discipline. Even here it may be suspected that the advent of new dynasties and the desire to break visibly with older régimes was an additional impulse. Certainly this was so when on six or seven occasions the Delhi sultanate was transferred to new foundations either in the vicinity or even far afield. And at Agra the great Akbar, one of the most intelligent minds in the history of despotism, built a splendid new – and frustrate – capital in a desert for a sentimental or superstitious fancy. His elaborate creation lived a mere seventeen years, appreciably less even than the short lifetime of the upstart Samarra.

In the move to Samarra were there factors other than the ostentation of a vain autocrat? There may have been. After the death of Harun ar-Rashid in 809, the designated heir to the khalifate had been murdered by an older half-brother whose mother had been a mere Persian slave-girl. The incidental siege of Baghdad had done much damage to the capital and had no doubt left much bitterness. During the proceedings, al-Mu'tasim's Turks had got out of hand and had murdered and pillaged. When in due course al-Mu'tasim assumed the khalifate he may well have thought that nothing short of a complete change of environment, with the attendant universal employment, could bring forgetfulness and renewed loyalty. He set to work on a large and imaginative scale.

Ya'qubi again tells us some of the details. Al-Mu'tasim assembled 'workmen, masons, and artificers, such as smiths, carpenters and all other craftsmen', including marble-workers. He collected teak and other kinds of wood, and brought palm-trunks from Basra. Elsewhere it is recorded that he sent to Egypt 'with orders that the columns and the marble should be taken from the churches'; those of Alexandria were pillaged, and from the pilgrim-church of St Menas in the desert behind Alexandria were removed its coloured marbles and its famous polychrome pavement. From all directions caravans laden with the loot of late antiquity converged upon the obscure site north of Baghdad.

At first indeed the upstart Samarra flourished as vigorously as its ambitious founder, with his eye upon worldly and other-worldly glory, could have desired. Surveying the trim lay-out of his Surra-Man-Raa ('Happy he who sees it') – the pun in which he wrapped a measure of continuity from the Aramaic Samarra with a suitable expression of personal satisfaction – he must have contrasted it happily enough with the clumsy aggregation of palace and suburb which he had left to decay far away in the south. Happily, too, he could not have thought that half a century later 'the very substance of the ambitious would be merely the shadow of a dream'. Surra-Man-Raa has for a thousand years been little more than ripples in the sand. In 892 a successor of al-Mu'tasim led his patient subjects back to the ruins of old Baghdad, and the Samarra episode was over.

Meanwhile, much had been done there, and the little that survives is of outstanding interest. The city had grown steadily, and we know the main processes of its growth. On arrival, al-Mu'tasim appears to have acted with tact and humanity; he paid the Christian monks whom he found there a substantial indemnity in a period when less civilized methods of sequestration would have passed without comment. He built forthwith a Friday-mosque and three palaces, one of these on the right bank of the river and linked with the main body of the town by a bridge of boats. The formidable and predatory Turkish mercenaries were quartered in a considerable territory away from the town, to the north, where (it was hoped) they would not unduly harass the Arab citizenry. Parallel with the Tigris, a monumental avenue – the Shari' al-A'zam or Great Street – formed the axis of the town-plan, and was prolonged as the great city spread northwards with the addition of new palaces, mosques and residential suburbs. These additions amounted in fact to a new city, built in 859–860 by the khalif al-Mutawakkil, a son of the original founder, and here the motive was self-confessed: to match the glory of his father. 'Now I know that I am indeed a king', he is recorded to have exclaimed, 'for I have built myself a city and live in it.' The new city was separately identified as al-Ja'fariya.

Before moving to his new palace-suburb, al-Mutawakkil had built at Samarra itself one of the outstanding buildings of Islam: the Great Mosque, of which the outer walls and the minaret still stand. They are of baked brick, originally disguised by a rendering of stucco. The walls are armed or buttressed by round-fronted towers on square pedestals, and were penetrated by sixteen doorways. Within were formerly quadruple colonnades round three sides, and a large sanctuary nine columns in

Aerial view of the Great Mosque, with the famous spiral minaret, the *Malwiya*, in the foreground

Part of the Jausaq al-Khaqani palace, overlooking the Tigris. The three vaulted rooms (*liwans*) were ceremonial apartments and were originally enriched by stucco ornament

28 The view towards – and from – the Great Mosque. LEFT: The Great
Mosque seen from across the Tigris. RIGHT: Looking out from the
pavilion on top of the spiral minaret. The openings in the wall at the far
end of the courtyard mark the position of the prayer-niche facing Mecca

depth and twenty-four in width at the southern end, towards Mecca. The *mihrab* or prayer-niche was square on plan, as was the early custom in Iraq and Persia; it was flanked by two pairs of columns of rose-coloured marble, and the spandrels of its high arch bore traces of gold mosaic. It is indeed recorded that the mosque had rivalled that of Damascus with its now-unsurpassed mosaics.

But the feature which still gives the mosque a high place in the world's architecture is the minaret, outside the northern wall of the main enclosure (there may once have been additionally an outer enclosure wall). The minaret, or tower from which the muezzin called the times of prayer, stands on a square foundation which is connected by a ramp and small bridge with the adjacent entrance to the mosque. Upon the foundation rises the tower itself, known as the *Malwiya* or Spiral, round on plan and encompassed by a spiral ramp 7½ feet wide. Above each circuit the width of the tower is diminished by the width of the ramp, which makes five complete turns in an anti-clockwise direction. The ramp becomes steeper as it rises in order to keep a constant height for the successive stages. At the top are remains of a little pavilion which rested on eight wooden columns.

Apart from simple tubular towers, Muslim minarets are of two main kinds. Those with simple diminishing square or round stages, as in the Ibn Tulun Mosque in Cairo and the Great Mosque of Kairouan in Tunisia, are commonly derived historically from the telescopic form of the famous lighthouse on the Isle of Pharos at Alexandria. The helicoidal type of Samarra and, be it added, of the Abu Dulaf Mosque built (on a smaller scale) just after it at neighbouring Ja'fariya, goes back rather to a type of ancient Babylonian *ziggurat* or temple-tower of which the most notorious was the Tower of Babel at Babylon itself. Herodotus has been quoted in this connection. He says that the tower of Babylon consisted of eight receding rectangular stages, reached by a path which wound 'round all the towers'. This feature was still visible in the twelfth century, so that the Arab architects may quite possibly have borrowed the notion thence, transferring it from the square to the circular plan.

Borrowing of this kind would be completely in accordance with Arab procedure. The Islamic Arabs started upon their conquering mission with no established architectural tradition of their own. They improvised as they went along, adapting their minarets from Alexandria or Babylon, their multi-aisled sanctuaries from the multi-aisled Christian churches which littered their path. With these general borrowings they took much detailed artistry, so that, for example, the sanctuary of the holy mosque of Kairouan is a veritable forest of Roman and Byzantine columns collected from the region. How far the Arabs were prepared on occasion to go afield for their material has already been illustrated by the story of al-Mu'tasim.

But, when all this is said, what matters most about the Samarra minaret is not its formal origin but its startling originality. Strikingly bold and simple in design, functional, elemental,

Typical wood-cut patterns (*Schrägschnitt*) found recently at Samarra

OPPOSITE: Characteristic stucco panel from Samarra, in the Islamic Museum, Baghdad. Although little of the stucco ornament of Samarra has survived, there is evidence that it was extensively used

The bastioned walls and commanding minaret of the Great Mosque

finely proportioned, comfortable to the eye – note again the steepening ramp and the sustained heights lightened by a rhythmic reduction of width: here we have in the ninth century many qualities which bridge the centuries. The *Malwiya* is truly a great and rather lonely masterpiece.

For the rest excavation and air-photography, with a few upstanding fragments, give some notion of the palaces, houses and shops that filled out the busy plan of Samarra and its extension, Ja'fariya. The houses were of one storey and show variants of a universal Eastern plan: rooms distributed round a rectangular courtyard, with the principal apartments usually at the end opposite the entrance save where they were duplicated at both ends to give alternative sun and shade. Sometimes a second court was allotted to the *harim*. Baths and drains were normal, and there were often wells. The material was commonly mud or mud-brick, except for drains and floor-slabs, which were of baked brick. Roofs were flat and of timber. Windows occurred and were glazed with bulging discs of coloured glass. Walls were often decorated internally with painting or a gypsum paste. Rarely the street-front of a house might consist of shops, as at Roman Ostia or Pompeii.

Of the numerous palaces which sprang up during the fifty-six years of the city's life, the best known is the Jausaq al-Khaqani or Palace of al-Mu'tasim. Its features included a triple-arched façade overlooking the Tigris, and it is conjectured that the central opening, larger than those which flank it, was used by the khalif for public audiences. The interior of the archways had been elaborately decorated with stucco ornament including vines and rosettes. Other vestiges of the palace include a square domed hall, probably the throne-room, with fragments of a fine marble frieze; domestic quarters, a great open court with a central canal and fountains; and a polo-ground with adjacent stables. The excavator remarks upon the magnificence of the ensemble: 'The dadoes of the walls were everywhere decorated with stucco ornament . . . In the throne-rooms the stucco dadoes are replaced by carved marble . . . The *harim* was decorated with fresco paintings of living forms . . . All woodwork, doors, beams and ceilings were of teak-wood, carved and painted . . . Amongst the epigraphic finds must be mentioned inscriptions on teak beams, many craftsmen's signatures in Greek, Syriac and Arabic'. In that last sentence lies the gist of the matter. Samarra represents the artistry of western Asia skilfully and powerfully combined in the service of Islam.

MORTIMER WHEELER

32

OPPOSITE: The *Malwiya*, one of the great monuments of Islam. From the summit the faithful were called to prayer

PERSEPOLIS

*The palace where Darius and Xerxes
immortalized their empire
on an array of sculptured terraces*

The ancient Greeks had no very clear knowledge of Persepolis until Alexander the Great's invasion of Persia and the final sack of this city in 330 BC. To the Greeks the three royal capitals of the Achaemenids were Babylon, Susa and Ecbatana. Today, however, Persepolis surpasses all these and other sites of the Achaemenian period in the importance of its extant remains.

Darius I abandoned Pasargadae, the old capital of Cyrus the Great, and planned his new residence at the neighbouring site of Persepolis, in the province of Fars. The reason for this move was probably none other than sentiment, for though Darius I (522–486 BC) succeeded Cambyses II as the Persian king of kings, he was not in the direct line of succession. His descent was traced from Ariyaramnes, the brother of Cyrus I. Hence the new Persepolis was designed to mark a fresh beginning as the spring capital of the new Achaemenian court; a citadel built on virgin rock and named 'Parsa' after the Persian homeland. The early Greeks too called it the city of the Persians, until Aeschylus ironically mistranslated this as 'Perseptolis' – the destroyer of cities – a misnomer which persists even today.

The Kuh-i-Rehmat (Mount of Mercy) stands in splendid isolation in the plain of Marv Dasht; the latter, 5800 feet above the level of the Persian Gulf, is watered by the River Araxes. A rock in the shape of a natural terrace, the Kuh-i-Rehmat served as a solid foundation for the buildings of Persepolis. Darius I's decision to construct his new citadel on an out-jutting spur of rock was undoubtedly made with a thought for defence as well as for its majestic setting. Moreover, in his choice of a natural rock terrace backed by a sheer mountain face, Darius I followed the architectural tradition of earlier, though less spectacular, Achæmenid citadels.

In the royal foundation inscriptions of Persepolis, set along the southern face of the outer platform, is the description of this new capital: 'I Darius, great king, king of kings, king upon this earth . . . upon this place this fortress built. Previously here no fortress had been built . . . I built it secure and beautiful

Aerial view of the great palace of Darius I
and Xerxes, about 510–460 BC

OPPOSITE: Sphinx flanking the winged symbol of the god Ahuramazda,
the Persian creator, from the staircase of the Palace of Xerxes

Darius under the royal umbrella, from the *Tripylon*
(ante-room) to the residential quarters of the palace

and adequate, precisely as I ordered.' The list of nations
mentioned in the text of these inscriptions indicates that work
began at Persepolis by 520 BC. The initial phase of the construction lasted about ten years (between 520 and 511 BC) on
this thirty-one-acre site. As at Pasargadae, the buildings at
Persepolis were constructed in the local grey limestone. The
extent to which this medium added to the time spent on construction is well illustrated in comparing Persepolis with the
Assyrian capital of Calah. The latter, though far larger in
extent, was built in half the time because of the exclusive use of
mud-brick.

The architecture of Persepolis is purely that of royal structures; the more humble buildings, built in less permanent
material, have not survived. Of the former, there are
residential palaces, administrative buildings and those reserved
for court ceremonial; there is no evidence of a structure
designed purely for religious purposes. The Persepolitan style of
architecture does not much vary to suit function, and similar
units characterize all types of buildings.

The main entrance to the site is set on the western side within
a recess whence a double reversed stairway leads to the main
platform 40 feet above. The width of the steps as well as the
shallow risers made the ascent usable by mounted horsemen
during ceremonial processions, a point undoubtedly kept in
view by the architects. Facing the upper of the two landings is
a Gate House giving access to the buildings on the terrace.
Four guardian bull colossi, sculptured in the Assyrian manner,
flank the doorways of the structure. These have become
perhaps the best-known sculptures to a visitor at Persepolis,
partly because of their prominent position and partly for their
monumental size (about 23 feet in height). Trilingual inscriptions placed above these guardian figures explain that Xerxes I
(son of the founder of Persepolis) constructed, 'by the grace of
Ahuramazda, this gateway of all lands'. There is evidence that
the Gate House also contained an altar which was placed
opposite the main doorway. A water-tank on the outer side may
also have been connected with the ritual performed at the altar,
within the main hall of the Gate House. Monumental gateways
with guardian animal colossi are included in the plan of several
citadels in the ancient Near East from Hittite times onwards.
Thus the style of Xerxes I's gateway at Persepolis is not an
innovation. However, in one essential it varies from its earlier
parallels – the absence of defence-towers flanking the approach
to the Gate House. A mud-brick fortress wall once abutted this
structure, and protected the area between it and the main
entrance to the terrace.

In architecture, as in every aspect of the visual arts, a strict
adherence to a set tradition was observed by the Achaemenids.
Stylistically, Persepolitan buildings are derived from a simple
type of wooden house-form which still survives in the peasant
dwellings of northern Iran. The structures are set on high
platforms and monumental staircases of divergent flights

Xerxes enthroned, in the western doorway of the
southern wall of the Hall of a Hundred Columns. The
throne-platform is 'supported' by subject peoples

Doorway into the Throne Room or Hall of a Hundred Columns, built by Xerxes and Artaxerxes

The Apadana reliefs

Scythian leading a horse (eastern staircase)

Lion-and-bull combat (eastern staircase)

Indians bringing tribute (eastern staircase)

OPPOSITE: Gandharans and Bactrians
bringing animals as tribute (eastern staircase)

Persian guards on the northern, inner flight of stairs
of the eastern staircase of the Apadana

Servants on the western staircase of
the Palace of Darius I

give access to the interiors. The essential ground-plan
consists of a columned portico which leads to a spacious hypostyle hall; on three sides the building is surrounded by suites
of narrow rooms and vestibules. The wooden roof is supported
by tapering columns crowned with addorsed animal capitals, a
feature characteristic of Achaemenid architecture. The carving
on the entablatures of buildings proves that they were based on
wooden and not on stone prototypes; indeed the dentil cornice
ornamenting the façades of Achaemenian rock-cut tombs
is directly derived from the use of wooden beams. Despite
clerestory lighting and the occasional use of windows, the
heavily columned interiors must always have been dimly
lit. Moreover, because of their immense scale even a comparatively small palace must have proved an uncomfortable royal
residence in the winter months. Perhaps these disadvantages
were to some extent mitigated when the court moved to a

different capital each season, the rotation being governed undoubtedly by the climate of the province to be visited.

Xerxes' Gate of All Lands leads to the Apadana, the largest structure at Persepolis. Though its foundation was laid in the time of Darius I, the Apadana was completed over a span of thirty years, in the reign of Xerxes I. Architecturally it is of considerable importance, for not only is it the most spacious of Persepolitan buildings (with the main hall alone about 200 feet square), but its plan is characteristic of less well-preserved Audience Halls at other Achaemenian royal capitals.

The two staircases which give access to the Apadana dominate the building; these are best remembered by the splendid reliefs covering the entire surfaces of their parapets and façades. The themes of the reliefs are identical on each staircase except for the fact that they are portrayed in reversed directions. Their total length is estimated at about 1000 feet. By virtue of their size alone, the Apadana sculptures are thus of major importance in the art of the period. They portray various themes and were not designed as a unity.

The central façades of the staircases have a pair of reliefs on either end showing a subject characteristic of Achaemenian art – the lion-and-bull combat, often referred to as the 'symplegma'. The sculptor carving these reliefs at Persepolis worked at a disadvantage, since the composition had to fit within the triangular spaces of the breast-walls. The reliefs thus perhaps best illustrate a point which constantly recurs in Persepolitan art: the fact that Persian art of this period is always subservient to architecture. All examples of such scenes of combat at Persepolis are restricted to the triangular spaces of staircase façades, and would appear to be designed primarily as space-filling devices for such architectural units.

Classical sources make reference to the Immortals, the personal bodyguard of Achaemenian kings, whose number was never allowed to fall below 10,000. Files of such guards embellish the staircases of the Apadana, which lays great emphasis on their portrayal by virtue of the ceremonial nature of the reliefs. The dominant theme of the Apadana reliefs is that of tribute-bearing processions. Arranged formally within horizontal registers, twenty-three foreign delegations are portrayed in procession, showing their individuality by national costume and not by the portrayal of their ethnic types. Each group is heavily laden with royal tribute, brought from the outlying satrapies of the Achaemenian Empire during the celebration of the spring festival at Persepolis.

The effect of the Apadana reliefs must be considered as a whole, with greater stress on composition and design than on the merit of their carving. These are not indoor sculptures and thus do not demand close scrutiny; moreover, the observer is dwarfed by the height of the reliefs; the carving on the top register is 10 feet above him. In their original state all Persepolitan sculptures were further embellished by the use of colour and precious metal for added detail.

Unused impost for a column at Persepolis. The impost terminates on each side with the vigorously carved forepart of a lion

LEFT: Inscription of Xerxes in Old Persian on the façade of the southern staircase of the Palace of Darius I

BELOW: Gateway in the palace from a water-colour drawing (c 1817) by Sir Robert Ker Porter, painter and traveller

43

Rock-cut tomb of Darius II (424–405 BC) at
Naqsh i-Rustam, near Persepolis

The buildings of Persepolis impress the onlooker, above all
else, by their size, as in the hypostyle hall of the Apadana, where
the columns alone are about 62 feet in height. These, nonethe-
less, retain the slender tapering proportions of their wooden
prototypes. This is made structurally possible because of the
use of wood in roof construction, for such columns would have
made poor supports for stone entablatures. A unique creation of
the architecture of this period is the style of the complex column
capital; addorsed animals (usually lions or bulls) form a saddle
to support the transverse beams of the roofing. Between these
animal capitals and the richly ornamented bell-shaped bases
are closely fluted column shafts set in careful alignment.

Windows play an important part in the buildings of Persepolis and these are not restricted merely to residential palaces.
Many stone frames of both windows and doors still stand upright in the palaces of Darius I and Xerxes I. In the latter alone,
there are nineteen windows in the walls of the main hall opening
on to surrounding apartments. In their cavetto cornices with
fluted decoration, there is direct evidence of Egyptian influence.
Sculptured reliefs are frequently inserted on the jambs of both
doors and windows, often portraying reliefs of royal combat or
the king followed by attendants, much-favoured themes in the
limited repertoire of Achaemenian art.

Nevertheless, art in itself is of secondary importance in the
Achaemenian period; it is architectural art in the main, in that
it is wholly subordinate to the shape and size of the structural
surfaces. Moreover, indoor reliefs have a limited use in Persepolis, for interior wall surfaces, almost hidden by heavily
columned halls, are not suitable settings for such sculpture.
Thus Persepolitan reliefs are predominantly reserved for the
decoration of stairway façades. Yet another reason why the art
of this period holds a position of lesser intrinsic importance is
because its sculpture is mainly decorative in content. It is this
which results in the constant repetition of themes and ornamental motifs, tendencies which figure prominently in the
nomadic arts of embroidery and textiles to which Achaemenian
reliefs are closely allied.

Of added interest in Persepolitan art is the extent of foreign
borrowing; the main direction of influence is from Assyrian and
neo-Babylonian art, with Greece and Egypt also exercizing in-
direct but not controlling influences. A capital as sumptuous as
Persepolis was primarily built as a centre for royal ceremonial;
to harmonize with this background its art too is highly formal,
technically perfect but stylized in portrayal. What the sculptures of Persepolis lack in variety of narrative, however, is fully
compensated for by fineness of detail.

Within these limitations, the Achaemenid Persians created a
new and cosmopolitan art, worthy of the achievements of royal
builders of a world empire, an empire signalled by Darius the
Great in his Naqsh-i-Rustam inscription: 'the spear of a Persian
man has gone forth afar; . . . a Persian man has delivered battle
far indeed from Persia'.   VERA S. KATRAK

OPPOSITE: Columns of the Apadana or Audience
Hall of Darius I and Xerxes

ISFAHAN

The opulent city of the Safavid kings of Persia,
containing some of the finest examples
of Persian Islamic building

Shah Abbas (1586–1629), from the *Travels*
of Sir Thomas Herbert, Baronet, who was Groom of
the Bed Chamber to Charles I of England

The phrase *Isfahan – nisf-i jahân* (Isfahan is half the world') is constantly on the lips of all those who have ever been there; yet the saying is of no great age, since it refers especially to the Isfahan created as his new capital city by Shah Abbas (1586–1629), when it saw its greatest prosperity and glory and was resplendent with that pageantry and panache which so impressed contemporary Western travellers. But the city is much older. Of the two sites from which it grew, Jayy (the Gabae of Strabo) was a residence of the Achaemenids of the fifth century BC and their successors the Parthians and Sassanians, the ruins of whose fire-temples can still be seen; the other site, on which most of the present city is built, Yahudiyya, if not founded as a Jewish settlement by King Nebuchadnezzar in the sixth century BC, as one popular tradition has it, may at least have been colonized by Jews at the instigation of the Sassanian king Yazdigird I, who had a Jewish wife; in the fifth century AD. Even today Isfahan is a cosmopolitan city; the Zoroastrians are now few, but the Jewish settlement is some 6000 strong, the thriving Armenian colony with its thirteen churches in the suburb of Julfa is rather larger, and there is a sizeable European community.

Isfahan has always owed its importance to its situation at the intersection of important trade routes (even today, although the motor-bus and aeroplane have replaced the camel), and to its river the Zayanda-rud, the 'life-giving stream'. Its wealth early attracted the Arabs, who conquered it in the early years of Islam – the exact date is uncertain, but it must have been between 640 and 644 – and it remained under the Caliphate before passing in the tenth century to the Buwayhid princes, under whose rule the Shi'a sect of Islam came to the fore in Iran, and later to the Daylamites, the Kakwayhids, and then in the eleventh and twelfth centuries to the Great Seljuqs.

The Mongols reduced the city in 1235, and it knew troubled times until the reign of the Mongol Il-Khan Öljeytü in the early fourteenth century, when some prosperity returned. This

OPPOSITE: The central bay of the sanctuary of the Shah
Mosque, richly decorated with the finest Safavid tiles

The entrance portal of the Shah Mosque, looking over the *maidan* towards the bazaar

Metal plaque on the main door of the Shah Mosque

The Shah Mosque, showing the wooden kiosk used by the muezzin

was increased under the Muzaffarids and the later Timurids in the fifteenth century, and its culture further advanced under the Turkoman Qaraqoyunlu and Aqqoyunlu dynasties. Then came the Safavids; Shah Isma'il, in 1502, united all Iran under one kingdom and one religion from his capital at Tabriz, and although the Safavid capital remained there or at Qazvin until 1591, Isfahan prospered under the early Safavids. When Isfahan became the Safavid capital in 1592 the ruler Shah Abbas decided to make it the first city of the world; he laid out its great squares and avenues, and built most of the great works described here. The later Safavids added to his work, although later dynasties more or less neglected Isfahan and transferred the capital to Tehran; a few interesting buildings remain of the Qajar period, late eighteenth and nineteenth centuries; and the present dynasty, the Pahlavi, has seen an enthusiasm for the preservation and the restoration of the great buildings of preceding ages.

Almost the entire run of the history of Iranian Islam is epitomized in the great Masjid-i Jami (Mosque of Congregation – often called, not quite correctly, Masjid-i Jum'a, 'Friday

OPPOSITE: One of the side courts of the Shah Mosque. The plain single pillars provide a welcome contrast of texture with the profusion of blue tile

A minaret on the sanctuary of the Masjid-i Jami (Mosque of Congregation), decorated in coloured tiles. The geometrical patterns on the minaret are stylized varieties of Arabic lettering

An interior court of the Masjid-i Jami showing Seljuq workmanship

Mosque'). Almost; for although we know that a mosque was built on this site in the time of the Abbasid caliphate, nothing of this early mud-brick structure, in the simple Arabian style, now remains. Its replacement must have been gradual, and there is still much to see of the first phase of this replacement under the early Seljuqs. On its median line (north-east–south-west) there are two tall domes of baked brick, the larger one on the south-west standing over the principal *mihrab*, the prayer-niche giving the direction of Mecca. Both retain their original brickwork with diaper patterns, large arched squinches, the sixteen-sided phase of transition with smaller blind brick arches, an inscription in Kufic characters below the dome, and the tall dome with eight internal brick ribs. The mark of the Seljuqs appears also in the columns supporting the side arcades, round with heavy square capitals, and with the characteristic ornamented brick-plugs. The arches they support are varied in their shape and decoration, a favourite device being the addition of a blind trefoil arch above the arched opening, giving an effective recession of planes.

It must have been in Seljuq times that the building assumed its present general plan, for the porches on each side of the central rectangular courtyard still show some Seljuq workmanship, though much added to and decorated later. North of the north-west porch a section of the Seljuq arcades was partitioned off by the Mongol Oljeytu after his conversion to Shi'i Islam in 1309, and he added to this section a *mihrab* in exquisitely carved stucco. Some fifty years later, under the Muzaffarids, extensions were made on the outside of the Seljuq arcades, one on the south-east to form a *madrasah* (Koranic school) and another to join the northern dome with the rest of the building; and in 1447 another such extension took place, by the Timurid Muhammad ibn Baysunqur, great-grandson of Timur, of the great winter hall, with transparent blocks let into its roof to admit light, on the north-west side.

In the time of the Turkomans there were many projects for the repair and embellishment of the mosque, some of which can be seen in the interior walls of the southern arcades; these are not definitely dated, but stylistically are very similar to those of another building of Isfahan, the Darb-i Imam, known to be of the last Qaraqoyunlu ruler who died in 1467. Certainly his conqueror, the Aqqoyunlu Uzun Hasan, decorated the porch of the south-western prayer-hall and added the heavy pendentives to the original Seljuq structure. The fine mosaic tile calligraphy and floral designs on the courtyard side of this are, however, Safavid work of the time of Shah Tahmasp, about 1532. Finally, the large hall in the extreme south-west corner of the mosque is the work of the great Shah Abbas, some fifty years later.

Shah Abbas's greatest work, however, was carried out some way south of the Masjid-i Jami, in the oblong Royal Quadrangle, an area of some 540 yards from north to south, 160 yards from east to west, originally used by the king as a polo ground – the heavy stone goal-posts still stand. At the south end of the quadrangle is the Masjid-i Shah (Royal Mosque), on the east the

OPPOSITE: The wares of a metal merchant displayed under one of the crossings of the great covered bazaar

mosque of Shaikh Lutfullah, on the west opposite this the royal palace called Ala Qapi, and at the north end the Qaysariyya Gateway leading to the royal bazaar. The old frescoes of the bazaar gateway, which depicted Shah Abbas's conquest of the Uzbeks, have now faded, but exquisite mosaic tiling still remains, including the representation of Sagittarius the archer. The bazaar is still active, all manner of merchandise being offered for sale beneath its covered arcades, but especially carpets and hand-woven and hand-printed cloth.

The mosque of Shaikh Lutfullah was the first of this group of buildings, its portal having been finished by 1602, although seventeen years passed before the completion of the building. The doorway is a harmonious composition entirely covered with mosaic tiles, in which turquoise preponderates; the dome, which rises from the mosque behind it, is also worked all over with mosaic tiling, but on a background of *café-au-lait* colour, and is perhaps the most perfect in shape of all the domes of Isfahan. The interior is similarly covered all over in mosaic tiling (except only for the marble floor), and consists of one large octagonal chamber. The *mihrab* is decorated with stalactite pendentives, and its design surprisingly includes the wine-cup.

The Masjid-i Shah at the south end of the quadrangle is set at an angle to its gateway, to comply with the prescriptions for the orientation of the *mihrabs* with the direction of Mecca. The great portal was completed by 1616, although the interior was not finished at Shah Abbas's death. The portal is in mosaic tiling throughout, the blues and turquoise again predominating, with a cluster of stalactite pendentives, and the outline of two peacocks in the floral sprays above the door. But it took four years to build the doorway alone, and the king ordered the bulk of the tilework of the interior to be done in the square painted tiles known as *haft-rangi*. The dome of the sanctuary stands on a tall drum with pierced openings to admit light, and is tiled inside and out. A tall pylon-like arch stands before it, flanked with two slender minarets – echoing those of the gateway – and the pylon is repeated in the other façades of the courtyard. The wooden pavilions, for the use of the muezzins, reflect the original Safavid style, but have been somewhat restored. We must not omit to mention the delicate brass plaques on the main gates of the mosque, with their bird motifs.

The palace standing opposite Shaikh Lutfullah's Mosque goes by the name Ala Qapi (Exalted Gate), built by Shah Abbas but completed by his successors. It has seven interior storeys – some of these only small mezzanine floors – approached by a spiral staircase; but from the quadrangle it appears to consist of two large floors, the lower of brick decorated with tile, the upper a large balcony with a flat roof supported on slender wooden columns fashioned from single plane trees, with stalactite capitals also carved in wood, supporting a painted and inlaid ceiling. On the floor of this balcony stage is a cistern, which must have afforded some measure of coolness to the king and his guests when they held banquets and watched polo matches in

Shaikh Lutfullah's Mosque from the *maidan*. The stalactite pendentives over the entrance doorway are perhaps the best proportioned in Isfahan

The *maidan* in the early eighteenth century, from Cornelis de Bruin's *Travels through Muscovy to Persia and India*

The Ala Qapi Palace

The Ala Qapi Palace, with its great balcony
formerly used for royal entertainments and receptions

BELOW : The veranda of the Ala Qapi,
with the Shah Mosque in the distance

OPPOSITE : Capital of a wooden column and
panelled ceiling of the balcony of the Ala Qapi

Seventeenth-century view of Isfahan, from the *Travels* of Adam Olearius

this great grandstand. The interior rooms are variously decorated; particularly noteworthy are the ceilings of a large pillared hall in the third floor, and the cut-out pots and vessels of the 'music-room' on the sixth floor, delicately worked in stucco, with some good fresco floral designs still remaining. The balcony commands a view of the royal quadrangle, but a panoramic view of Isfahan can be obtained from its roof.

The royal quadrangle was only one of Shah Abbas's great projects. Almost as important – and certainly now appreciated more by the Isfahanis – was the great avenue known as the Chahar Bagh (Four Gardens), some way west of the Royal Quadrangle, leading down to the river. It had two avenues of plane trees at the sides, and another central avenue, and the two roads, now a modern dual-carriageway, were once full of flower beds. A central avenue, now used as a shaded walk for pedestrians, was once a stone channel with streams and waterfalls. The great gateways of former times have now been replaced by the fine shops and other modern buildings. And yet the avenue is still one of great charm, the favourite walk and meeting-place of the élite of Isfahan. Near its southern end stands the Madrasa-i Chahar Bagh, the Chahar Bagh theological school, built in the time of the last Safavid king in the early eighteenth century, tall tiled arcades surrounding a central quadrangle through which a stream flows. The double dome, tiled inside and out, ranks second only to that of Shaikh Lutfullah's mosque, and the tiling of the whole building is very varied, there being examples of almost every Iranian style.

Between the Chahar Bagh and the Royal Quadrangle lies another Safavid building, the Chihal Sutun (Forty Columns) of 1647, its tall pillars of plane trunks reflected in a long pool outside, with behind a series of halls which formerly bore most delicate fresco paintings; many of these still exist, but some of the finest have unfortunately perished through incompetent 'restoration'. The palace is now used as a museum.

The smaller buildings of Isfahan are no less important, but here we can do no more than mention them. There are dozens of very fine tombs, from the early fourteenth century onwards, and the smaller mosques would be accounted marvels in a city without such dominating mosques as those we have described above. The minarets of Isfahan are justly famous, many of them dating from Seljuq times, some no longer attached to mosques but free-standing. The Armenian quarter of Julfa has its own celebrated monuments, not least the cathedral built in 1663, owing not a little to the imagination of the craftsmen of Isfahan as well as to the Christian influence from outside Iran; and the collection of drawings and portraits casts an interesting light on the life of this great minority.

No one can think of Isfahan without calling to mind its bridges. The old Shahristan Bridge is of Seljuq work on Sassanian foundations; Allahvardi Khan's Bridge is an impressive construction of thirty-three arches, with smaller arches flanking the roadway above. However, the pride of place is taken by the

Khaju Bridge, built by Shah Abbas II on the old road to Shiraz, its spans of side arches including covered footpaths, with semi-octagonal towers projecting towards the river on both sides to form rooms of retreat from the summer sun, these rooms and the spandrels of all the arches carrying fine geometrical tile ornament.

The Huguenot jeweller Chardin, who lived ten years in Isfahan in the late seventeenth century, describes the life of the city with much insight, ranging from lofty mosque to lusty tavern, and from his account we can recapture much of the spirit of the Safavid court in its heyday. Shortly after his time Isfahan was overrun by Turks, Russians and Afghans, falling into the hands of the latter at last after a terrible siege which broke the city's spirit. Nadir Shah expelled the Afghans and regained Isfahan, but himself ruled from Meshhed. Karim Khan made Shiraz his capital, and the later Qajars ruled from Tehran. Isfahan is now thriving again, its ancient textile industry having given place to a modern one, but fortunately restoration has been discreet. More than anywhere else in Iran, it retains much of the sparkle and panache of its glory under the Safavids.   J. BURTON-PAGE

The Khaju Bridge over the Zayanda-rud.
Its rooms overlooking the river were
fashionable retreats from the summer sun

SAMARKAND

Centre of Tamerlane's vast empire, once a city of flower-gardens and flower-like buildings and famous still for the tall, coloured dome of the conqueror's tomb

The buildings which Tamerlane and his successors left at Samarkand are now under the protection of the Soviet government. The Gur-i-Mir, the tomb of that great destroyer himself, is already restored. And so, very largely, is the Shah-i-Zindah where so many of his family were buried. The superb Reghistan, the loveliest group of academic buildings in the world, is still in the throes of restoration. Its three *madrasahs* (Islamic colleges), which were falling into ruin long before the Revolution, are having the exquisitely-patterned tiles of their façades and courts replaced, their leaning towers straightened. Soon the vast central courtyard will be almost as good as new.

There is a long-drawn irony in this (and a double-edged irony for those who find such restoration excessive). Tamerlane carried his conquests to the Volga. Now the settled Western peoples whose towns and countryside he destroyed have come to rebuild the nomad capital. The galloping bowmen of the steppes were irresistible, but the plodding cultivator must win in the end.

Samarkand's position in the fertile valley of the Zaravshan, close to the borders of 'the Steppe and the Sown', has had a dominating influence on its history. Culturally it was bound to owe most to the great civilizations to the south and east, but it was a tempting prize for the oriental nomads, and twice has been enveloped by counter-surges of power from the west. First that of Alexander the Great; then of the Russians under the Czars and Soviets.

During this long and fluctuating history, the main growing point of Samarkand has shifted by a few miles. The turquoise city of Tamerlane lies between a predecessor and a successor. To the north are the sad, grey-green mounds of Afrasiab, the most ancient city – once known as Maracanda, capital of the Achaemenid province of Soghdiana. It was destroyed by Alexander, taken by the Arabs in the early eighth century, and afterwards became a famous centre of learning under the enlightened Persian dynasty of the Sassanids.

A fanciful portrait of Tamerlane, from *North and East Tartary* (1785) by Nicolaas Witsen

OPPOSITE: The tombs of Olja Aim and her daughter in the Shah-i-Zindah. The lofty domes set on tall drums are characteristic of Timurid architecture

General view of the Gur-i-Mir. The mausoleum was originally built by Tamerlane for his grandson, and was completed in about 1405

When Ghenghiz Khan and his Mongols struck in 1221 the walls are said to have been defended by over one hundred thousand men, but the destruction was so complete that the city was reduced to insignificance until it was revived by Tamerlane. Now the dusty mounds of Afrasiab, looking remarkably like those of Nineveh or Babylon, are disturbed only by Soviet archaeologists who are cutting deep sections through the citadel and walls.

While the corpse of ancient Samarkand makes the quietest of neighbours, the new Russian quarter on the other side is growing fast, and before long is certain to engulf the oriental city. This part of the town was pleasantly laid out after 1871 at the time of the Czarist expansion. Now, under the Soviets, Samarkand is again a centre of learning. The University is very large indeed, and is putting up new buildings (unhappily of the most mediocre kind) along the enormous central boulevard with its garden full of forest trees.

The good, homely looking Soviet citizens shopping in the terraced Czarist shops contrast as much as shoppers can with those in the traditional Samarkand market near the Reghistan. There the customers, and still more the stall-holders, could come straight from illustrations of a Mongol or Tartar horde. Their slant-eyed, leathery, intricately wrinkled faces are embellished with little beards and thin, dangling moustaches, while many are dressed in padded coats and boots, with turbans, fur hats or black-and-white Uzbek caps. It would not be hard to pick out individuals who could have sat for the various pictures – probably none a true portrait – that have been given the name of Tamerlane.

The Conqueror was in fact born only about fifty miles from Samarkand, at Kesh, or Shahr-i-Sabz – the Green City. His father, chief of the Turkic clan of the Barlas, was the first of his line to become a convert to Islam. He enjoyed a studious life, and according to some accounts his son Timur (the variants of his name derive from Timur-i-Leng, Lame Timur) was a sound scholar of the Koran. However, he soon discovered his genius for war, and after a decade of ruthless rivalry with the dynasty of Ghenghiz Khan, won the throne of Transoxiana and leadership of Asian nomadism. He was crowned at Samarkand in 1369. Most of the rest of his life he gave to great sweeps of pillage and conquest, carrying his power westward to the Volga and the Aegean shores of Anatolia, southward over the whole Persian Empire to Baghdad and Kurdistan. He conquered northern India, sacking Delhi with hideous savagery, fought the Turks and Egyptians, capturing Damascus and Aleppo, and was preparing a campaign against China when he died in 1405.

Between those who have regarded Tamerlane as a butcher and wanton destroyer of civilizations, and those who have been able to admire him as a hero, one can accept Marlowe's phrase that he was 'Thirsting with sovereignty and love of arms'. Certainly at Kesh, his birthplace, and at Samarkand, the capital of his vast, totally unstable empire, he made a creative effort to

OPPOSITE: One of the glories of Timurid architecture: the great glazed dome of Tamerlane's tomb, the Gur-i-Mir

set aside his unbounded depredations. He is said to have brought ninety elephants to Samarkand to move stones for a mosque, and he himself describes how, after the capture of Delhi, he 'ordered that all the artisans and clever mechanics who were among the masters of their respective crafts, should be picked out from among the prisoners'. In this way, he says, 'Some thousands of craftsmen were selected to await my command.' So he saved from his own shambles an international army to build the huge and lofty buildings that his grandiose taste demanded.

The influence of these foreign workers on the architecture of what can be called the Timurid Renaissance is recognizable in some of the decorative detail in buildings at Samarkand. And Indian ideas in particular seem to have inspired the Stone Mosque there – now completely destroyed. But this eclectic element was superficial. Essentially Timurid architecture is in the pure Persian tradition.

At Tamerlane's death in 1405 his son Shah Rukh transferred the capital of the already disintegrating empire to Herat in Afghanistan. However, only five years later the Conqueror's brilliant grandson, Ulug Beg, became viceroy of Samarkand, and he and other cultivated members of the family maintained and developed the Timurid Renaissance there. Ulug Beg himself built his fine *madrasah* on the Reghistan, and made it famous for mathematics and astronomy. The handsome observatory he set up on a ridge near Afrasiab housed a giant Fakhri sextant, a part of which can still be seen today.

This fifteenth-century Samarkand must have been a place of wonder and delight. It had long been famous for the way in which two streams had been diverted to make it a verdant city of canals, with water available to every house. It had orchards, flower gardens, aqueducts and springs – and in Tamerlane's time great plantations spreading all round it. This is the setting in which the Timurid buildings – themselves brighter than flower gardens – must be imaginatively enjoyed. Such perfection could not exist for long. Another nomad incursion, that of the Uzbeks, overwhelmed Samarkand and its territories in 1507. The Timurid dynasty was scattered and made impotent.

It is fitting to choose the Gur-i-Mir, where Tamerlane himself lies buried, to represent Timurid architecture. In its present state it is, perhaps, rather austere and unappealing. But it certainly exemplifies what is one of the recognized virtues of this architecture: a strength of form which can carry the delicious Persian ornamental schemes, and the brilliant turquoise, green, yellow and gold of the tiles and faience mosaics, without being dominated by them. Then again the great feature of the Gur-i-Mir is the dome above the royal tombs, and it has been said that 'The most novel, and still the most triumphant, innovation of Timurid architecture was the tall, bulbous dome on the tall, cylindrical drum'.

Although it has been questioned, there seems little doubt that this famous mausoleum was built by Timur for his favourite

Detail from the so-called 'Throne of Tamerlane' in the Gur-i-Mir

OPPOSITE: General view of the Shah-i-Zindah, with the tombs of Tamerlane's nurse, Olja Aim, and her daughter in the foreground

The Shah-i-Zindah

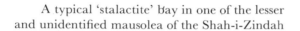

A typical 'stalactite' bay in one of the lesser
and unidentified mausolea of the Shah-i-Zindah

'A peaceful alley of the dead': the
upper path of the Shah-i-Zindah

64

Entrance to the mausoleum of Tamerlane's niece, Shad i-Mulk Aka
(*d* 1372). Panels of handsome relief tiles, a special feature of the region,
flank the arch and doorway

OPPOSITE: The flight of stairs and gate leading to the upper path of the
Shah-i-Zindah. The group of the four great mausolea rises beyond the gate

grandson, Sultan Muhammad, when he died of wounds after the battle of Angora. The battle was in 1402, and the mausoleum was dedicated within two or three years. Tamerlane's building was based on a traditional Persian plan deriving from the fire temple. The dome and its drum crown a mortuary chapel which is octagonal outside but square internally with doorways in each of its four sides.

The octagon is in the pale biscuit-coloured brick characteristic of Samarkand, netted in patterns of dark and light blue. The great dome swells to a height of 112 feet, and its sixty-four fat, powerful ribs are green, marked snake-like with lozenges in black and white. These ribs curve in a little to grasp the drum, which is charged with texts from the Koran in handsome Kufic lettering. There is no doubt that the dome of the Gur-i-Mir is perfectly satisfying and deserves its fame.

Originally the mausoleum had free-standing minarets flanking its main entrance, but in 1434 Ulug Beg had these linked with an arcaded screen, while at the same time adding a forecourt and entrance portal. The fine gateway still stands, and is embellished with all the prevailing motifs of the time: geometrical entrelacs, arabesques, foliate scrolls, stars and lotus palmettes, all in rich lapis blue and white, touched with green and gold. Today both minarets have been overthrown by earthquakes, and much of the forecourt has disappeared. The general effect of the Gur-i-Mir must also have been profoundly changed by the destruction of the mosque and *madrasah* which once stood beside it.

Returning to enter the central octagon, the interior of the mortuary chapel is sombre but magnificent. Above an alabaster dado there is a four-bayed frieze of the intricate cellular construction known as stalactite. This in turn is topped with a cornice in dark green jasper, elegantly inscribed with the genealogy and deeds of Tamerlane. The ceiling is an inner dome separated by a wide space from the huge melon overhead. Light tilts into the chapel through carved grilles.

Tamerlane's tomb, with its two great inscribed blocks of dark jade from East Turkestan, dominates those of his grandsons and other kinsmen. All the tombs are enclosed in a stone balustrade – and here it seems that the Indian craftsmen were allowed to express something of their own taste. The tombstones are not the true sarcophagi; these can be seen in a vault below the chapel.

If the Gur-i-Mir in its present restored and isolated form is lacking in feeling, the opposite is true of the related group of Timurid tombs known as the Shah-i-Zindah. This can best be described as a beautiful and peaceful alley in a city of the dead.

Central arch of the façade of one of the three fifteenth-century *madrasah*, or Islamic colleges, forming the great square of the Reghistan. The building is unusual in including animal forms in its decoration – the tigers above the arch are in orange tiles

It climbs up a ridge on the outer slopes of Afrasiab, and is entered through a portal built by Ulug Beg in the same year that he made his additions to the Gur-i-Mir. Immediately inside this gate the way leads past the mausolea of Tamerlane's nurse, Olja Aim, and her daughter, both with lofty turquoise domes, up a steep flight of steps and through an arch that gives a dramatically sudden access into the upper path. Here, standing in a group, are four of the finest tombs, two of them belonging to sisters of Tamerlane.

On the left is that of Tshujuk Bika Aka and three of her children. Like most of these graves, it consists of a square, domed chamber with a portal arch and a screen pierced by a narrow doorway. Inside there are blue-and-white stalactite bays below a handsome domed ceiling. The best feature of this building, however, is the exceptionally good carved and glazed relief tiles – a decorative form which is something of a speciality in Transoxiana. The dome of Tshujuk Bika's chamber is low and drumless – a primitive, unevolved version of the Timurid form. That of Tamerlane's younger sister, Shirin Bika Aka, on the other side of the road, is already (1385) higher and possesses a modest drum.

The path, of slabs and cobbles tended with an exquisite care unusual in Central Asia, continues to climb towards its central section where the mausolea are relatively small, low-domed and ill-preserved. Those which are built out on platforms above the slope command a prospect of the city with miles of shimmering countryside beyond. At its uppermost, northern end, the funerary way reaches its destination – a place where more tombs, including one attributed to a wife of Tamerlane's, cluster round the grave of Kasim ibn Abbas. Kasim was a holy man, reputed to have been the first to bring Islam to Samarkand, and his shrine (1334) was already a popular centre of pilgrimage in pre-Timurid times. The four-tiered tomb is in a small room off a lovely domed prayer-hall.

This building, so much the earliest in the Shah-i-Zindah, is of special interest as an illustration of the sources of the Timurid style. Already, for example, the architects are using the stalactite half-dome and squinch, and the carved relief-tile. Half a century later, the mausoleum of Shirin Bika can be recognized quite plainly as a miniature prototype of the Gur-i-Mir.

Pilgrims still occasionally visit the tombs and the shrine of Kasim ibn Abbas. Dressed in their best – perhaps a man in blue turban and long robe, a woman in dark velvet and their small girl in brightest crimson – they walk solemnly between the biscuit-and-blue tombs, below the turquoise domes and lighter blue sky. Shah-i-Zindah means the Living King, and refers to the legend that the holy man still lives on the hill and one day will return to his people. When Samarkand has become a modern industrial and university city with notable ruins preserved among its traffic, it is likely that something of the living Timurid past will endure only up here, in this calm alley of the dead.   JACQUETTA HAWKES

The lofty ruins of the Bibi Khanum Mosque: entrance to the main shrine

INDO-PAKISTAN SUBCONTINENT

Introduction by Mortimer Wheeler

A general review of the greater buildings of the Indo-Pakistan subcontinent involves two simultaneous lines of approach: one environmental, the other historical. At any given time and place, what was the nature of the landscape? And what were the origins, aims, equipment and quality of those who successively sought to use it? Of these the landscape is the most easily forgotten; yet scarcely a dozen sentences can be written about Indo-Pakistan architecture without reference to environment, and often enough that environment must today be drastically reconstructed, with such skill as we can bring to bear upon it.

For example, we speak casually today of the Northern Plains of India: that vast expanse of tillage or waste-land, often almost featureless, through or over which we may travel a trifle wearily for hundreds of miles on end between Delhi and Calcutta. It requires a deliberate effort of the imagination to recall that almost the whole scene is man-made. In the Middle Ages, with a population perhaps a mere tenth of today's total, much of this great region must have been covered as densely with jungle as in the days of the epics, when Rama and Sita and the Pandavas spent years of their lives in traversing 'the dark and pathless forest', the Mahavana. No doubt here and there were exiguous patches of desert, as there are larger ones at the present time. But much of this desert is and was the product of man's improvidence. In Rajasthan, timber has been cut without replacement, and the land-surface thus exposed has been stripped from the underlying rock by the monsoons. So too in the Ambala Siwaliks, where it is recorded that 'when they came under British administration they were thrown open to unrestrained wood-cutting and grazing, and the imprudent activities of the peasant proprietors have turned the range into a desert'. Examples need not be multiplied. It will suffice for present purposes to affirm that, whatever its modern aspect, a thousand years ago and less a large part of the subcontinent was a land of epic jungle and close horizons.

Thus it is that native Indian art and architecture, and native Indian religious expression, are subliminally of the jungle; rich and tangled, swarming, monstrous, sometimes sinister and often fantastically beautiful. Here is no room for the hard perspectives which gave to classical Europe its Parthenon and its sense of history. Where untouched by Persian or Western ideas and moods, the Indian tradition has almost no historical perspective. There is no perspective in the jungle.

We shall see in the following pages a little – not, of course, enough – of this habit of thought and expression. But when we echo the official claim that the Great Temple of Madura with its satellite buildings and gigantic gate-towers is encrusted with thirty-three million carvings (human and animal figures, mostly life-size or larger), the affinity of the jungle needs no further emphasis: unless to add those astonishing vegetable growths that are the temple-towers of Bhubaneswar, as it were tropical marrows or melons on end, enriched by the diversity and multiplicity which the tropics are liable to bestow upon their vegetation.

There are, needless to say, many qualities in Indian architecture other than an organic identity with a tropical environment. But this over-all aspect I emphasize here for a reason. There can be few episodes in the history of architecture more fascinating – I had nearly used that deplorable word *exciting* – than the sudden impact upon India of a whole range of ideas that were born of the desert and the mountains. I refer to the impact of Islam upon the subcontinent, first upon Sind in AD 711–12 from the direction of the Arabian and Mesopotamian deserts and then, after AD 1000, upon north-western India (West Pakistan) from the mountainous Irano–Afghan plateau. Here was something altogether new. Nothing could stand in greater contrast to the luxuriant and recondite jungle art and architecture of Hindustan than the solemn sobriety and open airiness of the architecture of the desert and the mountain.

The essential and simple function of Islamic religious architecture was to provide an oriented place of prayer, a screen-wall containing (after *c* AD 708) a *mihrab* or niche to

OPPOSITE: Sculptures on the left wall of the antechamber of Cave no. 7 at Ajanta drawn by Major Robert Gill (*c* 1824–1875)

69

indicate the direction of Mecca, generally supplemented by a prayer-hall and courtyard. These simple basic elements were capable of extensive elaboration, in which regional fashion emerged. Thus the Persian mosques freely adopted the dome, particularly over the bay confronting the mihrab, no doubt borrowing this feature from the premier Ommayad mosque (AD 705) at Damascus, and ultimately from the domed crossing in front of the high altar of a Christian church. With this often went a rhythmic arcading of the prayer-chamber, and the use of brightly coloured tiles wherewith the Persian architect sought to perpetuate the glories of the brief springtime of the plateau and to anticipate the more lasting glories of Paradise. And the use of the voussoired arch and lime-mortared rubble or brick-work – long familiar to the West but little known in pre-Islamic times east of Persia – freed the Islamic builder from the limitations otherwise imposed by mud-brick or inferior stone.

Briefly then Muslim architecture is first and foremost, with Islam itself, a product of the desert and the highland: of broad, bare horizons, broken if at all by the severe geometry of rocky ranges. In conformity with this setting the mosque, particularly in the Persian manifestation which mattered most to India, is a simple cube or group of cubes, with rigid outlines interrupted only by a sudden mountainous dome or spiky minaret. Within all this rigidity the surface may be variegated by tilery or polychrome masonry, but the geometrical framework remains the dominant note.

It would be difficult therefore to find a more completely alien landscape wherein to transplant this desert or highland growth than that of medieval India. Nevertheless the interesting fact remains that the two opposed traditions, Persian and Indian, were in great measure reconciled on Indian soil, and that in different and ingenious ways.

First, coloured wall-tiles were never fully acclimatized in the subcontinent save in Sind and the Punjab, both readily accessible from the West. At Tatta, in Sind, two lovely tiled mosques of the sixteenth and seventeenth centuries are pure Persian; and tiles are abundant at Lahore, where the pictorial mosaic panels on the exterior of the northern corner of the Old Fort are among the most remarkable in

Aurangabad, a copy of the Taj Mahal, from Louis Matthieu Langlès' *Monuments anciens et modernes d'Hindoustan* (1821)

The building of the Red Fort, Agra, in 1565, from a Mughal manuscript of Abu'l-Fazl's *Life of Akbar* (c 1597). The Red Fort was completed in 1568

Asia and stand to the credit of the Mughal emperor Shahjahan (AD 1632). But within a century of the Muslim conquest of Delhi, the use of tiles for variegation was supplemented or replaced in deeper India by a striking and original use of coloured stones and marble for the same purpose, a medium more attuned to the traditional skill of the native mason. Some part of the essence of Persian architecture had been replaced by a more homely mode.

A second and more significant innovation was the gradual break-up of the rigid, square outlines of Islamic design by the addition of pinnacles and pavilions, until in the fifteenth and sixteenth centuries the building-profile began to assume a bustling diversity which belongs to India rather than to Persia. The luxuriance of the jungle was tempering the austerity of the desert. Already by AD 1000 the Hindu architect (for example, at Khajaraho in central India) had learned to pile up pavilion on pavilion to 'support' the great spire of his own shrines with a tumultuous crescendo of varied form. And now this principle was gradually transferred to mosque and tomb so that, particularly in the latter, the final dome no longer stood in stern isolation but emerged as the inevitable culmination of a complex but careful co-ordination of subsidiary units. The extreme development of this Indo-Islamic style was reached in the time of Akbar the Great, whose famous palace and mosque at Fatehpur Sikri (AD 1570) are a riot of Hindu fantasy within and even traversing an Islamic framework. Here at last the desert and the jungle are imaginatively reconciled by the genius of a rare and catholic mind which found good in everything.

And in the sequel, though lesser emperors sat upon the throne of Akbar, this intelligent composition between the two disparate traditions largely endured. The seventeenth century is not, by and large, a very lovable century; it was prone to the malady of righteousness, and India was no exception. Aurangzeb, who succeeded to the Mughal empire in 1658 after much (righteous) blood-letting, was *par excellence* the puritan of Islam, in every sense the opposite of his great-grandfather, the liberal and humane Akbar. He purged and, as he thought, destroyed or suppressed all that related to Hinduism: 'Glory be to God who has given us the faith of Islam', observed his gratified historian. Yet when he built a fine new gateway in Lahore Fort, that he might have direct access to the great Imperial Mosque which he had raised outside it, Aurangzeb produced the most elegant Indianizing masterpiece of its kind in the whole subcontinent. The towers are lightly capped by little pavilions which are far more of Hindustan than of Islam; and the towers themselves, boldly fluted and clasped at the base by large lotus-petals, have a flamboyant originality which, were it not unique, would be utterly Hindu. Bigotry was defeated literally on its own doorstep; even an Aurangzeb could not, if he would, ignore the immanence of India.

Nevertheless there is much in Lahore that carries one's thoughts back to the Persian plateau. Reference has been made to the tilework which is more extensively, and sometimes more splendidly, represented at Lahore than anywhere else in the subcontinent; and Mr Burton-Page will have more to say about this later. He will show that in the seventeenth century there was a flourishing school of tileworkers in the city, skilled more particularly in the art of mosaic tilework, the small colour-units being cut to the required shape and fitted together to form the pattern. In Persia, this art was perfected by the fourteenth century; in India, perhaps the oldest example is a simple geometrical mosaic pattern on the early sixteenth-century tomb of Maulana Jamali near the Qutb at Delhi, though it was not until after the middle of the century, in Akbar's reign, that this type of decoration began to take root. The addition of yellow and green colours facilitated the introduction of attractive naturalistic patterns, based at first on the established art of the painter and culminating, as we shall see, in Wazir Khan's splendid mosque of 1634.

A significant accompaniment of the fashion for tilework was a tendency to restrict the Indianizing development of the buildings thus decorated and to approximate them more closely than was otherwise normal at this period to the severity of traditional Persian forms. The strength and assertiveness of mosaic tilework brook no rival. All that is required is a plain wall on which to hang it, as one might hang a Persian rug from a balcony on a fête-day. Hence, alongside new architectural enterprise there was a constant recurrence at Lahore to Persian convention. Once more, Wazir Khan's mosque is in the picture. Here there are indeed specifically Indian elements. The design is dominated by four great octagonal minarets each terminating in a semi-Hindu pavilion and the gateway has two oriel windows and two more pavilions likewise of Indian character. But for the rest the outlines have the simple austerity of a Persian mosque, and the building depends mainly for its interest upon the Persian mosaic tilework which these outlines frame. It is in effect a scaffolding for the display of richly variegated ornament.

Purists, as Mr Burton-Page remarks, may object to such use of a structure as a mere hoarding for structurally irrelevant decoration – though less so today than in times gone by. The objection is in any case without weight. There is in fact no visual conflict here between the architecture and the decoration. The convincingly functional lines of the former release the mind of the spectator for the non-structural interest of the latter; and the quiescent satisfaction which the total design thus produces is its complete justification and its glory.

If we thus end with a design which is more alien than Indian, we are merely emphasizing the thesis from which this little introduction began. The twin factors of environment and history still dominate the scene; only, Lahore is on the fringe of the mountains, and lies astride the Grand Trunk Road to inner Asia and the homeland of Mughal India – a frontier capital, in spirit nearer the highland or the plateau than the jungle.

The Tomb of Rukn-i Alam dominating the town of Multan

Multan, Pakistan

TOMB OF RUKN-I ALAM

A monumental mausoleum of the fourteenth century, built by a great Governor for himself but later given to his saintly spiritual guide

'The four notable things in Multan' says an old Punjabi jingle 'are dust, heat, beggars and graves.' The author recently re-visited Multan in winter, and found it unjustly calumniated: the first two commodities were absent, the third presented no great inconvenience, and the graves were the attraction which had taken him there – especially the five great saints' tombs of the early days of Islam in the subcontinent, the most magnificent of which is described here.

Multan is a site of great antiquity, the old capital of the lower Punjab even in the time of Alexander the Great, and celebrated for its golden image of the Sun God. This, and the temple of the Sun, were destroyed and rebuilt several times in the Muslim period since Multan first fell to Islam in the eighth century, when Muhammad ibn Qasim took it for the Caliphate; the traveller Thévenot describes temple and idol late in the seventeenth century, shortly before the Mughal emperor Aurangzeb destroyed the idol and built a large congregational mosque on the temple site – itself destroyed when it was being used as a powder-magazine by the Sikhs in the siege of 1848. The events of the Second Sikh War do not concern us here; but we must at least record that the shelling of the fortress and citadel during the siege damaged most of the old structures, and hence many details of the Multan monuments are no more than faithful reproductions of the originals. Fortunately for posterity, Multan is a city of craftsmen, and their strong sense of tradition has spared us the worst horrors of modernization in this rebuilding.

The old fort stands on a mound – a *tell* representing the decay of successive generations of occupation over the centuries – to the north of the city. Crowning this mound is the tomb of the saint called the 'pillar of the world', Rukn-i Alam, looking down on the rooftops of Multan, and visible for thirty miles around. It is recorded that it was built in the second decade of the fourteenth century by the governor of the Punjab, Ghiyasuddin Tughluq, as his own mausoleum; however, that fine old soldier was called upon to restore the prestige of Islam to the capital,

Text on the exterior of the parapet below the dome: 'There is no god but God. Muhammed is the prophet of God'

ABOVE: The middle storey, with an angle buttress in the foreground. Architraves, frieze and merlons are in the characteristic Multani raised tiles

LEFT: The walls of Multan, shown in this drawing by John Brownrigg Bellasis, were demolished in 1854 by General Cunningham, later the first director of the Archaeological Survey of India

Delhi, after the moral deterioration which beset it in the closing years of the Khalji Dynasty, and having become sultan Ghiyasuddin Tughluq Shah never returned to Multan. He constructed for himself a new tomb at Delhi, on a fortified outwork of his new capital Tughluqabad, and made over the earlier building to his former spiritual preceptor Ruknuddin, called also Rukn-i Alam, grandson of the great Baha' ul-Haqq who had introduced the Suhrawardi order into India and who himself lies buried in Multan.

This tomb is at once traditional and original in concept, the culmination of the Multan tomb-builders' art and the beginning of a new trend. There are in Multan four outstanding earlier tombs, the first a simple flat-roofed cubical building, the tomb of Shah Yusuf Gardizi, of about 1170, entirely covered with flat or low-relief tiles; the other three, the tombs of Shadna Shahid, Shamsuddin Tabrizi and Baha' ul-Haqq, which all date from the period 1260–80, are three-storeyed buildings, with square base, octagonal drum, and hemispherical dome, and with small pinnacles at the external angles. All are built of baked brick, most employ some bonding work in wood in addition, and usually glazed tile plays a prominent part in the decoration.

In one feature, however, the tomb of Rukn-i Alam breaks away from the tradition of these thirteenth-century tombs in that its lowest storey, the tomb-chamber, is not a square but an octagon. There is only one previous example known in the subcontinent of an octagonal chamber, that of the tomb of Nasiruddin Mahmud at Delhi (locally known as 'Sultan Ghari') of 1231, which is, however, a crypt rather than a free-standing structure; it seems unlikely that this particular tomb can have been known to the Multan builders, and we should rather attribute the octagonal base of Rukn-i Alam's tomb to the local genius. The other traditional Multan features all appear here: the lofty second storey which forms an octagonal drum, the hemispherical dome, the external angle pinnacles, and the use of wood in the structure; but it is further distinguished from the previous examples by its commanding position, its greater dimensions, and its superlative surface decorations, which all go to make it, in Sir John Marshall's words, 'one of the most splendid memorials ever erected in honour of the dead'.

The tomb stands within a large rectangular enclosure, in which are a few minor buildings and gateways of later date, and a profusion of the graves of those who were so fortunate as to lie within the shadow of the great saint's sanctity. Entrance to the tomb is by a door in one face of the great octagonal lowest storey. This stage has a diameter of 90 feet, but appears even vaster to the eye because of its style of construction. The walls have a pronounced slope or batter, emphasized by angle buttresses which taper sharply towards the top and which are carried up above the general level of the storey into small domed pinnacles. This storey is of shallow light-red bricks, and derives great aesthetic unity from stringcourses of tile-faced bricks, bands of brickwork in a raised diaper pattern with

Wooden lintel and soffit of the interior face of the doorway into the hall, looking up to the dome

the interstices filled with turquoise tiled tesserae, carved brick, brick calligraphy, and a heavy parapet with blind crenellations, all carried round the entire circumference including the buttresses. More ornate work in raised brick and tile surrounded the entrance doorway, the shape of the inner arch of which indicates some rebuilding in a later period.

The second storey, which externally at least is a tall octagonal drum, is smaller in diameter, thus leaving a circumambulation at first-floor level to which the upper part of the ground storey forms a parapet. This second storey has an arched opening in each face to admit light to the interior, each surrounded by a slightly projecting architrave carried up into a mock parapet and profusely decorated with carved brick and tiles; a further note of unity is brought to each arch by stringcourses of larger bricks set at an angle so that they present a zigzag projection, one over the spandrel and the other below the mock parapet. Each angle of the octagon is embellished with a similarly projecting panel, complete with brick-on-angle stringcourse and mock parapet, and the intervening wall is more sparingly decorated with rosettes and geometrical figures in tile designs. The whole storey is capped with an elaborate dado in carved brick and tile, and a parapet with blind crenellations, the shield-shaped merlons with carved brick calligraphy and a tiled

ABOVE: Entrance doorway of the mausoleum. The right-hand tower was damaged in the siege of 1848 and the rebuilding omits the more intricate patterns

BELOW: Detail of the outer wall showing the bands of decoration, the lowest repeating the name 'Allah' in oblong panels

border. Above each angle, set within the parapet, is a small domed pinnacle.

The third storey is the dome, a hemisphere only very slightly stilted and in no way constricted or bulbous. A heavy moulded decoration at the base is in a variety of the merlon design with rosettes alternating with the merlons, and there is a band of geometrical patterns above; but the whole dome is covered with a thick coat of whitewash which obscures the detail. The dome is crowned by a projection similar in shape to the pinnacles on the second storey; this projection and the pinnacles on both storeys all bear finials of similar design, enhancing the harmony.

The tilework of Multan is strikingly different both from the delicate mosaic tile of Lahore and from the heavier glazed terracotta tiles of the lower Indus country of which Thattha is the best example. The colour scheme is more limited: dark and light blue, turquoise and white only appear, as in the earlier work at Thattha. Here, however, the main patterns are in relief, sometimes as much as three-quarters of an inch above the background. This adds enormously to the richness of the tile-work, adding depth and a constant effect of light and shade even when the merciless summer sun is at its most blinding and when the sheen of a flat surface would have become dulled by the pervading dust of Multan in summer.

A drawing of the tomb from 'Mooltan, A series of sketches during and after the siege by John Dunlop, M.D., Assistant Surgeon of H.M.'s 32nd Regiment'

Upper part of the interior of the second storey

Detail of the drum of the dome

OPPOSITE: The Tomb of Rukn-i Alam from the fort

78

The composition as a whole is most satisfying. The batter of the lowest storey with its sturdy angle buttresses suggests the stability of the pyramid, for there is in this work certainly no feeling of weakness which, it must be admitted, is sometimes present to the senses in some of the octagonal buildings of Delhi; and this author would claim for the tomb of Rukn-i Alam that 'rhythmic grace' and 'poetry of composition' which Sir John Marshall – grudgingly, I think – denies it. This building seems to be the immediate inspiration of the octagonal series of tombs in Delhi, although the early examples there are too flat and mal-proportioned for Rukn-i Alam's tomb to have been a model; it was, however, successfully imitated, although on a smaller scale, in two very fine tombs in nearby Uchh, those of the teacher and the daughter of the celebrated 'world-voyager' Jalaluddin Bukhari, now sadly neglected.

The interior of the tomb is no less impressive. The wooden structural beams, just visible in places on the outside wall, are here very prominent in their function as lacing courses, and a heavy wooden lintel supports the arch over the entrance, together with a carved wooden soffit. Much of this woodwork seems to be original; shisham wood is durable, especially in this dry climate where seven inches of rain may fall in a good year. But the principal ornament is worked out in finely chiselled brick, with diaper patterns predominating, and with a fine sense of unity with the exterior realized in the brick-on-angle string-courses in the same relative positions as they occupy outside. The second storey, however, differs in its interior plan, for at the level of the arched windows there are squinches thrown across each angle of the octagon to convert it to a hexadecagon, blind arches with a very effective recession of planes – a device not used in Delhi until much later – as a foil to the less elaborate windows, blind and open arches being separated by pilasters which, though in brick, are so finely chiselled as to resemble woodcarving. These pilasters support the next progression in the phase of transition, the thirty-two-sided figure which carries the circular base of the dome.

The finest work in carved shisham wood has properly been reserved for the focal point of prayer at the tomb, the *mihrab*. The curve of the niche is filled with an arabesque on the merlon device, with the tympanum above carrying a simple geometrical pattern based on the octagon. Carved pilasters support the pointed arch, the spandrels above which bear the six-pointed star commonly known as the 'Star of David', which is certainly a familiar device in Ghaznavid woodwork. The surrounding architrave bears a carved inscription carried all round between two bands of scroll arabesque very similar to that of the great stone screen of the Quwwat-ul-Islam Mosque by the Qutb Minar in Delhi.

Central on the ground floor is the plain cenotaph of the saint honoured by this most noble mausoleum, which in its pomp stands as a splendid reminder of a king's tribute to a saint's glory.

J. BURTON-PAGE

OPPOSITE: Typical Multani raised tile work on the exterior of the tomb

The richly-carved *mihrab* or prayer-niche

RIGHT: Detail of the wood-carving around the *mihrab*

LAHORE FORT

An ancient fortress, rebuilt by the early Mughals,
which rapidly became their most brilliant court
and their richest intellectual centre

At Lahore they have their own variation of an Old Persian saying: *Isfahan nisf-i jahan – agar Lahawr nabashad!* ('Isfahan would be half the world – if there were no Lahore!'). But this is hardly fair, and could only refer to a Lahore in its heyday under the early Mughal emperors, the great city Milton had in mind when he wrote of 'Agra and Lahore of Great Mogul'. For Lahore is a comparatively recent city – we know little of it before Mahmud of Ghazni's conquest early in the eleventh century – and in no sense can Lahore be considered an epitome of Indo–Muslim culture as can Isfahan of Persian Islam. None the less it has known greatness at many times in its history, and such of its fine buildings as were spared devastation or plunder at the hands of the Sikhs are the witnesses of the most illustrious of these.

Early references to Lahore may indeed signify no more than a district of the Punjab, but we know of it for certain as a town in the times of the Ghaznavids, those rulers of Turkish stock whose empire extended from the Caspian sea across what is now eastern Iran, Afghanistan and Pakistan; in their coinage Lahore figures as a mint-town, the 'seat of the sovereignty', in the tenth and eleventh centuries. It seems to have been first the headquarters of their Indian military command, becoming later the seat of the governor of their Indian province. Lahore passed to the Ghorid princes on its conquest by Shihabuddin Muhammad Ghuri in 1186, and thence to their deputies, the so-called Slave Kings, who established Islam as a settled power on Indian soil and, becoming independent in the thirteenth century, laid the foundations of what became the Delhi Sultanate.

The centre of power shifted to Delhi, but Lahore remained the seat of a strong provincial governor, the key to the rich grainlands of the Punjab and strong through its position on the high road from Afghan country to the new Indian capital. This strength could at times be a disadvantage, for Lahore was a tempting prey on the natural route for any invasion, and it can have been no unimportant city which was sacked by the Mongols, the forebears of those who later were to contribute most to

Detail of the exterior façade of Jahangir's tomb; the wine-flagon is a recurrent theme in this inlaid sandstone design

OPPOSITE: A corner minaret of Jahangir's tomb chamber

The Masti Gate on the east wall of the fort, built by Akbar in 1566. The tall battlements and hooded machicolations appear nowhere else in the fort

Carved bracket supporting the eave-stone in Jahangir's quadrangle

its greatness, the Mughals. The contemporary historian tells us that in December, 1241 when these Mongols took Lahore by storm they fought in the streets, annihilated the citizens, and razed the city walls to the ground. But we may suspect that many of the citizens had merely removed themselves to a place of safety, for although references in the next few years are vague the city does seem to have had sufficient resilience to become again a place of some prestige even before its restoration by the Delhi sultan Balban in 1270. It regained its position and power gradually, but the plundering raids by the Mongols and by the local Khokars continued, by far the most severe of which was the devastation wrought by Timur in early 1399; this once more left Lahore desolate, for we read of Mubarak Shah's order in 1421 to replace the walls which Timur destroyed by a mud-brick fort in order to form a stronghold against a refractory Khokar.

Little can have been done to Lahore in the troubled times which ensued, although its position still gave it some importance, and we know that it was plundered by the first Indian Mughal emperor, Babur, in 1524. However, Babur did not stay, and his son Humayun, in both his regnal periods, was occupied at Delhi. The third emperor, the great Akbar (1556–1605, almost exactly contemporary with Elizabeth I of England), first turned his attention to Agra, where he remodelled the old Lodi fort as the first of the great Mughal fortress-palaces. But while Agra was still in building he set about according similar treatment to Lahore, doubtless with a view to showing the strength of the Mughal power in the most populous and fertile regions of his young empire. Thus Lahore regained much of its former glory, and Akbar's biographer Abu'l-Fazl describes it as a 'grand resort of people of all nations'. He rebuilt the city walls, which with their gates have now almost vanished, and rebuilt the citadel, with which we are principally concerned here, on the northern wall of the city. Excavations in the last decade have confirmed that the mound on which the fort stands is an accumulation of cultural layers extending at least to Ghaznavid times.

Akbar's fort was rectangular, about 1400 feet from east to west and 1120 feet from north to south. The existing east and south walls, and the inner wall on the north, all remain from his time, and the fine but neglected eastern gate is dated 1566; this is a severely functional creation, but not without an eye to beauty in the disposition of its blind arches. It owes its present name, Masti (a corruption of *masjidi*), to the mosque (*masjid*) of Maryam Zamani some hundred yards outside to the east, the earliest remaining mosque in the city (1614), with well preserved fresco painting and cut-plaster work. Of the interior buildings of the fort there is now little to show of what may conveniently be considered as a first phase, including Akbar's buildings and the earlier additions of his son Jahangir, but what remains is good and typical. The northern quadrangle, to which Jahangir's name is now attached (he did indeed complete it in 1618) shows a surrounding cloister built in the trabeate (beam-and-bracket) style, carved and sculptured in red sandstone, with rich columns and

The 'picture wall' below the Shah Burj; the animal scenes reflect
Jahangir's love of nature, and are reminiscent of contemporary
miniatures, especially those of the painter Mansur

A view from outside the fort
on the north, looking over the
outer wall of Sikh
workmanship to the inner
'picture wall'

Shahjahan's 'reign of marble'

The Diwan-i Khass (Hall of Special Audience), one of the most restrained examples in Shahjahan's 'reign of marble'. Rings below the eaves were used to support awnings and canopies in the hot weather

The Pearl Mosque, which depends for effect on pure white marble, relieved only by the coloured dado which replaces the parapet, the carved pilasters flanking the central bay, and the stringcourse carving on the plinth of the mosque floor

OPPOSITE: Interior of the Pearl Mosque, showing the single prayer-niche (*mihrab*), the steps used as a pulpit (*minbar*), and the spaces marked out on the floor in black marble for each worshipper

A general view of Lahore Fort from a minaret of the Badshahi Mosque, showing the courtyard and east gate of the mosque with the Alamgiri Gate beyond

elaborate brackets ornamented with animal sculpture supporting the eaves.

The second phase of building, under Jahangir and Shahjahan in the seventeenth century, is manifested by Lahore fort at its zenith. The Diwan-i Amm (Hall of General Audience), an open hall of forty columns in the southern quadrangle, was an early construction of this period, although the present structure is a rather crude reconstruction from the earliest British occupation in 1846 after Sikh bombardment had destroyed the original building. Happily this did not damage the great picture wall begun by Jahangir and completed by Shahjahan, running from the north-west (Shah Burj) gate along the outside of the northern (inner) wall, its blind arches filled with floral and geometrical designs and its intervening square and oblong panels with hunting scenes, polo scenes, elephant and camel fights, and a variety of human figures from monarch to menial in the characteristic costumes of the time, all worked out in encaustic tile mosaic

OPPOSITE: The Alamgiri Gate built by Aurangzeb to replace Akbar's earlier gate in the western wall, on the Royal Way between the fort and the Badshahi Mosque

in colours which are still fresh and brilliant. This technique is also a feature of Wazir Khan's Mosque.

Different decorative techniques appear in the Shish Mahal (Palace of Glass), built for his empress in 1632 by Shahjahan, though restored by the Sikhs. It has a fine marble dado, carved marble screens, stucco tracery, *pietra dura* (inlaid floral patterns in semi-precious stones on a marble background) especially in the spandrels of the arches of the multicusped arcade, and the mosaic work in convex mirror glass (the so-called 'Aleppo glass') which gives the building its name. Also notable is the elegant marble pavilion called Bangla (bungalow) or Naulakha, built by Shahjahan at the same time as the Shish Mahal, with delicate and costly *pietra dura* work; the curved cornice, derived from the characteristic roof shape of Bengal, became a popular fancy of Mughal building of the mid-seventeenth century. The upper parts of its walls are an inferior imitation of the Sikh period, as are the painting and the glass work.

Shahjahan's building has been characterized as 'the reign of marble'. Some have thought that the predilection for marble has led to vulgarity, and the charge is not entirely groundless taking Mughal work as a whole. However, the graceful Diwan-i Khass (Hall of Special Audience) is restrained and refined; the design of the *pietra dura* of the parapet derives from the pattern of battlements, and is one which has persisted from at least the Lodi period. Of the same time, 1645, is the exquisite Moti Masjid (Pearl Mosque), built entirely of pearly white marble with most restrained decoration. This is the earliest of the three Pearl mosques (the others are at Agra and Delhi forts) built in Mughal palaces. The domes owe their bulbous appearance to the *cavetto* moulding which crowns the drum of each.

The third phase of the building of Lahore fort is represented by the emperor Aurangzeb's additions, by far the best of which is the gate connecting the fort to the Hazuri Bagh (the central courtyard was originally a caravanserai) beyond which is Aurangzeb's great Badshahi (Imperial) Mosque, and by the additions made later by the Sikhs. The mosque, although not part of the fort, was planned in relation to it, and its domes and minarets dominate the north-west corner of Lahore city. In architectural features it follows the general pattern of the Mughal mosques at Agra and Delhi, but lacks their vitality. From a minaret one can look towards the fort over the Hazuri Bagh, with its central *baradari* built in 1818 by Ranjit Singh with material pilfered from other Mughal buildings at Lahore, and see in the near corner the tomb of Sir Muhammad Iqbal, poet and philosopher, erected in 1951. The Alamgiri Gate, on the fort side of the quadrangle, was built by Aurangzeb in 1673, replacing Akbar's western gate, with imposing fluted flanking towers with lotus petals at their base and crowned with kiosks of a Hindu type.

In addition to some Sikh work within the fort, the exterior northern wall should also be mentioned. This was added in the time of Ranjit Singh (1799–1839) after a northward shift in the course of the river Ravi which formerly ran close to the northern

OPPOSITE: Detail of the interior of the Shish Mahal (Palace of Glass), showing the mosaic work in mirror-glass which gives the building its name

The interior of the Shish Mahal, with the pierced marble screen of geometrical and floral patterns in the background

Looking through the arcade of the Shish Mahal, with its *pietra dura* work on the arches, towards the Naulakha

The emperor Jahangir and his consort Nur Jahan, who shared with him the burden of government. Their tombs stand close together outside the city

wall of the fort. Some minor buildings were added in the Sikh period, and the British military occupation saw the free adaptation and misuse of many buildings and a mushroom growth of barrack-rooms, huts, sheds and hovels, now happily removed. The Department of Archaeology of the Government of Pakistan, sensible of the value of the fort in the culture of Islam in the Punjab, spares no effort in its preservation and restoration.

One cannot speak of Lahore's greatness without some reference to the fine works of art which lie outside the fort. The exquisite mosque of Wazir Khan (1634), in the south-east of the city, deserves its own place in this book, but almost equally fine mosaic tile work is still to be found in the Chauburji Gate (to a vanished garden) on the Multan Road, of 1646; the Gulabi Bagh (Rose Garden) Gate of 1655, on the Grand Trunk Road towards the Shalamar gardens, with superb tile calligraphy; the tomb of Dai Anga behind this gate, 1671; and the tall square tower-like Sarvwala maqbara (Cypress Tomb) of the mid-eighteenth century standing in the fields behind it, which has the unusual feature of a grave chamber some 15 feet above ground.

Perhaps the best known of the Mughal monuments of Lahore is the Shalamar garden of 1642, an imitation of the original Shalamar gardens of Kashmir, lying to the east of the city. This has three large terraces at different levels (the often repeated statement that there were originally seven terraces has no support in the contemporary history written under Shahjahan's orders) with canals, tanks, terraces, pavilions and summer-houses, fountains and cascades in white marble, all set in a vast garden of flowering and sweet-scented plants; the Dutch ambassador Ketelaar, who visited Lahore in 1711, tells us that no less than 128 gardeners were employed in its upkeep.

To the north-west of Lahore, on the far side of the Ravi, lie the tombs of Jahangir, his consort Nur Jahan, and her brother Asaf Khan. The two last are in disrepair, but that of the emperor, although it suffered somewhat at the hands of the Sikhs at the end of the eighteenth century, is still one of the gems of Mughal architecture. Completed after ten years in building by Shahjahan in about 1637, it is a long single-storey building with four ornate corner minarets, standing in the midst of a large symmetrical garden of sixteen square flower-beds. The exterior walls, and the lowest stage of the minarets, are of red Mathura sandstone, with designs in white and black marble; the wine-flagon appears prominently in the decorative scheme along with geometrical motifs. The three intermediate stages of the five-storeyed minarets carry zigzag patterns in white and yellow marble, separated by bracketed balconies, and the top stages consist of marble kiosks. The flat roof originally carried a cenotaph open to the sky (or perhaps covered by a canopy, as was Akbar's tomb at Sikandra; but the structural evidence is not clear). On the ground floor immediately below the cenotaph is the true grave, with its delicate *pietra dura* work in floral designs, and, in consummately excellent calligraphy, the nine and ninety Names of God.

J. BURTON-PAGE

Western prayer-hall of the Badshahi Mosque, erected in
1673/74 by Aurangzeb's Master of Ordnance. The façade is in red
sandstone with marble inlay, the bulbous domes of white marble

93

WAZIR KHAN'S MOSQUE

A lavishly decorated mosque of the middle Mughal period which displays the finest mosaic tile-work and painted cut-plaster in the whole of the subcontinent

The great buildings of Lahore Fort are on the whole constructed in material not truly typical of the Punjab, for in this region building stone is rare, and when materials are imported – sandstone from Mathura, marble mostly from Makrana in Rajasthan – they are used in what is an imported style, the mode of the imperial Delhi and Agra. The regional style of the Punjab is essentially in baked brick and wood, with an exterior facing of coloured glazed tile, or of stucco, in the larger and more important buildings. For the source of the glazed tile decoration which is so prominent a feature of the buildings of Lahore, and is at its magnificent best in Wazir Khan's Mosque, we must look beyond the boundaries of Hindustan to the neighbouring dominion of Iran, where under the Safavid dynasty, especially under the great Shah Abbas in his capital of Isfahan, brilliance in mural decoration had attained its zenith.

True, glazed faience had been known in northern India at least a century earlier, in the early Sayyid and Lodi tombs at Delhi in the fifteenth century, persisting as an embellishment in early Mughal times; it was also known in Multan and in Sind from much earlier. But in north India the tile-work was little more than an occasional course of contrasting bright colour, in Sind and Multan a complete veneer of the exposed surfaces through being applied to one or more faces of the building brick itself. In Lahore, however, the tile-work is neither a mere protecting glaze nor simply an addition to other decoration: it is the principal and autonomous medium of decoration. Some have objected that undue attention to this form of embellishment has led to the ornament dominating and controlling the structure rather than being subordinate to it, and this criticism is not unjustified in the case of some buildings. But Wazir Khan's Mosque is gloriously beyond such cavilling; its composition could stand as a fine example of the architect's art even if its splendid tiles were effaced or removed.

Wazir Khan was the title given to a former royal physician named (Hakim) 'Ilmuddin Ansari, who had become a governor

Detail of the tile calligraphy on the façade of the entrance portal

OPPOSITE: The entrance portal on the east wall, with its rich display of mosaic tiling

95

of the Punjab early in Shahjahan's reign; his time, the second quarter of the seventeenth century, was one of peace and prosperity. The mosque which bears his name, set among the busy bazaars in the south-east corner of Lahore city, was founded in 1634 on a site said to be that of the tomb of a saint of the Ghaznavid period. It is essentially an open rectangular building with a large central open court, its main gateway towering on the eastern enclosure wall, a western sanctuary, domed, with five bays, and a tall octagonal minaret at each corner. The gateway in the eastern wall is a gem in itself, its surfaces relieved by two flanking oriel windows carried on richly carved brackets, with their roofs supported by pillars and brackets Hindu in style. The angles carry elegant pilasters with a zigzag ornament, and the surface is broken up into panels into which the tile mosaic is set; the Muslim creed – 'There is no god but God, and Muhammad is the Prophet of God' – is carried in tile calligraphy over the tall central arch. Further colour and life are constantly provided by the stream of humanity coming and going through the portal, for the mosque is a focal point of the religious life of this corner of the city.

The wall itself is of interest. There is no tile decoration here, and the plainer ornament – the brick capping in a design recalling battlements, and a simple string-course dividing the upper blind arches from the lower arched bays – is an admirable foil to the richness of the gateway. The lower arches were originally occupied by traders who would use them as booths for their wares, and would pay for them some rent which would be used towards the upkeep of the mosque.

Within the courtyard the eye is drawn to the symmetrical features of the building no less than to the profusion of colour. The north and south arcades each have a taller central hall; in

The south-east minaret from within the courtyard, showing the commonest floral designs

The geometrical band below the gallery of the minaret reflects the Ghaznavid tradition

The base of the north-west minaret, showing the delicate detail of floral and geometrical design in tile mosaic

The western sanctuary, with
its pylon-like central bay and
false arch with shallow
stalactite pendentives

A mosque-school in session
within the northern bay of the
western sanctuary

97

The separate nature of each petal, stem and leaf is evident in this mosaic tile-work from the courtyard. The damaged parts reveal the thinness of the coat of glaze

The interior of one of the domes in the western sanctuary, fresco painting on cut-plaster, achieving more delicate shading than is possible in tile-work

the eastern wall the corresponding feature is provided by the back of the great gateway. The sanctuary on the west has the central of the five bays similarly raised high above the level of the others, the apex of its great arch some 30 feet above the courtyard, double the height of the recessed inner arch, and with its pylon-like frame obscuring the dome behind it; there are five domes above the sanctuary, of the shallow pitch characteristic of the Mughals' predecessors, the Lodis. The central bay is the focus of the ritual of prayer, although all the bays are in use at the normal official hours of prayer. When there is less demand on them from worshippers, they are put to use in another traditional way: out come the desks, the children gather, and the mosque school is in session. To give further life to the scene there are always the pigeons.

The four great minarets, set slightly in from each corner, tower over the courtyard and the neighbouring bazaars, and the muezzin's call to prayer echoes from one of the balconies at the canonical hours. They stand on tall square bases, the height of the sanctuary façade; each base has a balcony atop, with a parapet supported by paired carved brackets and a door leading to the staircase of the minaret. Recessed panels on all sides of the minarets are filled with mosaic tiles, and the tile decoration is cunningly carried up on the underside of the curved support of the gallery at the top of each minaret, which in turn supports an eight-pillared kiosk.

We have repeatedly mentioned the mosaic tile of this mosque, and must now describe its nature and the underlying technique in greater detail. Firstly, it is not quite a 'mosaic' in the Roman sense, built up of tesserae of similar shape which are worked into a multicoloured pattern, but rather a means of working out a pattern in specially cut shapes of tile. Thus, in a floral design petals, leaves, stems, flower-centres and the shapes of the background are all separately made from designs prepared beforehand on the drawing-board; in a calligraphic design the shapes of the letters and the background are similarly cut out: each fragment is of one colour only. The other common form of tile decoration, in which the patterns are carried from one tile to another and each tile is of many colours and of a uniform shape, although well known in Iran and in Sind and Multan, occurs in Lahore in only one building, the tomb of Asaf Khan, Jahangir's brother-in-law.

In producing tiles of this nature the first step is the production of a *frit*, an easily fusible glass, by mixing powdered silicaceous stone, soda and metallic oxides, and firing the mixture. Some of this frit is then powdered and mixed with lime and sand to form the base of the tile; this base then receives a thin lining coat of lime and powdered frit suspended in a thick rice-water paste. Finally the coloured glass frit alone, ground finely and suspended in rice-water or thin gum, is painted over the lining coat, smoothed and polished when dry, and the whole may then be further fixed by light firing. The resulting tiles are then cut down to the precise shapes dictated by the pattern, and are then

OPPOSITE: Detail of the minaret, showing the decoration below the gallery: the *chenar* (Asiatic plane) tree on the flat panels and the cypress on the angles

ready to be fixed to the prepared surface. This process is, of course, repeated for each colour required.

The result is a kaleidoscope of colour, with yellow, orange, green, the blues and white predominating. The lighter colours tend to be not pure colours in terms of the spectrum, but mixed with some measure of white ('unsaturated shades'); the darker colours are used more sparingly, in borders and in tile calligraphy. The designs are for the most part floral. Some are naturalistic flowering trees and herbs – irises are a favourite subject – almost filling their panel; others are more formal – vases or ewers filled with sprays of flowers – while some areas, such as the spandrels of the arches, are filled with a more conventionalized floral arabesque. Geometrical designs are favoured for borders and for some panels, based on the square, octagon and hexagon. The *chenar* tree, the Asiatic Plane with its broad three-lobed leaves, a favourite device elsewhere in Mughal art, appears here high on the minarets; and this mosque sees for the first time, on the angle panels below the galleries of the minarets, the dark green cypress which was to become a popular device in later Lahore buildings.

Tile-work of this sort – skilled, exacting and time-consuming work on the part of master-craftsmen – was necessarily expensive. It was therefore used most where it could not only decorate but also protect. (The thinness of this protective coat of glaze can now be clearly appreciated from those places where the top glazed layer has fallen away.) But interior surfaces, not so exposed to the elements, did not need this protection, and a less costly form of decoration was used, fresco paint on cut-plaster. Cut-plaster is sufficiently familiar within the Muslim world, and eighth-century examples in Syria seem to indicate that its ultimate origin is Sassanian; its spread through Islam is attested by Ibn Khaldun writing of the building of the Alhambra, who tells us that the work there was executed by iron tools in the still wet plaster. In India this technique was combined with the skill of the fresco-painter. The wet plaster surface is marked out with a dry-point or burin to show the main outlines of the geometrical or floral pattern, and the water-colour or gouache paint is next applied, following the lines of the cutting but not, in the finer details, being confined to them. This technique occurs frequently in Lahore – examples of it in Maryam Zamari's Mosque outside the east gate of the fort are particularly fine – and good specimens of it grace Wazir Khan's Mosque also, where it adds rich colour in geometric and floral designs, with some fine pieces of calligraphy, to the interiors of the rooms in the north and south walls, and within the domes and below the soffits of the arches in the western sanctuary.

This mosque is perhaps the finest example in the subcontinent of the craftsman's skill lovingly worked out to the glory of God. The observer is surrounded by delicate and refined artistic beauty, but he cannot fail to be impressed, enlivened, and even awed, by the compulsion of a great monument to a great faith.

J. BURTON-PAGE

The interior of the mosque, with a *mihrab* on the right

OPPOSITE: The intertwined vine and cypress pattern of these fresco designs on cut-plaster inside the western sanctuary is a Lahore variation of an earlier Islamic decorative tradition

India

AJANTA

Rock-cut Buddhist monasteries set in a wild, remote glen of Central India and enriched by an unsurpassed display of painted walls and ceilings

The young British officers who in 1819 peered through the bushes on the northern side of the steep and tangled ravine of Ajanta saw an astonishing sight. The opposite cliff, extending in a crescent curve, was honeycombed with openings of diverse but man-made shapes, some fronted by pillars, others by the gabled ends of rock-cut halls. Even today the scene is wild enough. The noise of parrots and other birds is constantly in the air, monkeys lumber about among the caves and trees, deer graze in the vicinity, jackals whine as the days darken, and those who know the locality well speak of the occasional advent of wolf, black bear, leopard and tiger. Not least among the natural attractions, a useful stream cascades along the bottom of the valley.

The caves, twenty-nine of them, were carved out as monasteries and prayer-halls or temples for Buddhist monks, of whom there must from time to time have been not less than two hundred, excluding artisans. They represented successively the two main observances of Buddhism: the Hinayana or Lesser Vehicle of Salvation, and the Mahayana or Greater Vehicle. Details do not here matter, but the broad distinction was briefly this: Hinayana Buddhism was primarily a moral philosophy not altogether dissimilar from the Stoicism of the West, whereas Mahayana Buddhism was a religion. In the former the Buddha was an inspired teacher who preached the Middle Path between indulgence and asceticism, seeking an ultimate deliverance from accumulated sin in supreme detachment, *nirvana*. The Buddha was not a god, and the earlier Buddhism was a way of life, not a religion. By a process of evolution, however, natural to a country where reverence for the teacher is deep-seated, the Buddha gradually assumed the stature of a god to whom prayer might properly be offered, and this process received formal recognition in or about the second century AD, when the Mahayana persuasion became, at any rate for a time, the dominant mode.

For our present purpose, the outstanding difference between the two types of Buddhism was that during the prevalence of the Hinayana teaching the Buddha himself was never represented

Sculptures from the side shrines of the Buddhist monastery (*vihara*) no. 2, from a set of drawings (*c* 1846–50) by Major Robert Gill

Interior of *vihara* no. 16, sixth century AD, from James Fergusson, *Illustrations of the Rock-cut Temples of India* (1845)

OPPOSITE: Porch of the rock-cut temple (*chaitya*) no. 19, with its repeated figures of the Buddha

103

in art. His presence might be symbolized by a chair, a footprint, an umbrella, a riderless horse. About this symbol crowded in tumultuous masses the other participants in the scene; but there was no central commanding figure. In Mahayana Buddhism, on the other hand, the figure of the divine Buddha controls the assembly and is the focus of the composition. Both iconographically and aesthetically, the change was revolutionary.

At Ajanta the 'structures' fall into two corresponding series, with an intervening gap of some four centuries. They have been numbered from west to east: the earliest, nos. 8–10 and 12–13, towards the middle of the crescent, are of the aniconic Hinayana creed and are dated roughly to the second and first centuries BC or a little later. Of the second or Mahayana group, nos. 6–7 and 11 are of AD 450–500, nos. 14–20 are of about AD 500–550, and nos. 1–5 and 21–29 are of AD 550–650. Most, if not all, were therefore complete when the famous Chinese Buddhist traveller Hiuen Tsang came this way (as he seems to have done) about AD 640. The word 'complete' includes the internal paintings which hold a place of high distinction in the history of pictorial art.

First, the rock-cut 'architecture'. This was carved out of the native trap-rock by pickaxe and chisel, and was modelled for

ABOVE: Entrance to *chaitya* no. 19, about AD 550

BELOW: General view of the wild setting of the Buddhist monasteries

the most part on timber prototypes, sometimes (particularly in the earlier examples) with the addition of actual timber features. The general principles of rock-cut architecture were undoubtedly derived by the Indian Buddhists of the third century BC from an established practice in Persia and Media, where rock-cut 'structures' go back at least to the seventh century. This borrowing was in fact merely one of several which characterized the development of thought and expression in India during the century following the overthrow of the Achaemenid Empire by Alexander the Great and the consequent dispersal of Persian ideas and craftsmen.

The 'structures' at Ajanta are of two kinds: the prayer-hall or *chaitya*, and the *vihara* or residential hall. The *chaitya*-hall resembles an apsidal (rarely square-ended) basilica without a clerestory; that is, it consists of a nave divided from two aisles by a range of columns which at the inner end follow the apsidal form and there contain the shrine itself, the stupa, on a pedestal. In the Mahayana persuasion this bears a figure of the Buddha as the centre of prayer and ceremony.

An early form of the colonnade simulated a range of plain wooden posts, and of this simple kind are nos. 9 and 10 at Ajanta, probably of the second–first centuries BC. In both, the roofing ribs of the side-aisles are of stone imitating timber, but no. 9 and probably no. 10 originally had wooden ribs applied to the roof of the nave. These were later removed and so left broad rock-surfaces for the sixth-century painters.

The front of the *chaitya*-hall includes a large gable with an ogee outline derived from the bamboo roofing of the wooden prototype. Within the gable a window might have a timber lattice, and other timbers might be used for a gallery and other minor fittings, sometimes above a pillared portico. At first, as in Ajanta no. 9, the curves of the gable were bold and simple, and the whole pattern was near to the wooden model. Later, the scheme became increasingly elaborate and non-functional; the gable-opening tended to approach a circle, and its outer ogee frame developed 'ears' and other extravagances. Of the two Mahayana *chaityas* at Ajanta the more satisfactory, both in general proportion and in the balanced wealth of its decoration, is the earlier and smaller, no. 19, of about AD 550.

This ripe example of the Buddhist temple was approached through a balustraded forecourt with elaborately carved flanks, each containing a pillared side-room or chapel, the pillars capped by bowls overflowing with fruit and flowers in the lush Gupta manner. Alongside, the rock is enriched by a multitude of large and small relief-figures of the Buddha and worshippers. On the inner side of the court is the single entry to the prayer-hall, with a porch held by two free-standing and two attached columns, fluted and enriched by patterned bands. The capitals are also vertically fluted, derived at long remove from Darius's lotus-capitals at Persepolis but now more nearly resembling the *amalaka* or melon capping of a 'Northern' temple such as those at Bhubaneswar. The roof of the porch rises in two stages, each

The main shrine or stupa of *chaitya* no. 19

Part of the roof of *chaitya* no. 19, with stone ribs imitating timber and intervening painted Buddhas

decorated with lines of small *chaitya*-gables, internally circular and framing tiny heads. The flat top of the roof is continued laterally along the main face of the 'building' to form a minstrels' gallery.

Behind and above this gallery is the open gable of the *chaitya*, of horseshoe form internally and an ogee curve externally, with lateral 'ears'. The opening was perhaps originally barred by a timber grill. The faces of the rock flanking the gable are carved with Buddhas, pilasters, and horizontal bands, again bearing small decorative gables enclosing heads. The figures in relief often proclaim mass-production, but the general effect of the façade is of an elegance redeemed from frailty by a sufficiency of strongly marked 'structural' features.

In mere footage the interior is small; its length is scarcely more than 45 feet. But it gives a sense of grandeur far in excess of its size. On each side a line of ornate pillars, 11 feet high, upholds a panelled frieze covered with framed figures of the standing or seated Buddha, and the pillars themselves rise from deep shadow near the floor into the dramatic lighting which penetrates through the gable-opening. In the centre, where the colonnades converge to form the closing apse, the light falls on the main dome of the double-domed stupa or shrine, which is cut away in the form of a pillared niche to contain the principal standing Buddha. His head and body are also fully lighted, his feet remain in the shadow. Above the dome are three diminishing ritual umbrellas and a crowning vase which vanish again into darkness immediately under the roof. The whole scene is astonishingly successful theatre; rich and balanced, with a mystique apt to its function.

In more detail, the columns, square on plan below and circular above, are successively plain and fluted vertically or diagonally, with ornate bands and developed, almost vestigial Persepolitan capitals. Above these are spreading brackets, likewise derived remotely from Persian prototypes but each with a central Buddha and lively supporting figures, human and animal. Higher again, the strongly partitioned panels or metopes of the frieze might, by their uncertain vertical relationship with the colonnade beneath, offend an eye trained in the Graeco-Roman tradition but, catching the last of the daylight, form a satisfactorily emphatic base-line for the dark and lofty roof, with its imitative stone ribs and shadowy painted Buddhas.

The *viharas* or residential quarters are relatively numerous and are variations on the theme of a central court or hall surrounded on three sides by cells for the monks, with a colonnaded entrance on the fourth. Free-standing timber structures were again the basic model, but with the passage of time the rock-cutters moved into a tradition of their own, increasingly remote from these prototypes. In the Mahayana phase of the fifth–seventh centuries the work reached an increasing elaboration, culminating in no. 1 of about AD 500. This has externally an ornate verandah (and formerly a porch) sustained by columns similar to those of *chaitya* no. 19, with capitals and friezes

Front colonnade (porch missing) of the richly carved and painted *vihara* no. 1 (about AD 500)

The large relief of the preaching Buddha in the shrine of *vihara* no. 1

Vihara no. 1: rock-cut high relief showing the Buddha flanked by figures
of the Hindu god Indra and preaching the sermon in the deer-park at Sarnath

Painting in *vihara* no. 17, showing part of a crowd receiving alms in one of the Buddha stories (probably the Visvantara *jataka*)

One of the masterpieces of Indian painting: a Bodhisattva or probationary Buddha from *vihara* no. 1

enriched by small exquisitely cut figure-groups. Within is a hall 65 feet square containing a surrounding aisle with a colonnade of twenty pillars. Around the hall are the cells, with a central chapel at the back containing a seated Buddha flanked by figures of Indra. The whole interior, walls and ceiling, was elaborately painted.

The paintings here and in others of the Ajanta 'caves' are among the glories of Indian art. A surprising quantity of them has survived alike centuries of neglect and a century of miscellaneous conservation. They reached their apogee in the late fifth and sixth centuries, particularly in the crowded scenes illustrating the stories (*jatakas*) which gathered round the previous incarnations of the Buddha. These crowds, at first sight tumultuous and chaotic, are in fact constructed with as much care and zest from individual figures and groups as were Frith's documentary railway-stations or racecourses fourteen centuries later, and at a different level give the spectator something of the same simple and happy sense of discovery. Two segments from a long scene painted on the back wall of the verandah of *vihara* no. 17, dated epigraphically to the neighbourhood of AD 500, are here illustrated as typical.

The first (*left*), towards the left of the composition, shows petitioners for gifts from the king (off left, not shown in the illustration) who was the father of the proto-Buddha, the young prince Visvantara. The petitioners include, on the left, a brownskinned Brahman, who is enumerating his claims on the fingers of his left hand. Behind him is a dark-skinned guard with a whip,[1] to keep the crowd in order. Behind him in turn is an ascetic with outstretched hand; an Indian writer observes that 'his features are regular, but the general expression of the face betrays a cunning heart'. He is thought to be the avaricious Brahman Jujaka, to whom Visvantara had given, as an act of charity, his son and daughter who, here and on the left of the next section (not reproduced), are shown with unkempt hair, indicating hardship, but also dignified by umbrellas which betoken high rank. Further to the right (again not reproduced) are two chariot-horses, which Visvantara, with his fairy-tale generosity, had given also to the Brahmans; and a servant is displaying a necklace, towards which (since generosity is in the air) a one-eyed holy man, a Parthian with conical hat, and a woman with an infant across her hip, are stretching covetous hands. Near the door, an Amazon with scimitar and large curved shield is on guard.

The second illustration (*right*) is an extension of the scene. It appears to represent the swarthy figure of Visvantara himself under a Chinese-looking umbrella held by a woman, with three other elegant women about him. Further to the right, also under an umbrella, is his princess, confronted by a pale-skinned beggar holding a crooked staff. In one way and another, the whole panorama commemorates both the virtue of extravagant generosity on a princely level and the colourful diversity of mature Ajanta painting.

MORTIMER WHEELER

OPPOSITE: Painting in *vihara* no. 17, probably showing the young prince Visvantara (under an umbrella, left) with his princess (under the central umbrella) and attendants

BHUBANESWAR

*A town of many temples, displaying in rich
variety the architecture and sculpture of
north-eastern India through four centuries*

Bhubaneswar, in Orissa on the east side of India, is today a
burgeoning provincial capital and its new developments, however reticent, are inevitably regretted by sentimentalists who
knew the place in days gone by. The memory-picture is a vivid
one. Around the great tank which forms the centrepiece of the
site clustered the small teeming town on its rich, deep-red soil.
The horizon from any point was broken by the towers of some
of the thirty-five temples which give the place its special
character; and though the surrounding landscape was itself of
no great consequence, the scene as a whole and in detail was
one of astonishing beauty. Something of that beauty still lingers.

Amidst the flat lands on the outskirts of the town the passer-by
can observe the high earthen ramparts which represent its first
surviving phase. These are the vestiges of a remarkable fortified
township, square on plan with sides three-quarters of a mile in
length and with two monumental gateways placed symmetrically in each of them. The street-plan, though not yet verified,
must have been of a correspondingly symmetrical kind unusual
in India between the time of the Indus civilization before 2000
BC and that of the Indo-Greeks after 200 BC. Shishupalgarh, as
the Bhubaneswar site is known, has been ascribed by archaeology
to the third century BC and may more narrowly be attributed
with tolerable certainty to the Mauryan emperor Ashoka after
his famous victory over the Kalingas of these parts about 260 BC.
The controlled and rational plan would be an appropriate
reflection of one of the most orderly, interested and far-ranging
minds that India has produced.

But it was not until nearly a thousand years later that the
Kalingas themselves emerged as a culturally creative folk in
their own right. Towards the end of the eighth century AD they
began to find expression for religious and artistic ideas of considerable originality; more particularly in the famous temple-
architecture of which Bhubaneswar retains the most ample
surviving illustration. This architecture belongs to a general
category which has been labelled the 'Northern' or 'Indo-
Aryan' style. The latter is an archaic term with no place in

The Vaital Deul (about AD 850), a temple
combining Northern and Dravidian (Southern)
characteristics, lithographed by T. C. Dibdin
from a sketch by James Fergusson in *Picturesque
Illustrations of Ancient Architecture in Hindostan* (1847)

OPPOSITE: The Mukteswara temple (about AD 975), a strong but
somewhat 'top-heavy' example of the earlier Orissan style

A splendid example of early Orissan carving, forming the grill of a stone window on the Parasrameswar temple (late eighth century). The figures represent dancers and musicians in the style of a vigorous folk-art

modern thinking; it was originally devised to distinguish the style from the 'Dravidian' or 'non-Aryan' mode of Southern India, at a time when linguistic designations were loosely used in a variety of inappropriate contexts. The term 'Northern' on the other hand indicates with sufficient accuracy the distribution of the style as a whole, always with the proviso that within the vast expanse of northern and central India its local variations have a primary importance.

Among these local variations or schools of the Northern style, that of the Kalingas of Orissa, as represented abundantly at Bhubaneswar, is outstanding. Its principal features are as follows.

The shrine or *deul* is internally a plain (rarely decorated) square cell covered by a tower or spire or *shikara*. On occasion it stood alone, but in surviving examples at Bhubaneswar it was fronted, originally or later, by a square hall known as the *jagamohan*, to which the pious might bring offerings. Other buildings might be added in axial alignment: successively a *nat-mandir* or dancing-hall and a *bhog-mandir* or outer hall of offerings. All these adjuncts were of a single storey and normally had pyramidal corbelled roofs of varying height, sometimes with four internal piers to distribute the heavy weight. The *shikara* was the most lavishly ornate member of the complex. To the height of the walls of the *jagamohan* it was perpendicular, but above that level it inclined increasingly inward to a sharp shoulder where it was crowned by a fluted disc or 'melon', the *amla* or *amalaka*, beneath a *kalasa* or finial in the shape of a vase. The *amla* may have derived something ultimately from the vertically fluted Indo-Persian lotus-capital, but aesthetically its function was, by a combination of vertical and horizontal lines to form a satisfying cap to the strongly vertical decoration of the main body of the tower. The task was not an easy one. The more developed Bhubaneswar *shikaras* are bold and rebellious extravaganzas which depend for their success upon the firm, intelligent and imaginative handling of a multitude of detail.

The Bhubaneswar school is represented here mainly by three of its more mature creations, dating from the tenth and eleventh centuries. The oldest of the three, the small temple of Mukteswara, was built about AD 975 and has rightly been described as a gem of its kind. It lies on the outskirts of the old town, in an enclosure entered through a rich and remarkable gateway or *torana*. This is flanked by polygonal columns on square bases with decorative projections; the upper parts of the shafts are adorned with beaded swags, and the elaborate capitals incorporate elements of the *amla*. The arch itself, semi-circular below and segmental above, retains a faint reminiscence of the *chaitya* gables of classical Buddhist architecture, and the theme is emphasized by three small motifs – one at the summit, the others at the sides – based also on the *chaitya*. From each of the small gables a human face looks out; and reclining on the lateral curves of the arch are two leisurely, lovely and provocative female figures clad only in jewellery, no doubt in theory

Entrance-archway to the Mukteswara temple, built about
AD 975. The rich carving is framed by strong marginal lines

One of the two sumptuous female figures
flanking the arch of the entrance to the Mukteswara
temple. Below is a carving based upon the *chaitya*
gable, framing a human head

dvarpalas or doorkeepers. Projecting sideways from the haunches
of the arch are the heads of *makaras*, mythical crocodiles. The
whole structure is ornate, original and successful, the abundance
of its ornament firmly contained within its strong outlines.

The temple itself is only 45 feet long, and its tower or *shikara*
is rather less than 35 feet high – a mere baby of its kind. But its
proportions are admirable and it carries lavish decoration with
dignity. It has rounded corners, in which the *amla* element
recurs, and projecting faces, each of which bears a large and
vigorous figure-sculpture in relief. The dominant vertical lines
are tempered but not weakened by a variety of horizontal sub-
divisions, which subtly link up the aspiring character of the
tower with the strong horizontality that marks the staged
pyramidal roof of the adjacent *jagamohan*. The walls of the
jagamohan are lavishly ornamented with pilasters on pot-like
pedestals, and with a diversity of stonework that suggests a
possible origin in the early brickwork of the northern plains.

The second of our examples represents the culmination of the

Decoration on the Mukteswara temple, a good
example of the relatively simple, boldly carved
ornament of the earlier Orissan period

The Lingaraja temple

The great Lingaraja temple (about AD 1000), seen from across the large tank which forms the centre of the town's activities

ABOVE: The high tower or *shikara*, which represents the culmination of the Orissan style. To the right is the hall of offerings and scattered throughout the courtyard are small votive shrines
OPPOSITE: Detail of the tower, with its ornate gable-pattern and succession of small superimposed towers

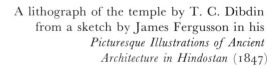

A lithograph of the temple by T. C. Dibdin from a sketch by James Fergusson in his *Picturesque Illustrations of Ancient Architecture in Hindostan* (1847)

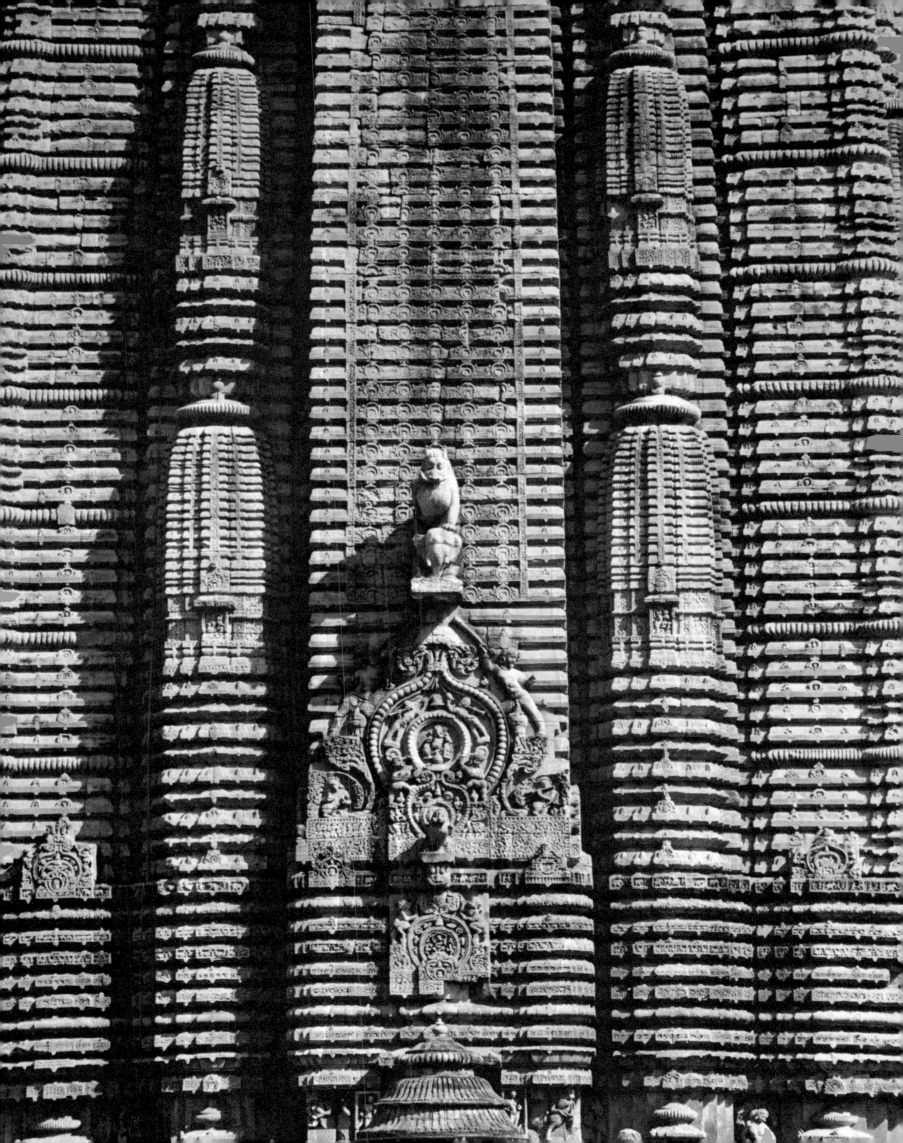

Orissan style. It is the Lingaraja, of which the great tower, more than 125 feet high, looms over the whole town. As though to emphasize this feature from within, the shrine or *deul*, here known as the *Shri Mandir*, has no roof of its own but is carried up within the tower as a gigantic funnel until closed ultimately by the *amla*.

The temple was built about AD 1000 within a large, high-walled quadrangle measuring 520 by 465 feet. This enclosure eventually accommodated a large number of small votive shrines modelled more or less upon the great temple and put there by the faithful much as at the height of the Buddhist period six or seven centuries previously small votive stupas (shrines) had tended to cluster round the main stupa of a Buddhist monastery.

The walls of the famous tower are vertical for one-third of their height, and up to this level are given a distinctive panelled design. Above this point the sides incline gradually and then more sharply inwards, ending in the *amla* and finial bearing the trident of the god Shiva. The upper two-thirds are recessed between rectangular and rounded ribs of which eight consist of superimposed reproductions of the *shikara* itself, forming a sort of vertical bead-reel motif. The strong upright lines are less broken by the pronouncedly horizontal crevices than is the tower of the Mukhteswara, and the whole design has an easy confidence which the earlier building had not quite achieved. The satisfactory effect is that of complete mastery, poised momentarily between phases of anxious effort and excessive facility.

Extending in alignment eastwards from the *shri mandir* are the *jagamohan* and three added halls, all capped by the strongly horizontalized pyramids of their kind, and all seemingly a trifle coarse in detail beside the masterly refinement of the *shikara*. Moreover, the varying height of these annexes produce an uneasy outline and may be thought to interfere with the unity of the group. Nevertheless, the temple as a whole ranks among the great buildings of India.

The third example is the Rajarani temple, which may be ascribed roughly to the twelfth century, perhaps about 1200. Here we have the almost baroque sequel to the Lingaraja, with all the excessive facility to which I have referred. The building was never finished, but the *shikara* is sufficiently complete for judgment. And what we find is this: the design has broken up into massive components which in the aggregate may be thought to give a vegetable rather than a structural semblance to the design. The robust model-*shikaras* of which the tower is largely composed above two ornate friezes of isolated human and animal figures form a chaotic though more or less circular cluster suggesting nothing so much as some gross tropical growth, remote from the restraint and seemliness of the Lingaraja. Moreover, the *shikara* is now completely out of keeping with the simple rigid horizontality of the adjacent *jagamohan*; the concept as a whole is an extravagance which has lost any pretence of unity.

The Rajarani temple (about AD 1200), one of the latest and most ornate of the Bhubaneswar series

Typical carvings at the base of the Rajarani temple

Elsewhere than at Bhubaneswar this baroque development was attended by greater success. In particular at Khajaraho in central India, some 450 miles north-west of Bhubaneswar, another school of Hindu master-builders was at work within a part of the same period (about AD 950–1050) upon a similar project with similar architectural and sculptural skills, but with strikingly variant results. Today, in a small space, about twenty-five temples remain there, from a former total at least three times as large, in a condition of almost uncanny dereliction. Again the great *shikara* with its aspiring lines and often luxuriant detail dominates the scene, while alongside it are ranged halls or *mandapas* with strong horizontal trends as at Bhubaneswar. But here the component parts of the design have been integrated by a variety of cunning devices.

First, the temple, instead of being masked in part by a precinct wall or other buildings, is set proudly upon a high, open platform as a single composition for all to see. Secondly the ancillary halls, perhaps three of them, are graded in a regularly descending sequence in such a manner as to lead continuously up to, and 'support', the main tower. And thirdly, the *shikara* and its halls are closely clasped together by the emphatic horizontal lines of a high and continuous basement-storey and by rich bands of sculpture of a particularly sensuous and exuberant kind which carries the eye easily and uninterruptedly round the endless intricacies of the plan. Of its kind, the resultant *ensemble* is superbly successful. Here was a unity of a sort that in its later phase Bhubaneswar missed. Nevertheless, the total achievement of the Orissan builders and sculptors had for two centuries or more been a very notable one and holds a high place in the history of the world's architecture.

Incidentally, at Bhubaneswar the unfinished state of the Rajarani temple, and particularly of its *jagamohan*, gives it a technical interest which is worthy of passing note. It had been intended that much of the carving should be done after the stones, in a rough condition, had been placed in position. On those of the *jagamohan* some of the designs had been merely outlined, others summarily blocked out. Such was the frequent habit of the Hindu builders; an eloquent illustration of it can be seen in the same province of Orissa, at Mahendragiri in the Ganjan district. Here two similar temples show, on the one hand, the nearly finished product and, on the other, the structure built up in preliminary fashion of great rough blocks upon which, save for the *amla*, the carver has not yet set his hand. Such, too, was the not infrequent habit of the classical Greek architect and sculptor; while 'the Median stone-masons, when making columns, doors, windows or stairs, used to build up an artificial rock of the size and approximate shape required, and carved the wanted object out of that rock' (E. Herzfeld). Whether in sculpture or in architectural detail, this procedure must have given to the carver a continuous and intimate sense of actuality which he might readily have lost, or failed to acquire, in the detachment of the studio.   MORTIMER WHEELER

The Parswanatha temple (about AD 1000), typical of the Khajaraho style, a combination of astonishing richness in detail with a dominant over-all design

OPPOSITE: One of the languid, sensuous female figures (a *yaksha* or an *apsara*) on the tower of the Rajarani temple in the rather self-conscious and fulsome late Orissan style

MADURA AND SRIRANGAM

*The soaring temple-gateways and fantastically exuberant carving of
South India in the sixteenth and seventeenth centuries*

The immense temple-precincts of southern India are liable to disconcert the inexperienced Westerner with their busy medley of the sacred and the profane, ranging from the most mundane chaffering to the most subservient adoration. In Hindu life today, particularly in the Peninsula, divine worship has not been arbitrarily abstracted from the general fabric of living; life is still one. It is easy to forget that there was a time in the Far West, too, when work and worship were organically integrated; when the Londoner, for example, had his public market in the nave of St Paul's cathedral. But it must be three or four centuries since that pioneer 'Puritane-one' marked the end of this sort of thing by hanging his cat on Monday for killing of a mouse on Sunday; and when with our modern cellular outlook we pass through the temple-gate of Madura to find within it a sprawling bazaar between ourselves and the dark recondite sancta, there is perhaps a momentary shock of readjustment.

For the Great Temple is almost a self-contained town within its high four-square boundary wall, some 850 feet from east to west and 730 feet from north to south. Behind the wall lurks a multitude of flat roofs broken here and there by small golden excrescences to mark the holy places. But the whole scene is dominated by the four mighty gate-towers or *gopurams* which loom symmetrically over it, one on each of the four sides. Seven others in descending scale can be observed in the interior; so that the points of ultimate focus, the shrines of the great god Shiva, here known as Sundareswar, and of his consort Minakshi, the 'fish-eyed', are in fact among the least obtrusive moments of the design. The reason for this withdrawal is simple enough. The main shrines were the first elements of the plan and have preserved something of their natal simplicity; only later were the courts and halls and storerooms and gateways assembled about them, each grander or more ostentatious than its predecessor. Dramatically and spiritually the inverted sequence is right. The flamboyant, noisy, semi-secular impact of the towering exterior yields gradually through a prolonged approach to

A pillar in 'Tirumalai's Chaultri' at Madura,
from a set of drawings made about 1810 by a South
Indian artist working for the first Surveyor
General of India, Colin Mackenzie

OPPOSITE: Mounted warrior on the colonnade of the Horse Court
at Srirangam. A vigorous example of the sculptural extravagance
of the late sixteenth century in southern India

the quiet and crepuscular dignity of the godhead in the final lamp-lit cell.

Before we enter the precinct, something more must be said about those gate-towers. They are a feature of the warm South Indian landscape, rich in hills and vegetation, and both their size and their infinite ornament fit them into it with the aptness of natural phenomena. Their plan is oblong, with the long axis at right angles to the passage. Above two basic vertical stages they taper at Madura to a maximum height of 150 feet but may elsewhere on occasion have been twice as high. The truncated top is crowned by an elaborate roof along the line of the main axis, with a baroque reminiscence of the Buddhist *chaitya* gable at each end of it. In the riper examples the sides of the tower assume a concave profile as they rise, giving them a satisfactory aspect of grace and stability which enables them to carry a fantastic load of decoration without sensible strain. This decoration, usually in brick and plaster for lightness, consists of crowded lines of figures or groups supported by horizontal mouldings which again help to stabilize the astonishing encrustation. It would be easy to condemn these towers as merely ostentatious and vulgar; certainly they contribute largely to the 'thirty-three million' carvings of which the temple-administrators boast; but in their setting, and with the controls of which architect and sculptor are fully aware, they are often unexpectedly successful.

The genesis of these gate-towers is not of great interest and need not here be recounted. In the mature form in which they became important they were a sudden growth, scarcely earlier than the beginning of the sixteenth century, where they were developed under the later kings of wealthy Vijayanagar on the Tungabhadra River. When in 1565 a Muslim army and a mad elephant combined to destroy the capital, the creative centre of the Hindu empire (or what was left of it) moved southwards, and it was Tirumalai of the Nayaka dynasty who, in 1623-52 built or rebuilt much of the Great Temple at Madura in the full maturity of the southern style.

Today the normal entry into the precinct is not through one of the main *gopurams* but through a secondary entrance in the eastern wall. This is fronted by a painted corridor flanked by statues of Minakshi which, like caryatids, support the roof. Here traders display their goods behind the goddess, and other traders share with the temple-elephants a much longer colonnaded corridor immediately within the precinct. The elephants, now a vanishing spectacle in India, even in the south, are still kept for ceremonial purposes, and on these occasions are elaborately painted and caparisoned. The internal-combustion engine is a beggarly substitute.

At the end of this second corridor a large brass door opens towards one of the lesser *gopurams*, through which access is obtained to the sacred *Teppa Kulam*, known as *Swarnapushpakarini* or *Pottamarai*, 'The Tank of the Golden Lilies'. A pillared verandah surrounds the oblong tank, and stone steps lead

OPPOSITE: One of the main *gopurams* or monumental gateways of the Great Temple of Madura. The luxuriantly ornamented pile rises aptly behind the screen of rich, tropical vegetation

Detail of an unfinished *gopuram* of the Great Temple of Madura. The motif is a late Indian elaboration of a theme earlier characteristic of the classical and post-classical West, where it took the form of animals within intertwining grape-vines

Entrance-lobby to the Great Temple of Madura, flanked by 'caryatids' in the form of the goddess Minakshi upholding a painted roof, with a continuous bazaar in the background

Part of the palace at Madura,
from a drawing by Thomas Daniell published in 1797

Courtyard of the palace of Tirumalai Nayak
(early seventeenth century), from a drawing made
about 1840 by Lieutenants Jenkins and Whelpdale
and an Indian artist, Ravanat Naig

down to the water where the faithful are forever washing themselves and their clothes. Cleanliness is a normal and ritual feature of Hindu life, and tanks are commonly an adjunct to places of worship. It may be that the famous tank or Great Bath which can be seen on the citadel of Mohenjo-daro in Sind (West Pakistan) carries the custom back into the pre-Aryan third millennium.

From the vicinity of the tank a small *gopuram* leads into the precinct of the temple of Minakshi. The pillars of the approach are lively carvings of monsters intermingled with epic figures of the *Mahabharata* – typical examples of exuberant seventeenth-century sculpture verging upon over-ripeness. A further *gopuram* opens from this precinct into that of Shiva (Sundareswar), with its attendant Nandi bull, the 'vehicle' of the god. Nearby is the treasury, which contains the variegated plate and jewels of the temple, a gaudy spectacle of very diverse values.

Finally, in the north-eastern angle of the enclosure is the vast Hall of a Thousand Pillars (the *Sahasrasthambha Mandapam*), which patient calculators have reduced to 997. It was built about 1550 by the founder of the Nayaka dynasty, and mounted on a spirited, rearing horse the king himself both adorns a pillar and greets the visitor at the entrance. Behind him are other lively pillar-sculptures of dancers and musicians. Ganesha, the elephant-god of good fortune, dances with ponderous agility, holding a doll-like goddess on his uplifted knee; and a lightly poised Sarasvati plays the stringed *bina* or *vina* which she is supposed to have invented. Her fantastically exaggerated body and wholly stylized drapery mark the end of an era, but it was a gracious ending. No doubt the great hall was used by the Nayaka dynasty as a place of ceremonial assembly; it is eloquent of the extravagant showmanship of these latter-day Hindu kingdoms on the eve of the colonial period.

Beyond these two *gopurams* of the Great Temple of Madura, the vista is that of a typical South Indian landscape, once thickly forested within a frame of abrupt hills

OPPOSITE: Interior of 'Tirumalai's Chaultri'
(about 1640), a large aisled hall outside the precinct
of the Great Temple of Madura

View across the roofs of the inner buildings of the great Vishnu temple at Srirangam towards a succession of *gopurams*. The golden 'dome' in the centre marks the central shrine

The Madura temple was an ornament of a capital city. Eighty miles to the north-east was one of the great temples of India, a city in its own right. The vast complex of Srirangam, on an island between two branches of the Cauveri River outside the subsidiary Nayaka capital of Tiruchirapalli (Trichinopoly), was the headquarters of the cult of Vishnu, one of the two principal gods of the Hindu pantheon. In its final form, the complex consisted of no less than seven successive rectangular enclosures, one inside another, with the single temple at the centre. The outermost enclosure was 2880 by 2475 feet, containing an area of more than half a square mile; and each enclosure is entered in turn from three or four quarters of the compass by a *gopuram* in descending order of magnitude from the outside inwards, twenty-one of them in all. The outermost gateway on the south side was never completed but would have approached the height of 300 feet – in this respect equalling, as has been remarked, Giotto's campanile at Florence.

Like Madura itself, Srirangam owed much to the beneficence of the Nayaka rulers of the seventeenth century; but epigraphic evidence shows that the Pandyas of the south were at work here in the thirteenth century, and the kings of Vijayanagar were enriching the place in the fourteenth and sixteenth centuries. The successive enclosure-walls are of different though uncertain dates, the three outermost being relatively late.

Amidst an innumerable assemblage of buildings of one kind and another, two are particularly noteworthy, both between the third and the fourth enclosure-walls (from the centre). One is, as at Madura, a Hall of a Thousand Pillars, some 500 by 160 feet with (in fact) about 940 granite monoliths – a somewhat dreary forest rather than a landscape. The other is the celebrated

126

OPPOSITE: The outermost *gopuram* on the eastern side of the great temple at Srirangam. The mass of ornament is controlled by strong horizontal lines, culminating in the baroque *chaitya* roof at the summit

Marketing in the Hall of a Thousand Pillars at Srirangam, a characteristic juxtaposition of the religious and the secular

Horse Court or *Seshagiri mandapam*, with its colonnade of rearing war-horses rising to a height of 9 feet and sustained in an ingenuous but sufficiently convincing fashion by responsive foot-soldiers and other figures. These vigorous animals, their jaws fiercely open and tongues lolling out, are surely amongst the masterpieces of Indian sculpture; they are here of the latter half of the sixteenth century, but have a long South Indian tradition behind them, traceable in some measure to the Pallavas of the seventh century. At Srirangam they are a legacy of the Vijayanagar empire, and have been regarded, not inaptly, as the reflection of an Indian Age of Chivalry at a time of renewed Islamic menace. 'Something of this temper, a feeling of exultant invincibility translated into the power of good over evil, seems embodied in the art of this period and to account for these colonnades of splendid cavaliers nonchalantly astride gigantic rearing chargers and engaged in furious combat with fabulous creatures, an episode singularly analogous to that of St George and the Dragon in the West' (Percy Brown).

The whole concept is indeed one of fairy-tale rather than religion. The real and the fabulous are inextricably involved, but there is an over-all sense of the secular. The thought behind these sumptuous, clever, exuberant sculptures is the glorification of a warrior class and dynastic triumph. There are even touches of secular humour, as when the forelegs of one of the horses is lightly supported by a stiff hood held by a woman who sits upon the shoulders of a complacent warrior with drawn sword. The strange group, skilful but childlike, is thought to represent a Brahmanical notion of the domination of man by woman. The

A female musician (possibly Sarasvati) at Srirangam, in the developed Vijayanagar style of the sixteenth century. Contrasted with the conventional wasp-waist and opulent breasts are the sensitively observed fingers of the hand playing the *vina*

sculptor had his tongue in his cheek, and his art had not much further to go.

It is, however, the whole tireless life and laden atmosphere of this temple-town that leaves its impression upon the mind of the intrusive and irrelevant visitor. He has first to make his way with alien idleness through a busy bazaar which spreads within the outer precinct-walls and merges eventually with gardens, store-houses, hostels and dwellings of the remoter interior. If his visit has been properly prepared, he may be honoured at one of the *gopurams* by the temple-orchestra with its noisy drums and shrill pipes and strings. Temple-elephants, gaudily painted and arrayed, may here contribute to the dignity of the ceremonial. Away in the background a rogue-elephant, approachable only by his familiar mahout, may be weaving and trumpeting insanely in his stable, his legs shackled heavily to the floor. Altogether, it is a vivid scene. Elsewhere, until merely a quarter of a century ago, the temple-prostitutes offered consolation to the weary or curious pilgrim, as had their forbears at Babylon and a thousand Asian shrines for countless ages: a tradition ascribed by anthropologists to the worship of Nature and Fertility, but by their more cynical confrères to plain nature. And among this teeming, variegated throng are the true worshippers, mostly humble folk, who may pause in their path to stroke some macabre image with a muttered prayer, and then move on to bathe and to approach the holy of holies as nearly as caste will allow. Only for good Brahmins is the way to the godhead and favour an easy one; for the intrusive and irrelevant visitor there is very properly no hope.　　　　　MORTIMER WHEELER

Monolithic piers of the Horse Court at Srirangam, with its lively fairyland of knights and foot-soldiers in the mature Vijayanagar style

Part of the second storey of the outermost *gopuram* on the eastern side

THE RED FORT

*The greatest of all the Mughal imperial
palaces and the seat of the Mughal Emperor
until the Rebellion of 1857*

What is now called Delhi is a conglomeration of cities rather than a single city. Half a century ago, before the building of the vast modern city which has been called a 'monument to the dry souls of clerks', it was customary to speak of the 'seven cities of Delhi', although in fact the number of centres of government in the Delhi area has been nearer double that number. Ceramic fragments of the fifth century BC and relics of the Kushans in the first two centuries AD. have been discovered in the *tell* on which the Old Fort stands; but the first settlement in Delhi's continuous history was a site nine miles south of that, a Tomar city of the ninth century, and the next a Chauhan Rajput fort six miles south-west of the prehistoric *tell*. This fort, the stronghold of the last Hindu King of Delhi, fell to the Muslim invaders from Ghor in the closing decade of the twelfth century, and this and other nearby sites remained the capital of the northern dynasties of Islamic India until the fall of the last Mughal emperor in 1858, except for a few occasions when isolated rulers favoured capitals in Daulatabad or Agra or Lahore.

Successively the governors of the Ghori kings, the Khaljis and the Tughluqs ruled from Delhi until the sack of the capital by Timur's Mongol hordes at the end of the fourteenth century; the Sayyid kings ruled a much reduced empire from Delhi, although their successors the Lodis preferred to move to Agra. The Mughal invasions in the early sixteenth century brought the capital back to Delhi in the Old Fort, mentioned above, started by Humayun and completed by the Afghan usurper Sher Shah. Humayun later regained his Indian empire and died in his Delhi capital; but his son Akbar, and his successors, preferred Agra and Lahore, especially the old Lodi fort at Agra which Akbar rebuilt.

Akbar's grandson Shahjahan reigned his first eleven years at Agra, but then decided to transfer the capital back to Delhi because, in the words of the French traveller Bernier, 'the excessive summer heat to which Agra is exposed makes it unfitting as the residence of a monarch'; moreover Agra was crowded and

Shahjahan, who initiated the building of the fort, from *Old and New East India* (1726) by François Valentyn

OPPOSITE : The Musamman Burj and water postern, from the river-side. The small balcony with its curved Bengali roof was added by Akbar II in 1808

the fort not large enough to accommodate the army, and doubtless the idea of founding a new city of Delhi in his own name appealed to Shahjahan's vanity. A site was selected, north of Humayun's old fort and on a bend of the banks of the Jumna, and the foundations of a citadel were laid there in 1639. That citadel was the new fort, called Lal Qila (Red Fort) to distinguish it from Humayun's grey quartzite citadel, for its curtain wall is built throughout of red sandstone from the Fatehpur Sikri quarries. The fort is an elongated octagon some 3000 feet from north to south, 1800 feet from east to west, and is really the citadel of Shahjahan's new town, Shahjahanabad (now often conveniently described as Delhi-within-the-walls), the walling of which was carried out while the fort was in building.

The east wall of the fort forms the river-front, where the principal palaces are situated. Formerly a narrow sandy foreshore lay between the fort wall and the river, the venue for the wild-beast fights so popular in the Mughal court; but now the Jumna's course runs further to the east. The wall on the river side is some 60 feet high, while the walls on the land sides rise to 110 feet above the level of the encircling ditch. On the flat land west of the fort is an open plain where the tents of the Rajas of the army were pitched. North of the fort and connected to it by a bridge is the walled fort called Salimgarh, built by a descendant of Sher Shah the Afghan as an outpost bulwark against the return of Humayun.

The wall of the fort, with its shallow circular bastions crowned with kiosks

There are two major gates, as well as a small postern and a water-gate. The Lahore Gate is now the principal entrance, an arch 40 feet high flanked with half-octagon towers each crowned by an open octagonal kiosk, with a row of seven small square marble-domed kiosks running over the arch between them. The fine effect of the gate has long been lost to a distant view, for later in the century Aurangzeb added a barbican before the gate to form a bent entrance; this displeased the deposed Shahjahan, for it is said that he wrote from his prison in the Agra fort to his son Aurangzeb, 'you have made the fort a bride, and set a veil before her face'. On the southern wall is the Delhi Gate – so called because it faces the old city of Delhi – of similar design but flanked by a stone elephant on either side of the central arch. Aurangzeb ordered these to be destroyed, with his customary religious bigotry, and the present statues date from 1903, erected to the order of that enlightened Viceroy, Lord Curzon.

The Lahore Gate was the royal way to the great Jami mosque built on an outcrop of the local Aravalli rock to the south-west of the fort; and due west of the gate lies the principal street of Shahjahanabad, the famous Chandni Chauk ('market of moonlight'). Within the gate is a roofed street, a vaulted arcade with arched cells for traders on ground and first-floor levels, leading

The Lahore Gate, the main entrance to the fort. The view of this noble gate from the main street of Shahjahan's city is blocked by Aurangzeb's barbican

OPPOSITE : Bird's-eye view of the Red Fort from a gouache (Lucknow, *c* 1770)

133

The Delhi Gate inside the barbican. The original elephants were destroyed by Aurangzeb, and these copies were erected by Lord Curzon

Pietra dura panels in the Diwan-i Amm, including the incongruous Orpheus with his lute. These were probably imported from a Florentine studio

to the Naubat Khana (watch house), where the royal band played five times during the day, at any royal entry or departure, and all day on Sundays and the day of the week on which the emperor was born. Beyond this entrance the first royal hall is approached, the Diwan-i Amm (Hall of General Audience), on the east side of a great quadrangle.

The Diwan-i Amm is a pillared hall open on the north, south and west, of red sandstone, its interior divided into three arcades nine bays wide, with engrailed arches supported by elegant pillars – the pillars being doubled on the outer faces. In a recess in the back wall is a marble baldachino, the Nashiman-i Zill-i Ilahi (seat of the shadow of God), standing on a square plinth of marble finely carved with floral designs, with a curvilinear roof of Bengali pattern richly inlaid with semi-precious stones. Behind the baldachino is a remarkable set of panels in *pietra dura*, said to have been designed by Austin de Bordeaux, a renegade French jeweller at the Mughal court. However, the black marble and most of the inlaid stones, and the designs, are of Italian provenance, and it has been suggested that the works were executed in an Italian studio and imported whole. There is certainly nothing Indian about the figure of Orpheus with his lute, although the floral arabesques between the panels are unquestionably of Indian style and craftsmanship.

Beyond the Diwan-i Amm stand the palace buildings proper, in an enclosed area along the river wall between two great octagonal buttresses. A canal runs from north to south through the palaces in a shallow marble channel; this 'canal of paradise' was Shahjahan's extension of a canal first opened by Feroz Shah Tughluq in 1350 to bring water to Delhi from a point on the Jumna, sixty miles northwards. The buildings along and over the canal are, from north to south, the Hira (Diamond) or Moti (Pearl) Mahal, a small marble pavilion of the latest phase of Mughal architecture; the Hammam (baths) of three main apartments with floors, tanks, slabs and the lower part of the walls of pure white marble inlaid with precious and semi-precious stones in delicate floral designs with arabesque borders, the mechanism for heating the water still preserved (ten tons of firewood were required to heat the baths in winter); the Diwan-i Khass (Hall of Special Audience), standing in its own courtyard from which it was screened by a red curtain, where nobles of the highest rank waited on the emperor, and where the notorious Peacock Throne of the Mughals once stood; next the Khwabgah (the royal dormitory), with a projecting tower, the Musamman Burj, leading off it and projecting out beyond the wall; the canal then passes through a screen bearing a representation of the scales of justice before flowing into the principal royal palace, the Rang Mahal (Palace of Colour) and the Mumtaz Mahal, formerly an apartment for the royal princesses and now housing the fort museum. Of these the Diwan-i Khass, Khwabgah and Rang Mahal must have special mention.

The Diwan-i Khass is a single-storeyed building showing the middle Mughal style at its most sumptuous, with massive square

OPPOSITE : The 'seat of the shadow of God', with the Florentine *pietra dura* balcony behind, in the Diwan-i Amm

The fort from the old foreshore of the Jumna River. The Khwabgah (royal dormitory) with the projecting Musamman Burj is on the left, the Diwan-i Khass in the centre, and the domes of the Moti Masjid (Pearl Mosque) can just be seen behind the Hammam (royal baths) on the right

The Hammam (royal baths), with *pietra dura* decoration on the walls and floor

piers supporting engrailed arches very deep in the soffit, and a flat ceiling decorated with gold leaf. *Pietra dura* work graces the panelled sides of the marble piers below the springing of the arches, the upper parts being gilded and painted; and on the north and south walls appears the most famous of all Persian inscriptions: *agar Firdaus ba-ruh-i zamin ast/hamin ast o hamin ast o hamin ast*, 'if there be a paradise on the face of the earth/it is here, it is here, it is here'. The openings on the river side are filled with finely carved screens. The Peacock Throne which once stood here was carried off to Persia by Nadir Shah in 1739 and there broken up (the Peacock Throne in Tehran is no earlier than the Qajar period, but may contain remnants from the throne of the Great Mughals); it appears, from contemporary descriptions, to have been a work of ostentatious and magnificent vulgarity.

The Khwabgah is really the central set of rooms in the Khass Mahal (Royal Palace), the walls formerly inlaid with precious stones, and leads to the Musamman Burj ('octagonal tower', sometimes fancifully contracted to Saman Burj, 'jasmine tower') with its finely carved marble screens looking out on to the old sandy foreshore where the animal fights took place, and where the emperor, continuing the old Hindu practice of *darshan*, showed himself to his subjects. The Rang Mahal was formerly adorned with rich colour decoration, with heavy piers and arches like those of the Diwan-i Khass, and a ceiling of silver gilded and ornamented with golden flowers. The canal here runs into a shallow tank seven yards square, its floor of marble carved into the shape of a flat full-blown lotus, on each point of which a jet of water flowed out – the waters no longer run – so that the petals and the foliage of the associated inlay work seemed to move as the water rippled. Even without its moving waters and precious stones it is still a thing of great beauty.

The fort was not at first provided with a mosque, Shahjahan making formal procession to the great Jami Mosque across the way. The pious Aurangzeb required a place of worship near his

OPPOSITE: The Moti Masjid (Pearl Mosque), with its Bengali cornice and marble floor marked out in oblongs as stations for worshippers

The Diwan-i Khass or Hall of Special Audience

The Diwan-i Khass, sumptuously ornamented in *pietra dura*, carved marble and gilding. The rings over the eaves and arches were used to support canopies

A nineteenth-century watercolour of the interior

OPPOSITE: Interior of the Diwan-i Khass: 'If there be a paradise on the face of the earth it is here, it is here, it is here'

139

Marble basin in the floor of the Rang Mahal

View from the Diwan-i Khass towards the Rang Mahal. The central channel ('canal of paradise') flows under the 'scales of justice' screen through all the palaces

private chambers, and caused to be built in 1659 the diminutive Moti Masjid (Pearl Mosque), a simple building in pure white marble with restrained decoration in *pietra dura* on the cornice. This cornice curves over the central bay of the façade in a way that would harmonize ill with Shahjahan's marble façades; but fortunately the mosque is in its own walled enclosure. The three marble domes, added after the Mutiny to replace those damaged in the siege, are too large for the structure and increase the incongruity.

South of the mosque enclosure is a large formal garden laid out with water-terraces, parterres, and a central pavilion. There are pavilions at each end of the central channel, named Savan and Bhadon, the Hindu names of the first two months of the rainy season, from which water used to flow into the water-terraces over cascades with niches where candles were placed at night.

Now the band is silent, the canal of paradise dry, and the brilliance, colour and panoply of the court of the Great Mughal lost for ever. But enough remains from Shahjahan's extravagant reign of marble to afford us a glimpse of that departed opulence. The Red Fort still stands for modern India as a symbol, and no one – even a survivor, like the author, from the last days of the British Raj – can fail to be moved by the impressive flag-hoisting ceremony at the Lahore Gate on Republic Day. It was the power of Islam that made Delhi the focal point of India; since the fall of the Mughal empire the British and the independent Indian governments have equally felt its prestige; but with the great Red Fort the dead Mughals still have the last word.

J. BURTON-PAGE

OPPOSITE : Pierced screen in the Musamman Burj

India

FATEHPUR SIKRI

The vast, deserted sandstone city near Agra,
built, occupied and deserted by Akbar
at the end of the sixteenth century

Sikri was a small village which found its way into the chronicles only because it had mosques there in the time of Alauddin Khalji at the turn of the thirteenth century. No more was heard of it until Babur pitched camp there before a battle in 1527. In 1568 Akbar founded a city there, which for a mere seventeen years was the glorious court of the Mughal empire, during which time it was accorded the honorific epithet 'Town of Victory' – strictly speaking Fathpur, though necessarily vocalized Fatehpur in India – in commemoration of Akbar's conquest of Gujarat. In 1585 Akbar moved his court to Lahore, and except for the great buildings which still stand the city fell into ruin, and became a village again:

> See the wild waste of all-devouring years!
> How Rome her own sad sepulchre appears!

Fatehpur Sikri is a site of outstanding importance for the history of Muslim art in India, demonstrating not only the persistence of local pre-Mughal features but also the architectural expression of Akbar's eclectic taste, and many buildings not distinguished structurally are important for the carved panels and fresco paintings they contain. The art critic Havell tried to see in Akbar's buildings at Agra and Sikri a deliberate synthesis between Hindu and Muslim styles; this author prefers to consider that Akbar drew much of his inspiration from Gujarat, where Hindu and Jain styles had long been absorbed in Muslim building. There are indeed direct borrowings from Hindu iconography in some buildings, notably the so-called 'Maryam's House', but much of the indigenous Indian element seems to have been imported already assimilated.

Akbar was attracted to Sikri for emotional rather than strategic reasons, since it was the abode of the Shaikh Salim Chishti, to whose intercession he attributed the birth there of his heir Salim, later the Emperor Jahangir, in 1569. Its walls, of sandstone rubble and enclosing the city on three sides (the fourth was occupied by a lake, now dry), were intended merely as

Shallow floral patterns carved in sandstone
on the central pillar of the Diwan-i Khass

OPPOSITE: The central pillar of the Diwan-i Khass
(Hall of Special Audience). The brackets supporting the
platform are echoed by the corner supports of the gallery

The north side of the great Palace Square, showing the Diwan-i Khass and, on the left, the 'Astrologer's Seat', with the 'Blind man's buff house' just behind it

enclosures, with some provision for the defence of the emperor's person, for Fatehpur Sikri was never a 'stronghold' capable of withstanding military operations; this function was fulfilled by Agra, twenty-six miles away, to which fort the court could retire in emergency.

The extant buildings consist of two blocks of palaces, a caravanserai and waterworks, and the great mosque. Many of the buildings are now known by names which are entirely arbitrary and have no justification beyond the usage of the local guides.

To the east of all the palaces is a plain sandstone building, the Diwan-i Amm, now devoid of decoration, within the cloisters of a large quadrangle, with the emperor's throne standing between two fine pierced sandstone screens. West of this is a large open court with the Diwan-i Khass (Hall of Special Audience) and Ankh-michauli ('blind-man's-buff') on the north, the Panch Mahal on the west, an ornamental pond and the Khwabgah on the south, and the 'Turkish Sultana's House' on the east.

The so-called Diwan-i Khass, which seems a strange function for such a curious building, is a square detached structure unique in Islamic architecture; externally it appears to have two storeys, but inside appears as a single vaulted room with a sur-

rounding gallery and a central carved sandstone column supporting a platform joined to the gallery diagonally. Akbar is said to have conducted religious disputations from his seat on the central column; but the building cannot be identified, as some have suggested, with Akbar's Ibadat-Khana, 'house of worship'. The shape of the heavy sandstone brackets supporting the platform recalls those of the Gujarat mosques, derived from balconies in local temple architecture. Outside the Ankh-michauli stands a small square kiosk, the 'Astrologer's Seat', the serpentine red sandstone struts of which are a direct imitation of struts found in Jain temples in Gujarat at Abu, Siddhpur, Modhera and elsewhere.

In the vast courtyard to the south of these buildings is a huge cruciform pachchisi board set into the pavement, more probably a relic of the eighteenth-century Sultan Muhammad Shah's brief reoccupation of Fatehpur Sikri than of Akbar's time. The royal apartments south of this include an ornamental pond, the Khwabgah (dormitory), and the 'Turkish Sultana's House'. The Khwabgah is a small square room the interior walls of which were formerly covered with fresco paintings, and has a balcony on the far side from which the emperor followed the

ABOVE: The Panch Mahal, a whimsical structure of no obvious ancestry

RIGHT: Columns on the first floor of the Panch Mahal

The Buland Darwaza ('Lofty Gate') of
the mosque from the south; the domes of
the sanctuary are on the left

The 'Lofty Gate' of
the great mosque

ABOVE: The great mosque from the south-east, showing the dominating
Buland Darwaza, from a drawing by William Daniell

OPPOSITE: The Buland Darwaza ('Lofty Gate')

Hindu practice of the *darshan*, showing himself to his people. The 'Turkish Sultana's House' – Akbar in fact is not known to have had a Turkish queen – is a single small chamber with a surrounding verandah, the most richly ornamented building in the city, carved externally all over with geometrical and arabesque designs and ornamented internally with scenes similar to Persian carpet designs carved on red sandstone panels, incorporating some figurations of Chinese provenance. Abu'l Fazl, Akbar's minister and panegyrist, tells us that Akbar's workmen could carve the local sandstone as skilfully as no turner could do with wood; this building certainly supports his statement.

West of this courtyard is the second block of palaces, commencing with the curious Panch Mahal, an open pavilion of five storeys with eighty-four columns on the ground floor, fifty-six on the first – all of different designs – then twenty, then twelve, and finally four on the top storey supporting a small kiosk dome. The open spaces between the columns were originally filled in with screens, and it has been suggested that the building was for the use of the ladies of the zanana. West of this is the building known as 'Maryam's House', a square building two-storeyed at one end, with the other end surrounded by a deep verandah with an eave-stone mounted on massive brackets, some of which bear unashamedly Hindu figures. Carried on four columns on the roof is a small sleeping-pavilion with verandah and inner walls which were once richly painted with frescoes: floral designs, hunting scenes, elephant fights and scenes from the Persian epic the *Shahnama*.

West again is the largest palace, called 'Jodh Bai's House', said to be the oldest in the city. It has a large open central court surrounded by single-storeyed rooms, with double-storeyed rooms in the centre of each wall and at each angle, although from outside the height appears uniform. Hindu influence is apparent here; the entire construction is by lintel-and-bracket, with the Hindu bell-and-chain ornament used on the pillars – another feature common in Gujarat. The arch is used sparingly in the inner building as a decorative device, although the eastern gateway has a wide four-centred arch with a fringe of stylized spearheads on the intrados, a device familiar in north Indian Muslim building since Khalji times. This appears also as a purely decorative device on the carved sandstone panels of 'Raja Birbal's Palace', a two-storeyed building with domes at two corners; these have inner and outer shells, the earliest use of the double dome in India outside Delhi. The carved decoration on all surfaces is exuberant, and the external brackets are particularly ornate.

North-west of these palaces are the citadel fortifications, including a great gate with two stone elephants flanking the outer archway, and a single massive bastion; but these represent no more than a conventional decoration of the palace area, as there is no indication that these token 'fortifications' were ever intended to be completed. A local tradition, tirelessly repeated in guide-books, that Shaikh Salim Chishti's disapproval caused the

Carved sandstone panels on the exterior of the 'Turkish Sultana's House', the most elaborately decorated building in the city

OPPOSITE : Fresco painting, depicting an elephant fight, in the northern verandah of the so-called 'House of Maryam'

149

The so-called 'Palace of Raja Birbal', more probably
a residence of one of Akbar's queens

Porch of 'Jodh Bai's House', the largest
and perhaps the oldest palace in the city

abandonment of works of fortification is without support in contemporary chronicles. Below these stand the caravanserai and waterworks, and lower still a single tower locally called 'Hiran Minar' (Antelope Tower) – but this is possibly a corruption of 'Haram Minar', a tower for the harem to watch the elephant-fights in the arena below.

South-west of all these buildings is the great mosque, its central quadrangle some 430 by 360 feet, its eastern (royal) gate looking from the palaces towards the great domed sanctuary of three interior square chambers supported by pillars of similar design to those of the later Gujarat mosques, but with arches of the same spearhead fringe character that we have observed elsewhere. The surface decoration in polished *opus sectile* work, however, is purely Muslim in character. This was the mosque in which Akbar's eclectic religion, the Din-i Ilahi, was first promulgated, with its ambiguous formula *Allahu Akbar* ('God is great' or 'Akbar is God'); and I am again reminded of Pope:

Who builds a church to God, and not to Fame,
Will never mark the marble with his name.

But the 'Divine Faith' died with Akbar.

The courtyard contains the necessary ablution tank, fed by an enormous reservoir under the paved floor of the courtyard.

OPPOSITE: The sanctuary of the great mosque

The great Akbar (1556–1605), who held court
in Fatehpur Sikri from 1568 to 1585, from François
Valentyn's *Old and New East India* (1726)

151

The Tomb of Shaikh Salim Chishti, the only
marble building in this sandstone city

Again this suggests the influence of Gujarat, where mosque reservoirs frequently provide a cool retreat in the heat of the day; the feature occurs nowhere else in north India. The courtyard, once symmetrical, has lost its balance by three additions, two tombs on the north side and a monumental gateway on the south. The sandstone tomb is that of Shaikh Salim's grandson Nawab Islam Khan, who for a time was made governor of Bengal by Jahangir. The other tomb, originally of sandstone, was faced with marble in the early years of Jahangir's reign, and is now a great marble casket enclosed by carved marble screens – another Gujarat feature – and with very wide eaves supported by fantastic serpentine brackets. Here again there are similar supports in some of the Gujarat temples, although the device is not unknown in Muslim work elsewhere, for example the Jami mosque at Chanderi in Central India. The tomb attracts a constant stream of pilgrims, Hindu and Muslim alike, and barren women frequently tie pieces of cloth on the perforations of the marble screens to secure the saint's intercession.

Dominating not only the mosque but the entire southern elevation of the hill on which Fatehpur is built is the Buland Darwaza ('Lofty Gate'), added by Akbar to replace the original south doorway; a great half-dome opening forms the portico, in the back of which the smaller doors open into the mosque courtyard – a most satisfactory way of solving the problem of how to give a large building a door in proportion to its dimensions but at the same time practicable as an entry for humans. The result towers 176 feet above the roadway beneath.

There are many other buildings still standing in Fatehpur Sikri: baths, stables, dwelling-houses, kiosks, offices, storerooms, guardrooms, and a mint, some still showing the traces of their former glory. Many lost it within a few years of Akbar's decision to move to Lahore, a decision prompted partly by the inadequate and brackish water supply but more compellingly by the political situation on the north-west frontier. But already in 1604 the Jesuit missionary Jerome Xavier found it 'totally demolished' and abandoned by its erstwhile population, and early in Jahangir's reign the English traveller Finch calls it 'ruinate, lying like a waste desert, and very dangerous to pass through in the night'. Except for occasional visits by later Mughal rulers, it remained so, a red sandstone city with no citizens, with no voices raised but the howl of the jackal and the scream of the peacock. The magic of Akbar's city, though, is still there to talk to us across the years; let us leave the last word with Ovid: 'Saepe tacens vocem verbaque vultus habet.' (Often the silent face has voice and words.)   J. BURTON-PAGE

Eave-brackets of the Tomb of Shaikh Salim Chishti

TAJ MAHAL

*The most famous of all the great buildings
of the east, the white marble monument to
the Emperor Shahjahan's love for his queen*

Mumtaz-i Mahal, the lady of the Taj

Everyone knows of the 'Taj'. It is for many the paramount symbol of oriental opulence and mystical beauty. Some admit no superior building in the world; others say the building is overrated. 'There is no . . . sense of partial failure about the Taj. A thing of perfect beauty and of absolute finish in every detail, it might pass for the work of genii who knew nought of the weaknesses and ills with which mankind are beset' wrote the American Bayard Taylor in 1853; 'there is something slight and effeminate in the general design' said Keene in 1909; and in recent years Aldous Huxley has complained that its elegance is of 'a very dry and negative kind', and described its classicism as 'the product not of intellectual restraint imposed upon an exuberant fancy, but of an actual deficiency of fancy, a poverty of imagination. One is struck at once by the lack of variety in the architectural forms of which it is composed.' Opinions of all kinds could be multiplied, and produce no conclusion; my own feelings when I first saw it nearly a quarter of a century ago were a bewildering mixture of awe at the vast marble mass of the tomb-chamber and amusement that the tall minarets really did look a little like factory chimneys. Perhaps we should refrain from attempting value-judgments on this occasion.

Certainly the Taj is a widely misunderstood, misinterpreted and misrepresented building. Its name is a corruption, even if an appropriate one; the name of the lady buried there was Arjumand Bano, entitled Mumtaz-i Mahal, 'Chosen of the Palace', but the local population know no difference between z's and j's, and from their 'Mumtaj' the name as we now know it has been formed. 'Taj', however, means 'jewel' – a happy coincidence, but nothing more. The 'Mahal' part, too, is grossly distorted by English mouths, as in north India this is pronounced more like 'mehl' – the artist Daniell was nearer with his 'Mah'l'. Again, it is not 'at Agra', but in a village outside the old town – though city growth may engulf it before long. It certainly was not built by a Venetian architect at the Mughal emperor's orders, even though a Spanish friar, who saw it under construction, says that

The Taj Mahal and its garden

The 'Persian' garden and the gateway,
from the south-east minaret

it was. Nor has the 'celebrated architect' Ustad 'Isa, variously described as of Persia, or Constantinople, or Shiraz, or China, or Qandahar, any better claim to be considered as its architect; there is in fact no evidence, at least before the nineteenth century, that such a person ever existed. And, most important, the memorial is not just a vast marble tomb with a minaret at each corner.

Arjumand Bano Begam was the favourite queen of Shahjahan, married to him in 1612, who followed her husband's fortunes and campaigns in personal companionship with him all over India. She shared in the responsibilities of state with him on his accession in 1628, and was renowned for her charity and her intercessions for clemency towards political offenders. She bore Shahjahan fourteen children, and on her death in childbirth in 1631 the emperor was prostrated with grief. They were then on a campaign in Burhanpur, in Khandesh, where the queen was first entombed. Early in 1632 her body was brought to the royal city of Agra to lie in a garden south-east of the city, where the foundations of her memorial were begun, not to be fully completed before twenty years had passed. The leading architects and engineers of the realm were consulted – it is possible that the Venetian Geronimo Verroneo was among the number, but unlikely that he had any voice on the final design accepted – and the plans must have been drawn up with meticulous attention to every detail. Artisans and materials were drawn from every part of the empire, and perhaps some craftsmen from outside. Some manuscripts, indeed, give lists of artisans and materials with their provenance; but these are of rather dubious authenticity and we have preferred not to use their accounts here.

Foundations for the tomb-chamber were sunk in the garden to the greatest depth the proximity of the river Jumna would allow; excavations within the last few years have shown that at least part of the sub-structure rests on deep masonry wells. Over this is a high marble terrace, on which the cenotaph-chamber with its four attendant minarets rests. But this is not the Taj, merely the focal point of it. [The Begam's memorial is one great complex: a long rectangular formal garden with an entrance gateway, enclosure wall with broad arcaded angle turrets, a river-front, canals running down the main approach-terrace and at right angles to it, a central marble platform and side pavilions of red sandstone.] The tomb and minarets occupy the river end of the enclosure, flanked by two sandstone buildings, one a mosque and the other an identical *jawab* ('answer') used as an assembly hall. Outside the great gateway lie other buildings which are also part of the scheme, in a fine courtyard. The whole conception is completely and perfectly bilaterally symmetrical.

The portal leading into the garden is itself an excellent specimen of Mughal art in Shahjahan's time. It stands a hundred feet high, its central chamber in the form of a half-dome, flanked by arcaded walls and octagonal corner-turrets crowned with

OPPOSITE: The Taj Mahal from the far side of the Jumna at dawn

open kiosks, in red sandstone with marble inlay. On the architrave of the doorway is a superlative specimen of Arabic calligraphy in black marble. The garden is a square, symmetrically divided and subdivided, with sandstone parterres for flowers, and a geometrically paved terrace divided by the canal in its marble basin with marble fountains playing; in the middle of the square is a marble platform with a central tank and more fountains; and beyond the garden square is the mausoleum itself, its reflection in the canal below.

The mausoleum is a square with truncated corners standing on a high marble plinth, the staircases of which are concealed within the plinth itself. Each face of the mausoleum shows a great central arch the parapet of which rises above the main building line, flanked by two smaller arches one above the other on each side; two similar small arches fill the angles cut off by the truncation of the square, each section separated from its neighbour by a slender pilaster which is carried up above the building line into a slender pinnacle. On the roof of the main chamber an octagonal open-domed kiosk stands at each angle, and in the middle the great white bulbous dome stands on a high drum. Except for its metal finial, the dome is almost exactly as high, 187 feet, as the façade of the chamber is broad.

Every component is of marble except for the decoration. The pilasters carry a chevron pattern in black and yellow marble bands, and the square panels at the lowest part of each face bear similar chevroned borders. All the spandrels of the arches on the faces are inlaid with *pietra dura* floral arabesques in semi-precious stones. The interiors of the outside arches are, by contrast, decorated solely with niches and blind shallow arches and cross-groining carved in pure white marble. Further marble carving runs round the entire foot of the chamber, and the alcoves of the four great arches are decorated with exquisitely carved flowers in low relief. The central chamber, then, expresses its contrasts by variations in the size and shape of the voids, and by variations in the material and techniques of its decorative embellishments.

A much stronger contrast is presented by the four detached corner minarets. Their encircling bracketed galleries are placed at the same height as the main levels of the horizontal features of the façade of the chamber; they rise to a height of 137 feet, above the level of the corner kiosks but below the height of the dome, and so effectively take the eye away from the severe pyramidal mass of the cenotaph-chamber. But their surfaces are different indeed, rusticated marble brick with the joints starkly emphasized in black, whereas the surface of the cenotaph-chamber is so smooth that the joints hardly show at all.

A further contrast to the entire central group of white marble – cenotaph-chamber and minarets on a common plinth – is afforded by the mosque on the west enclosure wall and its echo on the eastern wall. These are both of red sandstone with three marble domes, some *pietra dura* work in the spandrels of the arches, and chequered drums to the domes, and might have

South-west corner of the Taj Mahal, showing the *pietra dura* decoration on the spandrels and parapet and the inlaid chevrons on the pilasters

The carved plinth and lower part of the wall of the cenotaph chamber, with chevron inlay in black and yellow marble

OPPOSITE: The main approach to the Taj Mahal

159

Marble relief in the east alcove of the cenotaph chamber, perhaps the finest bas-relief marble carving in the entire Islamic world

OPPOSITE: Vault of the west porch of the cenotaph chamber. Unlike the exterior surfaces, the alcove relies solely on shallow carving in white marble for its decoration

The panelled sandstone and shallow domes of the mosque provide a foil, both in texture and colour, to the polished marble of the main building

received the attention they deserve had the central building not overshadowed them. The central group is intended to be seen between these two foils, but unfortunately the trees of the garden frequently grow to such a height as to obscure them from the gateway.

Within the central building is an octagonal chamber below the false ceiling of the dome, and in the middle of this is the cenotaph of Mumtaz-i Mahal, with that of Shahjahan by her side – an afterthought, obviously; for had the emperor at first intended this to be his own tomb he would have occupied the central position. We know that he intended his own tomb to be of a similar design to the Taj but in black marble, in a garden on the opposite side of the river and connected to the tomb of his consort by a bridge; there are indeed traces of the foundations for such a building across the Jumna. But Shahjahan's declining years, before his death in 1666, were spent as a deposed prisoner in the fort of Agra while his son Aurangzeb ruled in Shahjanabad-Delhi. The two tombs are enclosed by an octagonal trellis-work screen of white marble formerly encrusted with precious gems, thought to have been added by Aurangzeb – if this is so he must have shown more filial piety after his father's death than when he was alive. The cenotaphs are covered with *pietra dura* work of greater fineness and precision even than the other *pietra dura* of the Taj. The true graves lie in a crypt within the great plinth, immediately below the cenotaphs.

The materials concerned are, besides the red sandstone from Fatehpur Sikri and the spotless white marble from Makrana in Rajasthan, lapis lazuli, jasper, agate, heliotrope, sardonyx, chalcedony, plasma, cornelian, jade, onyx, coral, amethyst and turquoise – how Milton, with his love of resounding names, would have rejoiced in such a list! These all present the small-scale colour contrast, and *en masse* the contrast with the predominant white marble. But beside these contrasts of materials and the interplay of textures already mentioned, there is a further range of contrasts in the different ultimate provenances of the techniques. The dome, the arched façades with their half-dome openings, the minarets, the *pietra dura* designs of the spandrels, all bespeak a Persian ancestry; but the cupola roofs of the kiosks at the angles and the kiosks crowning the minarets, and the low-level encircling marble carvings, derive from the indigenous art. The four-square garden beloved of the Mughals is of Central Asian origin.

The effect of the memorial as a whole is, and could only be, the product of Islam in India. The river is one contributing factor to this; but the Indian climate has its own part to play in the total effect, for the white marble, dazzling in the full noon sun, may appear grey with the monsoon clouds overhead, or rosy or orange when lit by the slanting rays of the sun at dusk or daybreak. Nowadays there is a stream of picturesque humanity constantly visiting, adding its own counterpoint of colour.

The Taj grew naturally out of two earlier great monumental tombs of Mughal times. The first is the tomb in Delhi of the

OPPOSITE: The central dome seen from the south-east minaret

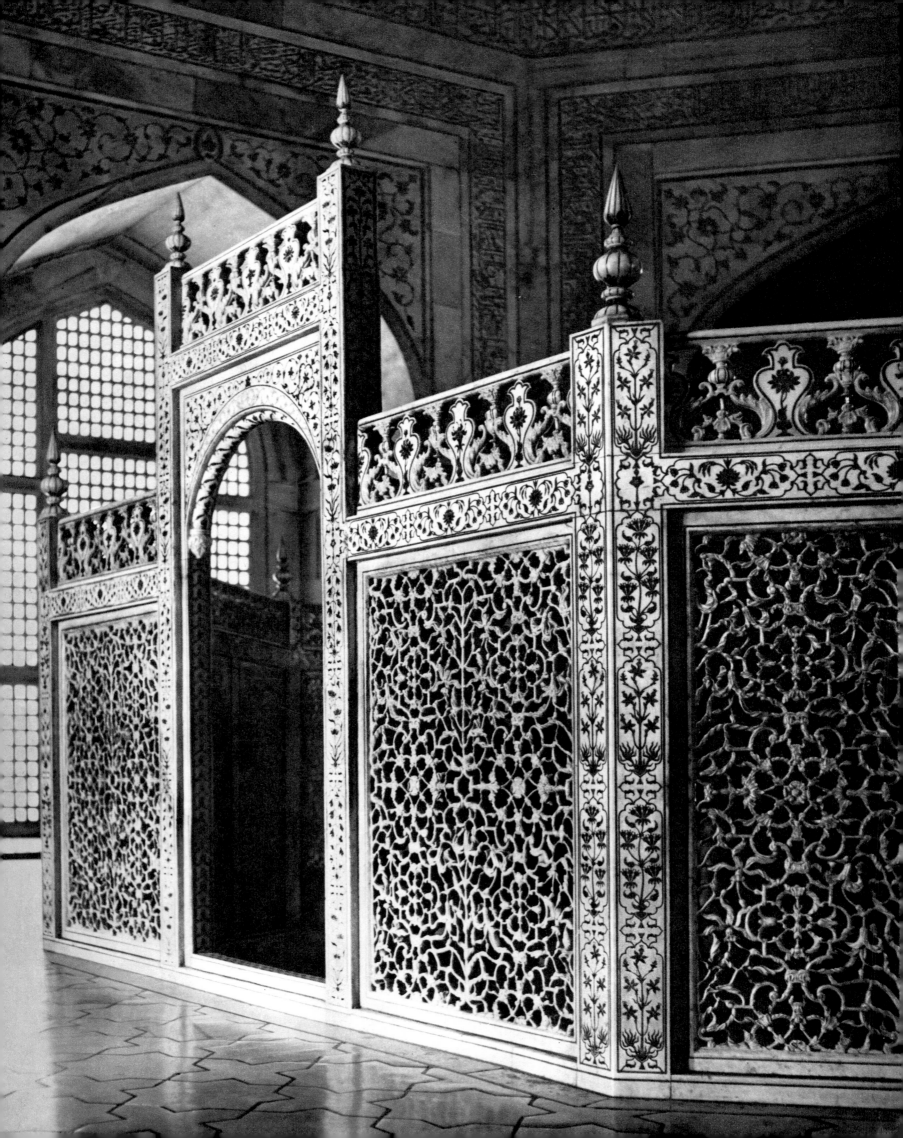

Emperor Humayun of seventy years before, inspired partly by the tomb architecture of Samarkand and Bukhara and partly by that of Qazvin in Persia where he and his consort spent their years of exile. Also in Delhi, but completed just before the Taj, is the tomb of Abdurrahim Khankhanan, the dome of which approaches that of the Taj more closely, certain proof that the tradition of the earlier design had been kept alive. With the Taj, however, something died. Less than thirty years after the completion of the Taj, Aurangzeb caused to be erected, outside his Deccan residence of Aurangabad, a mausoleum for his wife Rabi'a-ud-Daurani, based directly on the Taj. This, which locals who have never been to Agra call 'the Taj Mahal of the Deccan', is about half the size of the Agra building, but so cramped in its proportions and its fussy skyline as to be a travesty rather than a copy. Central canal, fountains, cypress rows, corner minarets, formal garden, tall plinth, all appear here in meretricious profusion, a sad reflection of Aurangzeb's tastelessness. Another imitation, smaller still, in the grounds of the Husainabad Imambara at Lucknow is even worse. But in Delhi at least the tradition did not wholly disappear, for one of the last great monumental tombs, that of Safdar Jang, who died in 1753, which it is the fashion to depreciate as 'enfeebled and decadent', is a restrained, dignified and artistic successor to Humayun's tomb of two centuries before.

Perhaps these other tombs, taken as a whole, enhance the Taj; perhaps not. This is something the reader must judge for himself. Great the Taj certainly is, but he would be rash who claimed perfection for it. I have heard it described as having a Mozartean grace – but for me it is too predictable ever to approach the Mozartean heights; I would settle for Boccherini.

J. BURTON-PAGE

Aurangzeb, the bigoted emperor (1658–1707), whose petty piety extended the Mughal empire to its greatest extent and its least repute

OPPOSITE: The magnificent octagonal screen enclosing the cenotaphs of Mumtaz-i Mahal and Shahjahan was erected by the emperor Aurangzeb

The mausoleum of Rabi'a-ud-Daurani, Aurangzeb's queen, at Aurangabad. Its attenuated corner pinnacles, weak engrailed arch, cramped skyline and disproportionately solid minarets all compare unfavourably with the Taj Mahal, which it imitates

165

NEPAL

*Himalayan neighbour of India,
with a distinctive individuality
in its art and architecture*

King Bhupatindra Malla

The best of Nepalese architecture is concentrated in the Katmandu Valley, an area of less than two hundred square miles. Although the vast mountainous regions of outer Nepal remain inaccessible to the traveller who is not at heart a mountaineer, Katmandu can be reached easily by air from India, and now the temples and shrines of this central valley attract visitors from all over the world. So Nepal has become famous for its 'pagodas', temples which are usually square in shape and surmounted by a set of tiered roofs, normally only two or three and very rarely as many as five. The term 'pagode' was first used by Portuguese traders in India in the sixteenth century, referring to the typical Indian temples of those times. As 'pagode' or 'pagoda' it has since become an exclusively Western term for any kind of tiered-roof temple; the Indians and the Nepalese have no special name for this distinctive kind of temple.

Although the Katmandu Valley preserves some of the finest examples of this type of architecture, the style is certainly of Indian origin. Not only in its architecture, but in its religious and social forms, this central valley of Nepal preserves many of the conditions which were typical of northern India 1000 years ago. Nepal was not the only borrower. Until its progress was destroyed by the advance of Islam, many influences of the great Hindu-Buddhist civilization spread from north-west India across the Karakorams and the Pamirs to Central Asia and even China. This same civilization spread easily to Nepal and thence onwards to Tibet.

Buddhist monasteries and Hindu temples were being founded in the central valley of Nepal at the very latest from the fifth century AD onwards. We know from stone inscriptions that there were royal endowments of monasteries in the area of the present-day town of Patan and in the northern part of present-day Katmandu. Also from inscriptions it is known that a third town, now known as Bhatgaon, was already existing in the sixth century, and this too probably developed around a

OPPOSITE: Bhupatindra Malla enthroned on
his pillar in the main square, Bhatgaon

small group of Buddhist monasteries, for these are still concentrated in the ancient north-east corner of the present town. It is likely that the inspiration for these developments came from the great Buddhist university cities of northern India: Bodhgaya, Nalanda, Odantapuri and so on. But just as in India of the first millennium AD, Hinduism and Buddhism developed together in Nepal as different religious aspects of one and the same culture. Hsüan-tsang, a famous Chinese pilgrim who visited India in the seventh century, refers to Nepal in the account of his travels. He was informed that there were about 2000 monks, both Mahayana and Hinayana, and that Buddhist monasteries and Hindu temples touched one another. He adds too that the people were excellent craftsmen.

By AD 1200 Islam had destroyed the great religious centres of northern India, and Buddhism rapidly disappeared from the land of its origin. The Katmandu Valley suffered from Muslim invasions in 1346 and 1349, but despite the destruction of shrines and temples, which is attested by still-existing inscriptions, there was no sudden break in Nepalese cultural traditions. India continued to exert a strong influence and, with the eclipse of Buddhism in India, religious influences were inevitably Brahmanical. The kings of Nepal had usually been Hindu in the old tolerant Indian way, acting as benefactors to Buddhist monasteries as well as to Brahmanical temples, but from the fourteenth century onwards, although still tolerant, they began to become increasingly caste-conscious.

During this period the two main cities of the central valley of Nepal, each with its own royal dynasty, were Patan and Bhatgaon. Katmandu was then a dependency of Patan, and yet another small town, Kirtipur, had come into existence in the twelfth century as a kind of southern outpost of Patan. While both Patan and Katmandu were still filled with Buddhist monasteries, Bhatgaon became more and more a Hindu city. Nowadays there are still more than forty monasteries (known locally as *baha*) in Patan, and more than thirty in Katmandu. In Bhatgaon there are now only six or so, all in a rather sad condition.

These Buddhist monasteries regularly consist of a main courtyard, on one side of which is a temple easily distinguished by its two- or three-tiered roofs. Covered passages lead into subsidiary courtyards, rather in the manner of Oxford and Cambridge colleges and, different as are the architectural styles from these Western counterparts, one can imagine the towns of Patan and Katmandu as being rather like medieval Oxford. Nowadays there are no proper monks in these old monasteries, but the present inmates are the descendants of the original religious brethren (known locally as *ba-re*) and many of them function as priests. Thus these *ba-re* have now become a caste, a kind of Buddhist equivalent of Brahmans.

The Hindu temples, which are cared for by Brahmans proper, may stand in courtyards, but more often on tiered platforms in the public squares. Since they are free-standing,

The Bhairava Temple in Kirtipur, one of the oldest tiered-roof temples in the Nepal Valley

The main stupa in Kirtipur, dedicated to the Five Supreme Buddhas, whose shrines are set into the dome

OPPOSITE: Carved struts supporting a tiered roof at Bhatgaon

169

The 'Five-Tier' Temple (Nyata-pola), Bhatgaon

they are far more spectacular than their Buddhist counterparts. Noticing only these temples, the visitor may overlook the fact that these tiered-roof temples are merely one special feature of Nepalese architecture, and that they usually form part of a whole complex of buildings, as in the Buddhist monasteries and in the old royal palaces. These last were conceived in conventional monastic style, as a haphazard collection of interlinking courtyards. One even sees over the old doorways of their courtyards ornamental embossed plaques (*torana*) portraying divinities, whose rightful place should have been over doorways of shrines. The most common divinity portrayed in the royal palaces is the Great Goddess (*Bhagavati* or *Kali*) in her triumphant five-headed ten-armed form, surrounded by Indian mythological creatures, the sacred bird *Garuda*, serpent divinities and ocean monsters.

Built of brick and wood, these buildings were comparatively fragile, and although they certainly represent very ancient styles, those that can be dated back in their existing forms to the fifteenth century are very rare indeed. Most of them, like the old royal palaces of Patan, Katmandu and Bhatgaon, date from the seventeenth and eighteenth centuries. What is so extraordinary about Nepal is that types of architecture, as well as social conditions, which were typical of pre-Muslim India have continued to flourish there up to very recent times.

The most typical Buddhist shrine is the stupa or relic mound, and there are thousands of these throughout Nepal of a whole variety of sizes and shapes. Patan, as the prime Buddhist city, still has four such great mounds on its outskirts, one for each point of the compass, and these are traditionally (but doubtless falsely) ascribed to the great Indian emperor Ashoka of the third century BC. Some of the smaller stone stupas can be dated by their styles to the fifth century AD and quite possibly earlier, for it is likely that Buddhism and Hindu culture began

OPPOSITE: Lattice-work on the
old royal palace, Bhatgaon

A stone temple of typical Hindu design

The terra-cotta temple at the western end of the square

Stone figures guarding the approach to a temple

The main square, Bhatgaon

OPPOSITE: Looking eastwards across the square, with the terra-cotta temple in the foreground

The Golden Gate in the main square

Embossed plaque (*torana*) depicting the
Great Goddess over the Golden Gate

to penetrate this remote Himalayan valley in the early centuries
A D. There are in fact interesting canonical accounts (inevitably
undated) describing how the first Buddhist monks found their
way to Nepal in the company of Indian traders. With the
complex developments in Buddhist doctrine, some of these
stupas have become very elaborate with shrines at the four
main points and the four subsidiary points of the compass,
containing images of the supreme manifestations of buddhahood
(*pancatathagata*) and the four protecting goddesses. At the
southern end of the Kirtipur Hill there is a splendid example
of this developed form of stupa.

Another style of temple, built of stone or terra-cotta with a
high tapering roof, also came from India to Nepal. The most
important of these is the 'Great Buddha Monastery' (*Maha-
buddha-baha*) in Patan, which was built in the seventeenth
century as an intended copy of the famous temple which towers
above the original tree of the Buddha's enlightenment at
Budhgaya in central India. There are some fine examples of
this style of temple in the main square of Bhatgaon, especially
the beautiful little terra-cotta temple at the western end of this
square, but unless urgent efforts are made to restore it, it will
not stand there much longer. Guarding the steps that lead up to
some of these shrines are stone figures, representing wrestlers,
horses, rhinos and man-headed lions.

All the crafts of building, wood-carving, metal-work and
stone-work continued uninterrupted until the eighteenth
century. Then in 1768 this central valley of Nepal was invaded
by the fierce and ambitious ruler of Gorkha, a small principality
in the mountains some 50 miles west of Katmandu. The petty
kings of the central valley failed to support one another and
were overcome by treachery on all sides. The peoples and
buildings of Patan, Katmandu and Kirtipur suffered terribly
from this invasion and from the cruel repression that followed.
Bhatgaon, however, was largely spared thanks to secret arrange-
ments that had been made with the conqueror, and also perhaps
to its comparative remoteness.

This city of courtyards and temples lies towards the eastern
end of the valley, some ten miles distant from Katmandu and
Patan. It is reached by a rough open road, and one leaves far
behind the tawdry aggressiveness and the ugly modernity
which mars so much of present-day Katmandu. Bhatgaon has
been neglected during the last two hundred years, but it has
not been spoiled. Patan, which lies so close to Katmandu,
being primarily a Buddhist city, suffered most from the scorn
and repression of the Gorkha conquerors, and its people have
hardly yet learned to hold their heads high again. Bhatgaon,
despite its poverty, has retained its sense of independence,
and so, despite the neglect, it still gives an impression of hope
and vitality. Compared with the other three ancient towns of
Nepal, its main buildings seem even clean and well cared for.
Standing in its main square one faces the great Golden Gate,
surmounted by the plaque of the Great Goddess, and on a

subsidiary roof over the gateway still stand the royal insignia in all their pride, ceremonial umbrellas, flags, jewels, lions and elephants, all in exquisite metal-work. On both sides wooden eaves and the elaborately carved lattice-work of the windows stand out as intricate patterns of black and white against the terra-cotta tones of the brickwork, while on the top of a high pillar in front of the palace the instigator of these labours, King Bhupatindra Malla, sits in prayer on his lion-throne.

The new Gorkha rulers abandoned the ancient town courts for new palaces, built in the surrounding countryside by nineteenth-century Italian architects in a brash stucco Italian style. Thus in the nineteenth century, after 1500 years of continuous practice, the traditional building crafts were abandoned by royal patronage in favour of pretentious Western styles. Finally, the twentieth century has brought with it modern concrete houses of crude Indian design. Here and there in the old cities one may occasionally see some builders at work on an old temple, carefully replacing fine wood-carvings (which no one can do nowadays) with new brickwork. An occasional private benefactor pays for the repair of a favourite temple, but such benefactors are all too rare.

As far as the great Buddhist stupas are concerned, the most generous benefactors have been the Tibetans. It is they who have revetted and repaired the great stupas of Shimbu (*Svayambhu*) and Bauddha, painting them every year and redecking them with coloured prayer-flags. Shimbu stands on a hillock to the west of Ḳatmandu, and traditionally it is supposed to be the oldest shrine in the valley, having been founded by the Great Bodhisattva Manjusri, who is said to have slashed apart the surrounding ring of mountains with his sword, thus draining off the lake that was once here so that men could settle in the valley. Bauddha stands just about in the centre of the valley beside the ancient trade-route that descends from Lhasa to Patan. One now enters its precincts through a nineteenth century stucco arch, while the eyes of all-seeing buddhahood gaze down demandingly from above the vast concrete dome. In Tibetan tradition this great shrine is associated with Padmasambhava, the great miracle-worker who came from India to Tibet in the late eighth century and, quelling the local demons, made Tibet a safe place for Buddhism.

Religious ties between Nepal and Tibet have always been strong. It was Nepalese craftsmen who helped to build some of the first Buddhist temples in Tibet, and for centuries Nepalese craftsmen and traders have kept workshops and offices in Lhasa, while year-in, year-out, Tibetans have come down on pilgrimage to the great Nepalese shrines. Now these same Tibetans have come in their thousands as refugees, and the temples around the great shrines resound with their prayers and their helpless deliberations. Who now will care for these great stupas, one wonders, if the Tibetans can no longer afford to do so? Will they go with the tiered temples into almost universal neglect?

D. L. SNELLGROVE

Bauddha, one of the two great stupas of the Nepal Valley

Nineteenth-century stucco gateway leading into the precincts of Bauddha

SOUTH-EAST ASIA

Introduction by A. H. Christie

The main external cultural influences upon South-East Asia have originated in the Indian subcontinent. This is nowhere more apparent than in the history of the region's architecture up to the time when western European styles began to be adopted for official and commercial buildings at the end of the nineteenth century. But although the historical monuments of South-East Asia derive from Indian originals or from the traditions of the *Shilpishastras*, the Indian architectural manuals, the various areas of South-East Asia saw the evolution of distinctive native styles which owed much to the local tradition of construction in wood and bamboo. These materials remain the most usual for domestic architecture to this day and were always considered fitting for any buildings except temples and pagodas. Royal palaces and monasteries, as well as the homes of nobles and peasants, were all in wood, and it is in this medium that the region's artisans achieved some of their most characteristic and effective buildings.

In one part of the region, however, another foreign influence predominated. From the beginning of the Christian era to the end of the ninth century the Tonkin delta and the coastal region to the south of it was under Chinese suzerainty. Here architecture developed under strong Chinese influences which persisted after the Viet-namese had thrown off the imperial domination of China and embarked upon an expansion of their own which led them to the Mekong delta and westwards towards Cambodia and Laos. The court remained profoundly Chinese in its cultural traditions, and the last imperial capital, at Hue in Central Viet-nam, had its 'Forbidden City' and its altar for the Sacrifice to Heaven and Earth, its dynastic temples and imperial tombs like any Chinese dynasty. Here, as elsewhere in Viet-nam, the Chinese influences are manifest and indisputable, but elsewhere in South-East Asia there are other, more subtle traces of elements in the architecture which seem to stem from China. This is scarcely surprising since the region had been of interest to the Chinese for both political and commercial reasons since the beginning of the

Christian era; Chinese traders had settled there; Chinese emperors claimed suzerainty over its rulers; Chinese Buddhists visited it, often for considerable periods.

The reference to Buddhists serves to emphasize the proximate cause for the strong element of foreign influence in the architecture of South-East Asia. There can be little doubt that the beginnings of building in brick and stone are directly connected with the propagation in the region of two faiths of Indian origin, Hinduism and Buddhism. The exact reasons for their spread into South-East Asia, and indeed the chronology of their early expansion there, are still uncertain, though the blocking of the Central Asian land routes by nomadic tribes which led to the development of Indo-Chinese maritime communications is clearly an important factor in this. But, whatever the reasons for the expansion of these alien religions, their adoption by local rulers and their socio-political significance led to the demand for buildings appropriate to their celebration.

The bamboo shrines which had served to house the spirits of the native South-East Asian faiths (when these had not been content to inhabit some curious stone or take up residence in some distinctive tree, practices which persist alongside more sophisticated ones to this day), were not suited to the rituals needed to celebrate Shiva, Vishnu or the Buddha. Nor did they sufficiently dignify a court which had resident Brahmins and a king with an impressive Sanskritic name and titulary; temples in stone or brick with statuary and narrative reliefs were the only possible shrines for the emerging kingdoms of fourth- and fifth-century South-East Asia. And for these shrines India, whence came the deities which they were to house, furnished the models upon which they were constructed.

What developed, however, was no mere school of provincial architecture, but a series of styles which achieved at their best buildings of distinction and merit which must rank among the great buildings of the world. It was once the fashion to ascribe such structures to Indian colonists but it is now clear that they represent not the flowering of

opposite: A view of Borobudur from
Javasche Oudheden (1854), after a drawing by
Adrianus Johannes Bik (1790–1872)

177

Indian culture overseas, as Sylvain Lévi, Tagore and Majumdar held, but a genuine new development that sprang from a complexity of Indian and local traditions. Later, when Islam began to be adopted by the people of some parts of Indonesia and the eastern littoral of the mainland, the building of mosques was at first in the strictest Muslim traditions. But even here, despite the existence of a much more rigid set of conventions and proprieties than either Hinduism or Buddhism has sought or been able to impose, there have developed traditions and treatments which are peculiarly South-East Asian. Finally, any account of the region's architecture should note, if only in passing, the construction at Tay Ninh, South Viet-nam, of the metropolitan cathedral of Cao Daism, an exotically eclectic building, which was designed some thirty years ago with the aid of a *corbeille-à-bec*, an architectural innovation which does not appear to have been widely adopted.

Two basic types of building of Indian origin are found in South-East Asia. The first consists of a shrine designed to house the statue of a deity. The structure at its simplest consists of a single cell just large enough for the statue, but allows for a great variety of related structures more or less integrated into a temple complex, with surrounding walls and moats representing Earth's peripheral mountains and Ocean as conceived in Indian cosmologies. The second type consists essentially of a solid shrine, reputed to contain some sacred relic; such a shrine is not designed to be entered but rather to be circumambulated with the worshipper's right side nearest the monument.

The religious buildings of South-East Asia which serve Hindu or Buddhist ends are essentially of one or other of these patterns. But there are local differences which are not without interest. Thus in the island of Bali, which is nominally Hindu, the temples can clearly be seen to derive from the first of these types, yet the cell is in many ways less important than a set of empty thrones set upon ornate towers; these constitute the true seats of the gods who may be invited with appropriate rituals to be seated on their proper thrones to take part in some rite or attend some festival. Similarly the ritual of circumambulation may be elaborated until it becomes a sort of pilgrimage in miniature, or the reliefs upon the walls and the shrine itself devised to recite the life of the Buddha so that a turn round the monument enabled the pilgrim to repeat the great events of the Buddha's life in the manner of a Christian visiting the Stations of the Cross.

In any case, however simple the central shrine, whether cell or solid stupa, it tended, particularly in the case of centres of high religious repute, to be surrounded by a complexity of shrines and ancillary buildings, monasteries and rest-houses, libraries and chapels. There were also myriad stalls which catered for the worshippers' bodily needs and housed the fortune-tellers and astrologers, the image and souvenir vendors, and the flower and incense sellers who form an essential part of every religious centre and place of pilgrimage.

Of the architects of the buildings which we have been discussing we know nothing: a few scattered inscriptions throw some light upon the existence of contractors and craftsmen connected with the building industry. The existence of a royal works service seems to be attested in Cambodia, and it is clear from both literary sources and inscriptions that royal patronage was a main source of employment for builders in brick and masonry. Various considerations affected the form which the buildings took. The limitations imposed by materials and methods were considerable. The total absence of building stone in the neighbourhood of Pagan and the unsuitability of that available to the Cham builders of Central Viet-nam led to the development of sophisticated brickwork which had then to be covered with stucco and plaster to simulate the stonework of the tradition from which the temples of these two areas derived.

The absence of the true arch, except in Burma where the arch attested at Hmawza in the seventh–eighth century made possible the superb barrel-vaulting of the eleventh–thirteenth-century buildings at Pagan, precluded the development of wide cloisters or extensive roof areas unless uneconomically supported. (An interesting example of the limitations imposed by the corbelled arch is furnished by the great road bridge near Siemreap in Cambodia, one of the few secular buildings from the Khmer Empire to have survived and to be still functional.) The lack of satisfactory bonding systems in Cambodian masonry meant that the structures were not particularly stable; a particular point of weakness is the junction between two walls at right angles, since usually no attempt is made to interlock the stones at the point of juncture.

The primary consideration in the design of South-East Asian buildings, in materials other than wood, was religious, for almost all the buildings had not only a religious function but were also required to express by their symbolism some religious concept. It is interesting to note the observation in a medieval Javanese text that 'the body of the Buddha is a stupa'. The stupa itself epitomizes the concept of the *Mahaparinirvana*, a mortuary monument which commemorates the moment when, for the Buddha, death itself as well as life ceased to exist. The Hindu temple, especially in South-East Asia where a native mountain cult predisposed the inhabitants towards the Indian idea, is a Meru, a microcosm of Sumeru, the world's axial mountain whose peak served the gods and demons as a churn stick when they churned Ocean to make the nectar of immortality. This theme was a favourite with the Khmers who portrayed it in their reliefs and, on an almost cosmic scale, in the figures which surround the temple complex of Preah Khan (AD 1191).

The single tower, perhaps raised upon a single platform, could well symbolize the world axis and at the same time house the deity. There was no need for space within the shrine; Hinduism was not a congregational religion. To the tower might be added a simple shrine before the door of the main cell to house the deity's *vahana*, the sacred animal upon which the god rode. From this it was an easy step to create three towers side by side to house, for example, the three gods of the Hindu trinity, each tower on its own platform, then all three on a common terrace, perhaps of several tiers in the interest of scale.

Gradually the tradition developed of a complex, quincuncial lay-out which reached its apotheosis in the great temple of Angkor Wat, discussed below. It is interesting to note, however, that among the Chams the idea of thus integrating the various units did not appear to exist; in Champa we find complicated temple sites, but each tower appears to have been set up without any attempt to relate it to its neighbours.

Somewhat similar symbolic considerations appear to have obtained among the Viet-namese, but here the underlying tradition was neither the Hindu nor Buddhist cosmological symbolism but the Chinese geomantic tradition. Some secondary influences can, however, be ascribed to Mahayana Buddhist theories which reached Viet-nam partly through China and partly, though this is seldom recognized, from the Chams who were their neighbours to the south and whose territory and much of whose culture the Viet-namese gradually absorbed as they expanded southwards.

Side by side with the architecture which we have been discussing there has always existed in South-East Asia another, indigenous tradition which exhibits different local variations. This is building in wood and bamboo, often upon piles and quite often on a large scale. In parts of Borneo a single longhouse serves as habitation for a whole village. Nor are these structures necessarily mere huts of grandiose size; in parts of Indonesia and the Philippines we find buildings of dignity and distinction which are the descendants of similar structures illustrated on bronze drums belonging to the prehistoric cultures of South-East Asia and of early date. Wood, too, was the traditional material for the king's palace though here it might be richly ornamented with gilded carving, scarlet lacquer and, more recently, mirror-work. The same tradition served for the monasteries of Buddhist monks which, despite the Buddha's injunctions urging austerity for his followers, were often embellished by generous laymen and royal patrons.

In parts of South-East Asia it seems that work in wood is the true native tradition; Burma seems to be a case in point. But the work in low relief which is part of the glory of Angkor Wat and other temples of the Khmer capital leaves no room for doubt; this is the work of men who truly understood the nature of the stone-carver's art, as did the artisans who decorated the temples of Java. If there is any truth in Sylvain Lévi's statement that the greatest flowering of India's genius is to be seen overseas, in Angkor Wat and Borobudur, then it must be added that those who cultivated the seed of Indian genius and brought it to this flowering were natives of South-East Asia who gave it a form which is theirs alone.

The cleaning of the ruins of the central temple of Chandi Sari, Prambanam (1807), from a drawing probably by a Javanese artist

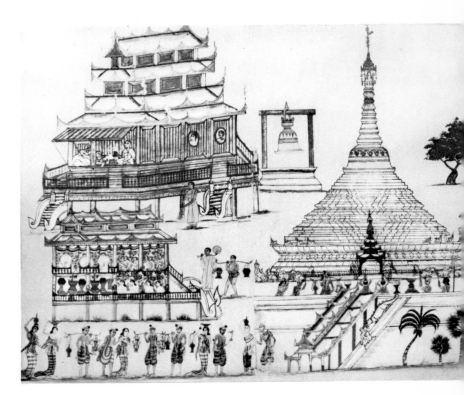

'A Burman Temple and Monastery' (*c* 1825), from an album of Burmese drawings

ANGKOR WAT

*The great Khmer temple-palace
with its magnificent
narrative bas-reliefs*

The following account of the Cambodian capital is taken from the writings of Chou Ta-Kuan, who was a member of a mission sent there by the Mongol emperor Timur in AD 1296:

'The wall of the city is some twenty li in circumference. There are five gates, each with a subsidiary gate on either side. There are two gates in the eastern side and one in each of the others. Outside the wall is a great moat which is crossed by great bridges. On either side of the bridges are fifty-four stone giants, like stone generals of terrible aspect. The five gateways are identical. The stone parapets of the bridges are carved in the semblance of nine-headed serpents. The fifty-four giants hold the serpents as though preventing them from escaping. The gates are surmounted by five Buddha heads in stone, facing west: the centre head is gilded. The sides of the gates are carved as stone elephants. The entire wall is of ashlar construction. The stones are most carefully and solidly arranged and there is no sign of vegetation breaking through. The wall is without battlements. On the rampart palms have been planted in a few places. There are empty wall-houses at intervals. The inner side of the rampart is like a ten-feet high ramp on the top of which there are gates closed at night and open during the day which dogs are not allowed through. The gates are guarded.

The wall is square with four angle towers. Criminals whose ears have been cropped are not allowed through the entrances. The centre of the kingdom is marked by a golden tower flanked by over twenty stone towers and hundreds of stone cells. On the East there is a golden bridge with two golden lions on either side and eight golden Buddhas placed in the bottom of the stone chambers. One li to the North of the golden tower is a copper tower of greater height which is a truly impressive sight. At its foot are a dozen stone structures. Another li farther North is the king's palace in whose private apartments is another gold tower. It is these monuments, in our opinion, which have given rise to the laudatory accounts of Cambodia's wealth and glory which merchants have lavished on the country since their arrival there. If one leaves by the South gate one finds a stone tower about half a li outside the wall. According to tradition this was erected by Lu Pan in a single night. About a li from the South gate is Lu Pan's tomb which is about ten li in circumference. It contains several hundred stone structures.'

Wooden figure of a worshipper from Angkor Wat, now in the National Museum, Phnom Penh

OPPOSITE : Window pillars and low relief motifs
on the surround, from a gallery at Angkor Wat

This was not the first visit to this region by Chinese officials; much of our knowledge of the history of the Khmer Empire, to use the Cambodian name for themselves, depends upon Chinese historical records. But Chou Ta-kuan was an observant visitor, and his account of the country and its people gives a lively and convincing picture of a realm whose territory once reached from the coast of Viet-nam to the Burmese–Thai frontier and from the Gulf of Siam to the marches of China.

A hundred years before Chou's visit the Khmer capital had been sacked by the Chams, a people who then occupied the central and southern coastal areas of what is now Viet-nam. After their attack the capital was substantially rebuilt by King Jayavarman VII (AD 1181–1219), an ardent Buddhist, who constructed the walled citadel known as Angkor Thom with its gateways surmounted by the great heads which Chou described. His 'tower of gold' is certainly the Bayon (whose towers repeat the head theme of the gates); this served to establish the Bodhisattva Avalokiteshvara, perhaps portrayed in the king's image, at the kingdom's centre. The 'tower of copper' seems to be the Baphuon, a structure which appears to have marked the centre of an earlier capital in the eleventh century AD.

To the north again was 'the palace' which is the Phimeanakas. This much-discussed building was almost certainly completed by King Suryavarman I some time after AD 1002. It was known as the Hemashringagiri, The Mountain of the Golden Horn, and whatever its function it can scarcely have served as a palace. Its modern name, which means Flying Palace, suggests that it was connected with the king as a divine being, however, for in Indo-Khmer tradition, divine beings frequently have flying residences. Chou repeats a tradition that it was in this tower that the king slept:

. . . all the natives claim that in the tower there is a spirit in the form of a nine-headed serpent who is lord of all the soil of the realm. It appears each night in the form of a woman. The king must spend the first watch of each night with her and have intercourse with her. Even the king's principal wives dare not enter. He emerges in the second watch and may then sleep with his wives and concubines. If the serpent spirit does not appear it is a sign that the king's death is at hand. If the king fails to keep his tryst, some evil will occur.

It will have been noticed that there has been as yet no overt mention of Angkor Wat, although this has today become the best known of the Khmer monuments and the eponym for the entire region of Siemreap where the successive capitals were built. It is included in Chou's account, but so disguised that it is not at once recognizable. According to him, south of the south gate is a stone tower, erected in a single day by Lu Pan. This is the Phnom Bakheng, which stands upon a natural hill in the middle of a walled enclosure, greater in extent than Angkor Thom. Phnom Bakheng was the central shrine which housed the palladium, the *deva-raja* of Yashovarman I (AD 889–900). This god-king, to translate its Sanskrit title, was a Shiva-linga, and its installation at Phnom Bakheng marked the re-establishment of the capital at

OPPOSITE: The southern gateway of Angkor Thom. It is believed that the representations of Avalokiteshvara over the gate are also representations of King Jayavarman VII, the builder of Angkor Thom

A somewhat imaginative illustration of the jungle-clad ruins which confronted nineteenth-century explorers of Siemreap, from L. Delaporte's *Voyage au Cambodge*. It is only recently that the mysterious faces on the walls of Angkor Thom have been identified with Avalokiteshvara, the compassionate future Buddha

Stone figure of Jayavarman VII (AD 1181–1219), who built Angkor Thom (National Museum, Phnom Penh)

Siemreap after a period in which it had been located at Roluos, still within the general neighbourhood of Siemreap, but farther south on the road which leads to the present capital at Phnom Penh.

The move to Phnom Penh was not to take place until AD 1434, after the sack of Angkor by Thai invaders who had learned their military craft as mercenaries of the Khmer. They are shown as such on the bas-reliefs of Angkor Wat which, in Chou's account, is the tomb of Lu Pan, the architect of Phnom Bakheng. Chou Ta-kuan gives us, in fact, a thoroughly muddled account of a number of stages in the history of the Khmer capital from the end of the ninth century (Phnom Bakheng) to the end of the twelfth century AD (Bayon), and adds to the difficulty by attributing two of the buildings to the Chinese god of architecture.

But although this last fact would seem finally to condemn Chou's account, it adds in reality to its verisimilitude for it echoes the Khmer tradition that Angkor Wat was built by the Divine Craftsman whom the Hindus call Vishvakarman and whose name Chou Ta-kuan sinized into its Chinese equivalent. It does seem likely, however, that his knowledge of the great temple was strictly limited, whether because of its sanctity which must have closed it to foreigners or because it was already out of cult at the time of his visit. None the less, his narrative holds the essence of the matter in many of the questions which concern the nature of the Khmer state and its rulers. Even the curious history of the king's ritual bedding with the land-owning serpent spirit has its place in the theory of Khmer kingship.

The essence of the matter lies in the concept of kingship as being embodied in a palladium, the *deva-raja*, which is housed in the centre of the kingdom. Countless inscriptions testify to this belief from the ninth century onwards and to the need to create a central mountain as the kingdom's axis. This theme is also known to India, where it may indeed belong to the Mesopotamian tradition of the *ziggurat*. As Indian influences grew in South-East Asia, what seems to have been a native tradition of a sacred mountain became identified with the Indian theme of Sumeru, the axis of the world. The concept translated into architecture gives rise to the temple with a tall central block, enclosed in walls and flanked with moats, to form a microcosm which houses the kingly essence and makes of its temporary tenant, the king, a true *chakravartin* or world ruler. The temporary tenancy is exemplified by the need for the king to renew his usufruct by his union with the true owner of the land, the serpent-spirit. (The serpents flanking the gate bridges of Angkor Thom stem from another tradition but their adoption, like the Khmer preference for images of the Buddha seated on the coiled serpent, is probably due to the pre-existence of a native serpent-cult.)

It is from this hybrid culture that another idea took root in the Khmer kingdom to be exemplified both in its art and in its nomenclature. For since the ruler was intimately linked to the

OPPOSITE : Buddha figures from Angkor Wat, which was originally a temple dedicated to the royal cult of Vishnu but later became used as a Buddhist shrine

divine he could be identified with the god by the form of his name during his lifetime and assumed to have become merged with the god after his death. The king's name, the name of his capital and the name attributed to the image deemed to house the royal essence, were all devised to illustrate the link between the ruler and his deity; after his death the king's name was changed to indicate the deity within whom his spirit was then lodged. And the dynastic temple which housed his royal essence seems to have become his mortuary shrine; here the principal deity seems to have been held to represent the apotheosized king.

Such a temple was Angkor Wat. The great central tower, still 215 feet above the approach road despite the loss of its finial, is Sumeru; the moats, 625 feet wide, which surround the outer walls are Ocean. The walls, forming a rectangle 1,425 by 1,640 yards, are the peripheral mountains of the earth. The scale is vast: the sandstone coping, almost 10 feet high, outside the moat is more than 6¼ miles in length. The entrance to this microcosm lies on the west side, a fact which has led some writers to stress its funerary nature since most temples have their main doorway on the east. A wide stone causeway, with a handsome serpent balustrade, crosses the moat and leads to an inner enclosure whose laterite and sandstone walls (890 by 1,090 yards) have entrances in three sides. The main one is an impressive monumental ceremonial gateway *gopura*, some 220 yards in length, whose three pavilions are crowned with towers. This gives access to another ceremonial way, also flanked by serpent rails. There were buildings on either side, in what may be termed a quadrangle, and at the end a ceremonial tank on either side in front of the entrance to the next enclosure (295 by 370 yards), some 380 yards from the last.

At this point the nature of the sanctuary changes and we appear to enter the temple proper. Linked galleries join the various elements of the buildings and the whole rises on terraces to the central tower which is the inmost shrine of Angkor Wat. Immediately within the gateway is a huge cruciform platform which may have served some ceremonial function at the temple entrance. This leads to a further enclosure which, like that surrounding it, was furnished with a covered gallery. The outer is 205 by 235 yards, the inner 110 by 125 yards; each is furnished with corner-towers and steps in the middle of each side leading outward. The inner terrace is about 45 feet above the level of the second main enclosure. Another 45 feet above this is the third platform, 245 feet square, with a galleried surround whose outer walls are 215 feet long. Each corner of the gallery has a high tower. In the middle is the central tower, the image house, from which the statue is missing. This rises from a subsidiary platform set on the third terrace, and is reached by exceedingly steep stairs in stone.

Such is the building which Chou Ta-kuan noted as the tomb of Lu Pan. Few visitors can have failed to understand the tradition which ascribed it to some Celestial Architect; Pierre

The north library at Banteay Srei, twelve miles north of Angkor. The temple was dedicated to Shiva in AD 967

OPPOSITE: Detail of the representation of the Buddha's footprint, showing some of the 108 magical signs. Such footprints, ancient objects of worship in Asia, seem to be thought of as 'sealing' the land as the Buddha's property

187

The great temple of Angkor Wat

North-west corner tower of the central quincunx

The main enclosure of Angkor Wat from the south-west

Looking west from the central quincunx at the inner side of the second cloister

Aerial view of Angkor Wat from the north-east

Detail of a bas-relief depicting a battle scene from the *Mahabharata* in the west gallery, Angkor Wat

Relief of Vishnu on his sacred mount Garuda, from Prasat Kravan, a brick temple dedicated in AD 921

Loti, Paul Claudel, and many others came under its spell. The soberest scholars have been moved to raptures by its majesty and its ornaments. Few, however, have concerned themselves with its patron, the Khmer King Suryavarman who initiated its construction early in his reign (AD 1113–50) and appears twice in its reliefs under his posthumous, apotheotic name, Paramavishnuloka. It is almost certain that the missing statue of the central tower embodied the king as the god Vishnu, perhaps in some syncretistic form, for there is evidence that the king, a notable builder, was also interested in religious reform and attempted to unify at least the official worship of the state. It is fitting therefore that Angkor Wat should illustrate the final evolution of the temple form as it developed in the Khmer world from a single shrine through a complex of loosely connected towers to the ultimate sophistication of Suryavarman's foundation which is, incidentally, probably the world's largest religious structure.

The wonder of Angkor Wat does not repose in its lay-out and its architecture alone, though the manner in which the unknown designer managed the ritual approach to the inmost shrine and his treatment of the symbolism of the temple are worthy of the highest praise. It is the manner in which the ornament, both the purely decorative, as in the scrolls which adorn the pillars, and in the great narrative bas-reliefs which fill the galleried cloisters, is integrated into the building and the sculptors' virtuosity displayed to full advantage without being allowed to dominate which distinguish Angkor Wat from so many of the other great buildings of the Khmer Empire. The false windows and doors (required in all Khmer temples for reasons both of symmetry and of orientation since all temples serve the four quarters of the world) are among the finest surviving examples of Khmer masonry. The delicate, shallowly carved swags of foliage, among whose leaves forest birds play, and the countless *apsaras*, divine dancers, who adorn the pilasters and outer walls of the galleries aid the microcosmic conceit without distracting the attention from the central shrine of the god-king. The style of the carving has been described as that of the embroiderer, and the whole effect is certainly comparable with that of tapestry-covered walls. And although the manner of the great series of reliefs is more assertive, here too restraint has been exercised; they complement the architecture and glorify both god and king without in any sense dominating the building.

Not all the narrative reliefs are of the same date: indeed it is changes in style and technique here which enable one to be certain that the building was not completed in the king's lifetime. It has further been argued that the reliefs are intended to be viewed in the course of a circumambulation counter-clockwise and that this proves the funerary destination of the monument. But though the panels are to be read from left to right the systematization of the major themes is not wholly clear and the argument is not, therefore, necessarily convincing. What is certain is that the reliefs are all Vaishnavite in their intention and that even those where the king is shown portray him under the rubric Paramavishnuloka, the name in which he is identified with the god Vishnu.

Of the scenes represented, two (those on the two flanks of the north-east corner-tower) were executed after the rest though they may well have been outlined in the original construction period. These represent Vishnu on Garuda and Vishnu's battle with Bana in which the god is shown in his form as Krishna, long a favourite subject for Khmer sculptors. The southern half of the eastern gallery is devoted to the Churning of the Ocean, the event in which gods and demons joined forces to extract from the waters, using Meru as churn-stick and the World Serpent as churn-rope, the ambrosia of immortality. This motif is one which the Khmers had adopted as a major theme and it is to be found portrayed three-dimensionally at Angkor Thom, where the gods and demons on either side of each gateway are using the central temple itself as their churn-stick while the serpent's body surrounds the whole enclosure.

Along the western gallery are shown two scenes of warfare taken from Hindu classics. To the north is the Battle of Lanka in which the monkey armies under Hanuman help Rama (a form of Vishnu) recover his wife Sita from the demon ruler of Ceylon. This is taken from the Ramayana. To the south we have the episode in the Mahabharata which deals with the great battle between the Pandavas and Kuravas whose intention is also Vaishnavite. Along the southern gallery are first a double-register scene in which the king, from a mountain, issues orders to his army (upper register) and takes part, with his escort, in a military march-past (lower). Beyond this, on the other side of the southern porch are scenes of heaven and hell (in which, as is so often the case in medieval Christian art, the hell scenes show far greater inventiveness and variety). It has been suggested that the order here implies that the king, shown with his escort, has passed through the afterworld to enter Vishnu's heaven (perhaps with the help of the ambrosia obtained from the churning scene which follows next) to be adored in the central tower in the form of Paramavishnuloka.

Pierre Loti, known as the Pilgrim of Angkor, wrote romantically of:

. . palaces in which lived those prodigiously luxurious kings of whom we know nothing, who have passed into oblivion without leaving so much as a name engraved either in stone or in memory.

The Khmer themselves attribute Angkor Wat to the Divine Architect, Vrah Bisnukarman. The labours of French archaeologists and scholars have revealed, if not the names of the individual artists and craftsmen, at least that of the king who inspired this masterpiece as his dynastic temple and his mortuary shrine. And it can scarcely be held that this knowledge diminishes one whit the immensity of this architectural achievement in twelfth-century Cambodia.   A. H. CHRISTIE

Divine dancer (*apsara*) from the inner side of the enclosure wall

Detail of the frieze above the dancers on the inner side of the enclosure wall

191

THE SHWE DAGON

*The best-known Burmese temple,
a lofty golden spire rising
above the city of Rangoon*

For the Burman to have obtained the right to be addressed by a title such as Founder of a monastery, Donor of a Buddha figure or Builder of a pagoda is to be recognized as having fulfilled one of the fundamental Buddhist virtues: that of giving. By giving the layman acquires merit, and such merit may outweigh any wrongful acts. Thereby the giver progresses one stage nearer to the ultimate attainment of *nirvana*, the state in which the otherwise inexorable laws of *karma* no longer operate. The attainment of *nirvana* is the ultimate hope of the Buddhist; the *Mahaparinirvana* of the Buddha marked the ending of his earthly career. He taught the doctrine, the *dharma*, upon which Buddhism rests, and founded the monkly order, the *sangha*, which continues to observe his teachings and to make them available to the laity.

The Three Jewels, The Buddha, the Dharma and the Sangha, are the heart of Buddhism and the laity serve them in many ways: by the provision of food for the monks; by the building of pagodas and monasteries; by the presentation of statues of the Buddha and the commissioning of paintings or reliefs which exemplify points of the teaching or act as reminders of right behaviour. It is a curious fact, however, that in all the canonical books of the Buddhist law there is little or no sanction for much of this activity. The tradition of building a pagoda, or having a statue made or a picture painted, rests almost wholly upon tradition rather than upon scriptural injunctions.

One version of the Buddhist Canon contains a story which sets out the reasons for having upon the outer wall of the monastery a picture of the Wheel of the Law. This symbol commemorates a crucial moment in the history of the Buddha's teaching when he preached the first sermon in the Deer Park at Banaras and 'set in motion the Wheel of the Law'. It also symbolically epitomizes that Law. The text makes it clear that the painting is intended to help in the exposition of the doctrine in the absence of the Buddha, first while away on journeys to teach the doctrine and later after his own attainment of *nirvana*. Similarly, there is

Guardian figure in gilded wood from the Shwe Dagon. The style is post-classical; the costume survives in the traditional theatre

OPPOSITE: This pavilion at the Shwe Dagon, with its lavish use of gilding and lacquer, exemplifies traditional Burmese architectural style in wood. The individual spires, as well as the building as a whole, are treated as manifestations of the Cosmic Axis, the tiers being separate heavens

The Shwe Dagon, from across the Royal Lakes

Detail of shrines on the north-east corner
of the Shwe Dagon enclosure

a story that an image of the Buddha was made, in somewhat miraculous circumstances, in order that his appearance should be recorded for posterity; it is often asserted of other images of great repute that their efficacy stems from the fact that they are faithful copies of this first portrayal.

The provision of buildings for monks and for cult practices is well established, yet here too the basic teaching is hard to find. There can be little doubt that morphologically the stupa is, in western prehistorical terms, a round barrow. In essence the stupa consists of a hemispherical mound, enclosed within a palisade, containing physical remains and surmounted by a mast which bore, perhaps, some kind of pennant to draw the attention of passers-by. The fact that the Buddhist stupa is supposed to house some sacred relic in no way invalidates the general similarity, no more than does the tradition of the stupa as a place of pilgrimage; the great barrows were almost certainly the centre of tribal cults and therefore the foci of seasonal migrations.

According to the great Chinese pilgrim Hsuan Tsang, who visited the Buddhist lands during the period AD 629–45, there was a tradition alive in Bactria in his day that the Buddha taught his first two lay disciples, the merchants Trapusha and Bhallika (Tapusa and Palikat in Burmese), to whom he had presented a lock of his hair and his nail-parings, how to build a suitable shrine for these gifts:

He took his three garments, folded them into four and piled them up on the ground, beginning with the largest and finishing with the smallest. Then he took his begging bowl and inverted it upon the garments. Finally he stuck his beggar's staff on top and said: that is the way to make a stupa.

This text is of course late, but the tradition which associates relics, the Buddha and stupas is early enough to make it part of the basic Buddhist pattern. The use of the stupa, usually in association with the tree or trees in whose shade he died (and which is the same as that under whose shade he was born), as a symbol for the Buddha's attainment of *nirvana* and as an iconographic representation of the historical event of his death is attested from the earliest monuments. A further substantiation is to be found in the tradition of the War of the Relics, immediately after the Buddha's death, when all those who had been associated with him in his lifetime claimed some portion of his remains as a sacred relic. There is, too, the tradition that the Emperor Ashoka built 80,000 stupas throughout his realm to house Buddha relics. Philosophically the association of Buddha and stupa is most neatly stated in an aphorism from a medieval Javanese text: 'the body of the Buddha is a stupa'.

The stupa and the rite of circumambulation, *pradakshina* in the direction of the sun, are therefore established Buddhist forms, but the development of the image led to the need for an image house. From this it was an easy step to a temple, but it must be admitted that by no means all Buddhist schools adopted the temple (properly, since the Buddha was not a deity and should not, therefore, receive worship). There is some evidence to suggest that, although strictly speaking not even the Buddha's image should have been worshipped, the stupa too, or a small, model stupa enclosed in a shrine, was in fact regarded as a kind of deity and offered appropriate treatment. (Such a development seems to be reflected in the Javanese source which has already been cited.)

In any event, there rapidly emerged in Buddhism a series of practices which were scarcely to be distinguished from the worship of a Hindu deity. These led to the development of Buddhist temple architecture which naturally derived its inspiration from Hindu sources. For long periods in Burma, both stupa and temple existed side by side. However, an interesting synthesis is also to be seen in such buildings as the Ananda Pagoda at Pagan (*c* AD 1105) which, although resembling a temple from the outside, seems in fact to stem from a stupa (now forming the apparent cult centre of the building, but solid with no cella). This structure has been surrounded by a series of circumambulatory passages, square in plan to conform to the outline of the base upon which the temple stands. These have been roofed over to create the superficial impression of a conventional temple to house a god.

The earliest surviving buildings in Burma, dating from perhaps AD 700, include shrines to house an image, shrines with a solid core on whose four faces an image could be displayed in relief, and stupas which show some affinities with those of the Ganges Valley in India. These buildings are attributed to the Pyu, a people related to the Burmans and who entered Burma before them. At one time they occupied most of the area of the central plains. Their culture, which is gradually being revealed

The *hti*, the gilded finial of the Shwe Dagon, conceived as a royal parasol. The stupa is treated as if it were the person of the Buddha to be shaded by such a parasol

The Mingalazedi Pagoda at Pagan, built in
AD 1241 and a magnificent example of classical
Burmese religious architecture

by archaeology and the study of Chinese sources, clearly contributed to the development of Burma and Burmese Buddhist architecture, as did that of the Mons, a people inhabiting both lower Burma and parts of Thailand where at one time they were the dominant people over a large area in the centre and south of the country.

Both the Mons and the Pyu markedly influenced the great efflorescence of religious building which occurred in central Burma, at Pagan, in the eleventh, twelfth and thirteenth centuries. Here, in the space of perhaps a dozen square miles along the bank of the Irawadi in an arid semi-duneland with few trees and almost without rain, there were built more than six thousand temples and monasteries in brick. Of these only one, it appears, was Hindu and very few Mahayanist. Almost without exception the buildings of Pagan, such as the Mingalazedi

Pagoda, are dedicated to the service of Theravada Buddhism. Nor must we forget that there were thousands of other buildings in wood: monasteries, royal residences, and houses and huts for the laity. Of these there remain no sign. But it was here that the synthesis of earlier Mon and Pyu styles took place in an area in which the Burmans gradually became predominant. This gave rise to a culture which thenceforward could be properly described as Burmese, a culture in which Buddhism played a central role.

All the laity could play some part in the support of the religion by their help in establishing buildings for its service. The great stupas were often royal foundations, as the inscriptions make clear, but it was, and indeed still is, possible for the humblest peasant to contribute by adding a fragment of gold leaf to the dome or to one of the figures that adorn the shrine, or by providing a water-pot for the refreshment of pilgrims. The more wealthy might add small stupas around the base of the main edifice or shrines to house statues and edifying groups depicting scenes from the Buddha's life.

Another type of shrine might also be found to house the nats, those semi-divine spirits, not all of them benevolent, who represent perhaps elements surviving from the beliefs of Burma's pre-Buddhist days. The best example of this is to be found at the Shwe Zigon Pagoda at Pagan built by King Kyanzittha at the end of the eleventh century and often considered the national shrine of Burma. Here the nats are housed in style, for, according to tradition, the king insisted that their presence at the pagoda would bring the nat-worshippers to the stupa where they might more readily be persuaded to adopt Buddhism. (In fact, Burmese Buddhists almost all treat the nats with considerable respect and many make offerings to them.)

Although the Shwe Zigon is so important in the history of Burmese nationalism, it is not perhaps the best known of Burma's stupas to the outside world. This must surely be the great Shwe Dagon which stands on a small hill immediately behind the city of Rangoon and dominates the city and its approaches. Burmese tradition tells how two brothers, Tapusa and Palikat, received from the Buddha eight of his hairs which they brought to the Golden Land Suvannabhumi and enshrined under the Shwe Dagon Pagoda together with relics of three previous Buddhas (although Buddhas appear to escape the cycle of birth, death and rebirth, there are in fact cycles of Buddhas also). Thus the tradition; but so far as is known the pagoda is of no great age, and certainly its present form is modern. We know that in AD 1362 it was repaired by a king who also raised its height to 66 feet. By the middle of the next century its height had been doubled and by AD 1768 it had reached the height of 321 feet: this is the present structure with the addition of a *hti*, the ornamental spire with umbrella crowning the Burmese stupa, which was presented by King Mindon to mark the holding of the Fifth Buddhist Council at Mandalay in 1871. The presentation was in fact an assertion of Burmese Buddhist nationalism against the

Temples and monasteries of Pagan

A view of the desolate waste of Pagan by Colesworthy Grant, an artist who visited the Burmese court at Ava in 1855. The site once contained more than 6,000 brick-built temples, stupas and monasteries; it was here that the synthesis of Indian, Mon, Pyu and Burman elements took place from which later Burmese architecture – and indeed Burmese culture – stem

197

The base of the great stupa of the
Shwe Dagon, with its lesser shrines and
guardian beasts

An impression of the Shwe Dagon by Lt Joseph Moore,
of His Majesty's 89th Regiment, in 1825. The bell
is reputedly the second largest in the world

198

British as well as an act of piety, and the authorities refused to allow the king to attend the ceremony. His envoys therefore presented the *hti*, whose jewels were worth £62,000 at that time.

Almost two hundred years earlier, an English merchant, Ralph Fitch, had visited Burma and wrote among other things of his impression of the Shwe Dagon:

About two dayes journey from Pegu [then capital of Burma] there is a Varelle or Pagode, which is the pilgrimage of the Pegues: it is called Dogonne, and is of a woonderfull bignesse, and all gilded from the foot to the toppe. And there is a house by it wherein the Tallipoies which are their priests doe preach. This house is five and fifty paces in length, and hath three pawnes or walks in it, and forty great pillars gilded which stand between the walks; and it is open on all sides with a number of small pillars, which be likewise gilded: it is gilded with gold within and without. There are houses very faire round about for the pilgrims to lie in: and many goodly houses for the Tallipoies to preach in, which are full of images both of men and women, which are all gilded over with golde. It is the fairest place, as I suppose, that is in the world: it standeth very high, and there are foure wayes to it, which all along are set with trees of fruits, in such wise that a man can goe in the shade aboue two miles in length. And when their feast day is, a man can hardly passe by water or by land for the great presse of people; for they come from all places of the kingdome of Pegu thither at their feast.

The shade trees and the long approaches are still there, each approach with its elaborately carved entrance of gilded wood crowned by spires, which occur again and again on the mass of small shrines and lesser stupas which huddle in the shade of the Shwe Dagon itself. The platform upon which the main stupa stands is vastly greater than it was in Fitch's time; it is now a great rectangle, 900 feet long and 685 feet wide, which rises nearly 170 feet above the base of the hill. Chinthés, Burmese leogryphs, guard the shrine and its entrances, and there are urns containing the ashes of monks preserved after ritual cremation.

There are no services; as Fitch remarked, 'they have none other ceremonies nor services that I could see, but onely preaching.' The monks expound the doctrine as the Buddha enjoined; the laity listen and thereby acquire merit. Their own acts of worship, if one may use the term in a system in which there is no deity, consist of obeisance to the stupa, perhaps the affixing of a piece of gold leaf, the taking of omens, the circumambulation of the shrine. They may also consult one of the many astrologers who conduct their business in the pagoda precincts, talk with friends and picnic. For a visit to the pagoda is a holiday and at times of festivals to visit a shrine is a family excursion. And over all looms the great golden spire, the reminder of the vanity of existence and the truth that it is only by the attainment of *nirvana* that fulfilment is possible. It is ironical that Fitch wrote: 'If they did not consume their golde in these vanities it would be very plentiful and good cheape in Pegu.'

A. H. CHRISTIE

Worshippers at one of the shrines which surround the main stupa

Detail of carved wood ornamentation at the Shwe Dagon, a good example of Burmese skill in wood-working

BOROBUDUR

*An ornate temple which represents a
uniquely Javanese translation of religious
ideas into architectural terms*

The great monument which stands surrounded by volcanoes in the middle of the Kedu plain in central Java is, without question, one of the noblest buildings to have sprung from the Buddhist faith and is worthy to rank among the world's finest religious foundations. It is, therefore, somewhat ironical that neither its date of construction nor indeed its builders are precisely known, while its doctrinal interpretation is open to considerable doubt. But despite these problems, Chandi Borobudur conveys, even to the most casual visitor, an extraordinary impression of the ultimate tranquillity which Buddhism affords to its believers. That it does so is an architectural achievement of the highest order and testifies to the successful manner in which structure and decoration have been treated together to produce a coherent whole.

The monument shows every sign of having been planned as a unit and wholly lacks that somewhat fortuitous air which is characteristic, if not unattractively so, of so many buildings in the Indian tradition. Great ingenuity is manifest in the lay-out and indeed in the siting of the building, for what appears at first view to be a true stupa, treated perhaps in a slightly unconventional manner – a point to which we shall return below – is in fact a galleried structure built around a hill which forms the core of the monument. Various other features also serve to distinguish Borobudur from other Javanese monuments: the first of these is that it is the only stupa in Java which is rich in other types of Buddhist monument. It is, it seems, a unique product of genius, and it is this uniqueness which makes its interpretation so difficult.

First, however, we must analyze the structure to show how its architect set about his task. The basic lay-out of the building is simple: four square terraces set upon a basement platform and surmounted by three circular terraces which support a stupa. (We may note here that there are indications that the building was never finished and it has been argued that the original plan called for a much larger terminal stupa: there is no real evidence

The entrance to the first terrace on the south side, from a drawing commissioned by Sir Stamford Raffles, who instituted the first scientific study of Borobudur during the British occupation of Java in the Napoleonic Wars

OPPOSITE: Monster-capped archway leading upwards from the second terrace to the austerity of the central stupa

for this, but we must certainly envisage some form of finial above the surviving structure.) The four square terraces are each provided with an exterior wall so that there is an enclosed pathway around each level of the monument. A staircase with lavishly-decorated archways leads to the top of the monument from the middle of each side of the square.

We have spoken of square terraces, but in fact each side of these has a doubly recessed corner to provide a far more complex outline. This contributes immeasurably to the whole effect of the building by providing marked contrasts of light and shade upon each façade, as well as within the circumambulatory galleries, and avoiding the monotony of overlong horizontals in a building whose sides at the base are 160 yards in length. This broken outline is repeated in the platform and its basement, part of which is an addition of uncertain function, but both these levels lack the exterior wall of the stupa proper. The extension to the lower part of the platform is aesthetically unfortunate for it tends to make the whole building appear a little squat. It has been thought that it was added because the whole structure showed a tendency to slide during its construction and that the encasement was added to bond the whole supporting platform. There is evidence to support this view, for when the monument was restored it was discovered that a series of reliefs, some 160 in number, lay concealed within this casing and that some of these had not been completed, as though some emergency had involved the abandonment of that part of the design.

The now-concealed reliefs on the basement platform are the only obviously narrative motif on the exterior of the building. This is not to say that it is unadorned. On the contrary, the whole is covered with carved garlands and swags and other motifs, while the richly carved gateways are each topped with a monster-head and have *makara* designs at the foot of the pilasters. This motif of *makara* (a kind of mythical sea monster) and head is a favourite theme among Javanese sculptors, though its origins are Indian. The tops of the walls are crowned with accent pieces and on each façade of the building there are ornamented niches crowned with small stupas which house life-size Buddha figures.

The basement reliefs have been shown to have been drawn from a religious text, the *Mahakarmavibhanga*, which deals with the Buddhist system of rewards and penalties for right and wrong actions, a system subsumed in the term *karma* which has been translated loosely as fate. Both the nature of the text and the illustrations of it which are found on Borobudur make it clear that it is addressed primarily to laymen whose function in Buddhism is, in part at least, to gain merit by supporting the monks. The occurrence of this text in illustrations on the outside of the monument, if this was intended as an object of pilgrimage for the laity, would seem most appropriate. But a more complex theology begins to emerge when we consider the Buddha figures enshrined in the niches on the façades.

On each side of the monument there are ninety-two statues arranged in four rows which correspond with the four terraces.

The seated Buddha, 9 feet high, of Chandi Mendut

OPPOSITE ABOVE: The intricate mass of Chandi Borobudur, from the west side

OPPOSITE BELOW: Chandi Mendut, one of several small temples associated with Borobudur

The figures on each side are distinguished by a different position of the hands, and it can be shown that each group represents one of the so-called *dhyani*-Buddhas – Akshobhya, Ratnasambhava, Amitabha and Amoghasiddha – who are associated with the four cardinal points, east, south, west and north, on which sides of the monument they occur. Above these fourfold ranks there is a fifth line, common to all sides of the monument, whose niches house Vairocana, the *dhyani*-Buddha associated with the zenith. There are sixteen of these figures on each side so that each façade has 108 Buddhas, a number which is considered auspicious in Indian numerological systems.

Further, upon the circular terraces which are otherwise undecorated, there stand a number of small stupas of a type which is found only at Borobudur. These stupas, which are constructed with half-open walls, number thirty-two, twenty-four and sixteen on the three successive terraces. Each houses a figure of yet another *dhyani*-Buddha, Vajrasattva, who is generally accepted as being the highest of these Buddhas and is indeed treated almost as a supreme deity in some schools of Buddhism. The uppermost circular terrace serves also as the base for the terminal stupa which is some 52 feet in diameter. An incomplete Buddha figure is said to have been found in the central stupa when it was being restored, but this is by no means certain. In any case it seems very doubtful whether its presence there, if authentic, had any esoteric significance.

Although the exterior of the monument is superbly ornamented and theologically significant, it is within the walled terraces that the finest examples of Javanese stone-carving are to be found. Here, as the pilgrim made his circumambulations beginning from the middle of the eastern side (as can be determined only by a study of the reliefs which we are about to discuss, since there is no distinction to make the entrance to the monument apparent), his way was flanked on either hand by hundreds of narrative reliefs. These number almost 1500 and would extend for some three miles if placed end to end. Each of the four square terraces is thus decorated, but as the pilgrim mounted to the first of the circular ones he would note at once, so marked is the contrast, that the reliefs cease and only the half-concealed figures of Vajrasattva – each in the attitude of preaching, the *mudra* known as 'The setting in motion of the Wheel of the Law' – express symbolically the doctrine which the monument attests.

Before considering further the religious significance of the monument, we must describe the contents of the reliefs. On the inner wall of the first terrace there are two sets of 120 panels each. The upper series tells the story of the Buddha's life up to the time of the preaching of the first sermon at Banaras, the event to which, when used specifically, the *mudra* of setting in motion the Wheel of the Law relates. The lower series contains a number of *avadana* or moral and edifying stories. On the outer wall of the first and second terraces are illustrated *jataka*, which deal with events in previous lives of the Buddha.

OPPOSITE: Relief carving at Borobudur: musicians play for the royal entertainment

An angle of the third terrace, east side. The relief carvings on the inner wall deal with the search for true Enlightenment

Relief carving on the first terrace illustrating a ship with tripod masts and heavy outrigger, characteristic of those which sailed Indonesian waters in the early centuries of the Christian era

The lively skill of Javanese workers in bas-relief
is well exhibited in these carved panels on the
inner walls of the lower galleries. The
representations of animals and plants furnish
valuable evidence for the natural setting of the
temple in eighth-century Java, while the details
of buildings provide an important source for
the history of Indonesian building in
perishable materials. Styles of dress, weapons,
jewellery and a host of other aspects of
Javanese material culture are also displayed
in these carvings

On the inner side of the second terrace a series of panels begins which seems to be based upon a text known as the *Gandavyuha*; this deals with the travels of the Bodhisattva Sudhana in his search for transcendental wisdom. In the course of his journeyings he visits sages, gods and the Bodhisattvas Manjushri, Maitreya and Samantabhadra. It is the repeated representations of the last two of these upon the inner walls of the third and fourth terraces respectively which has led to the view that the same text is being illustrated there. The uncertainty is in part because, whereas the earlier reliefs are carved in great detail and with many nuances which aid in the identification of their subjects, the later ones are far more restrained and stereotyped. This change fits logically with what seems to be the theological and intellectual progression of the series and the emergence finally upon the undecorated circular terraces.

The pilgrimage can be seen as an account of the history of Buddhism and of the doctrine which the Buddha expounded. On the exterior of the platform are depicted the inexorable laws of *karma*. As he enters the first of the circumambulatory terraces the pilgrim sees the way in which the Buddha, prepared for his role by a succession of previous lives (the *jataka* and *avadana* panels), is born to his last existence, receives enlightenment and preaches the first sermon in which he expounds the doctrine which releases men from the laws of *karma* and which the monument epitomizes. Also, as a stupa, the monument symbolizes the moment of the Buddha's own achievement of *nirvana*, an event which is not otherwise illustrated at Borobudur. But the doctrine has more esoteric truths to reveal than the simple historical teaching of Gautama; the story of Sudhana's search for these is now recounted in a stylized and restrained manner, for we are beyond the point of folk narrative and moving into the realms of metaphysics. This becomes clear on the circular terraces, where the reliefs cease, and thence at the central stupa where even the *dhyani*-Buddhas have disappeared. Yet, if we consider the *dhyani*-Buddhas upon the façades and the circular terraces as being in a sense the spiritual shell surrounding the whole monument, then it can be seen as a cosmos, a universe of which the central stupa with its lofty mast, now missing, is the world axis, the Sumeru of the Indian cosmologies.

As a testament in stone Borobudur is remarkable, but even without its religious implications the art of the carved reliefs would ensure it of a high place among the world's great buildings. Although the general manner is to depict types – Brahmins, princes, gods, ascetics – rather than individuals the treatment is naturalistic and poses are often remarkable in their expression. The buildings are those of medieval Java, and thus a valuable source of information for the archaeologist. The flora and fauna are those of the Javanese countryside most lovingly expressed; in particular the monkeys and the elephants are most admirably portrayed. And all, save the original inspiration of the texts illustrated, is Indonesian. There is nothing here of India.

A. H. CHRISTIE

Archway from the main terraces to the first of the circular platforms with their latticed stupas

A figure of the Bodhisattva Vajrasana in an attitude of preaching the Doctrine, originally enclosed by one of the latticed stupas

OPPOSITE: The central stupa, austere and undecorated apart from the stylized lotus base and the string course of the drum, with some of the surrounding latticed stupas which house figures of the Bodhisattva Vajrasana

CHINA

Introduction by S. H. Hansford

The selection of three or four of the most important buildings on the soil of China is a matter of some difficulty. Hardly a trace remains of the architecture of the formative years of Chinese civilization, and very little from periods prior to the last three centuries. Throughout their long history the Chinese have built with perishable materials, chiefly with wood, which provided the structural framework, much as steel has done in recent times. Stone suitable for building is to be found in many parts of China, and the massive carvings of animal figures excavated at An-yang, a capital city dating from the second millennium BC, may have been made as architectural ornaments. But the only considerable exceptions to the use of wood in the actual structure are certain stone pagodas and bridges, and of course walls, the most famous of which is the Great Wall of China.

There are, however, documents which throw light on building activities all through China's past, and conjure up visions of a marvellous succession of architectural splendours in the last two thousand years. The documents comprise tomb monuments dating from the first centuries of the Christian era and pottery models of houses made for burial with the dead; paintings and sculptures at Buddhist cave shrines of the fifth to tenth centuries; old Japanese buildings in the Chinese style; and descriptions of cities and palaces in Chinese books. Archaeological exploration has revealed little as yet, apart from the great size of the ancient walled settlements.

All the evidence points to the conservatism and continuity of tradition with which we are familiar in other Chinese arts and crafts. National and local histories record the scrupulous care with which established traditions were followed when a capital was rebuilt or a new site laid out. Even foreign conquerors, leaders of more-or-less nomadic peoples who were doubtless obliged to employ Chinese architects, followed the same courses. Classical writings like the *Shih ching*, The Book of Poetry, tell with awe of the princely palaces and ancestral shrines in the feudal states

of the Chou confederacy, from the middle centuries of the first millennium BC onward. Allowing for the poets' and chroniclers' desire to glorify their royal masters, it seems unlikely that architecture lagged behind other arts of the period, whose splendid works in durable materials like bronze and jade have come down to us.

In other ancient writings, especially the ritual texts *Chou li* and *Li chi*, there are numerous references to a part of the palace complex called the *Ming T'ang*, the 'Hall of Light', or 'Hall of Splendour'. Descriptions of it are obscure and contradictory, but it seems to have combined the functions of an audience chamber and a temple in which the Son of Heaven offered worship to the cosmic forces that were supposed to maintain his authority, and so demonstrated his harmony with them. The Chinese have not made such clear distinctions between sacred and secular usages as are customary in the West, so that such a dual purpose is not improbable. The possession of a *Ming T'ang* was at first the prerogative of the sovereign, but by the fifth or fourth century BC it had been assumed by the great feudatories. The hall was doubtless the noblest or most conspicuous building in a royal or princely capital, the idea has fascinated succeeding generations, and several emperors of later times have attempted to reconstruct a *Ming T'ang*, with an appropriate ritual, to buttress their authority and their claim to a divine right.

A great impetus was given to architecture through the conquest and unification of the Chinese world by the king of the Ch'in State, who proclaimed himself Shih Huang-ti, 'First Universal Emperor', in 221 BC. From now onward walled cities and seats of government were planned and laid out on a truly imperial scale. The Emperor rebuilt his capital at Hsien-yang, where it extended for many miles along both banks of the Wei River in the present province of Shensi. It is recorded that whenever he had conquered a principality, he erected in his capital a replica of the palace destroyed, and that each of these buildings was kept staffed and provisioned, ready for the Emperor, should he wish to

OPPOSITE: 'A view of the Temple serv'd by Eunuchs, and of the delicious Round Island it stands upon', from *The Emperor of China's Palace at Pekin, and his principal Gardens* (1753)

occupy it; also that the richest families throughout the empire were ordered to build mansions in the capital and dwell there with their belongings. The conqueror's reforms included the unification of the coinage, weights and measures, script, clothing, and so on, and it may be that his purpose was to evolve an eclectic architectural style that should combine the best features of variant styles existing in different regions. He built two vast imperial palaces, one on each side of the river, but these were destroyed when the city was sacked and burned soon after the Emperor's death.

In the world at large the 'First Emperor' is remembered as the builder of the Great Wall of China. This tremendous work of engineering has been hailed as an Eighth Wonder of the World, and claimed to be the only work of man on our earth that might be visible from the moon. Various estimates have been made of the length of the present Great Wall, dependent upon whether all or any of the numerous loops and branches are included. The shortest distance along the main rampart, from Shan-hai Kuan on the Gulf of P'o-hai in the east to Chia-yü Kuan in the north-west of Kansu Province, is approximately 1700 miles, but the total length of the whole system cannot be much less than 2500. Two misconceptions have had wide currency – that the project and construction of a great defensive wall against barbarian invasion were originally ideas of the First Emperor, and that his wall is substantially the one existing today and often visited by tourists from Peking.

All towns and villages of ancient China were enclosed and defended by walls, and most of them still are. There is ample evidence in the classics and in ancient historical writings that the princes of several of the feudal states, including the Emperor's own native kingdom of Ch'in, had walled their whole territories against their neighbours or against the barbarians to the north and west. It was these walls that the Emperor repaired and joined and extended at enormous cost in human labour, life and suffering, to enclose his empire. Similar enterprises have been undertaken and completed by several dynasties since then, the last by the Ming in the fifteenth century, and theirs is the present Great Wall of China.

Its main rampart is of about the same length as the first wall, but follows quite a different course. Moreover, while the first was probably a massive barrier of pounded earth, punctuated by gates, forts and watch-towers of masonry, the present wall was faced through most of its length with brick or stone, and topped with a pavement and crenellated parapets. It can be seen as completed and in a good state of preservation near Nan-k'ou, about thirty miles north of Peking, where the road passes through it into Inner Mongolia. Here the wall is 25 feet thick at the base, and composed of great granite blocks to a height of 20 feet. Above this and to a height of 50 feet it consists of large and heavy bricks of excellent quality, held together by hard and durable mortar. The roadway at the top is 14 feet wide, level enough in parts to drive a car on, but consisting elsewhere of flights of massive steps. There are drains at frequent

The Great Wall of China

intervals to carry off the rain-water. Every few hundred yards are watch-towers 30 to 40 feet square, and about 40 feet high. At times when the wall was fully manned, garrisons of hundreds of thousands were quartered in fortified camps in the rear, where they were encouraged to engage in agriculture by systems of land grants.

It is clear from descriptions of buildings in Chinese historical writings of the past two thousand years, voluminous and remarkably objective as they are, that architecture of awe-inspiring size and beauty was considered indispensable to effective government. The Han Dynasty which succeeded that of the Ch'in, and particularly its most famous sovereign the Emperor Wu (140–87 BC), embarked on an ambitious programme of palatial building for administration and imperial pleasure. Conventions were early established for the planning of both cities and palaces. In the latter the main buildings, apart from watch-towers and belvederes, were single-storeyed, of rectangular plan, and laid out symmetrically on a central north–south axis, with subordinate buildings disposed symmetrically to east and west. They were approached through a series of massive gateways and spacious rectangular courtyards, until the great audience hall was reached, raised on a terrace and approached by a short flight of steps. This arrangement must have ensured that the suppliant, whether prince of the blood, provincial governor, or tribute-bearing emissary, arrived before the throne in a suitable state of physical and mental exhaustion. In other great halls beyond the first, to which the favoured courtier or visitor might be admitted, he would be overwhelmed by the lavish decoration in painting and sculpture or by the service of an extravagant banquet.

The impact of Buddhism, which reached China early in the Christian era, brought some new elements to the national architecture. The first Buddhist temples were probably secular buildings, mansions donated to the apostles of the new faith by rich converts, but the need to accommodate great images of bronze or wood led to the erection of pavilions of two or more storeys, adaptations of the native watch-tower or belvedere, which were thus perhaps ancestors of the wooden t'a, or Chinese pagoda. Being

the principal centre of worship such a pavilion, or tower, or pagoda was placed in the front courtyard facing the gate of the mansion, on the main axis of the buildings and with the relatively low rectangular halls directly behind. It was this tower, or pagoda, that gave the secular buildings their religious character. By the fourth or fifth century, however, another kind of Buddhist tower, which the Chinese also call *t'a*, and which we call pagoda, was making its appearance. This was inspired by the Indian stupa, not the early form as seen at Sanchi and Bharhut, but a reliquary tower of masonry like the famous stupa erected by Kanishka I near Peshawar, and imitated by similar structures in Chinese Turkestan, ruins of which may still be seen.

It seems that the origins and functions of the two kinds of tower or pagoda were gradually lost sight of and confused, new symbolisms were attached to each, and some of their distinctive features were interchanged. When temples came to be designed specially for the service of the Buddha, a lofty main hall, the 'Buddha Hall', containing the altar and images, became the centre of worship, and the pagoda lost its pre-eminence and had to be displaced. By now, however, it had become the distinctive feature of a Buddhist temple, like the tower or spire of a Christian church, and could not lightly be abandoned.

The Chinese preference for symmetry was satisfied, in some of the larger temples, by the erection of two pagodas placed to the left and right of the entrance gate, from which the axis now led direct to the main hall. In others, or in less affluent times, one pagoda was deemed sufficient, and it was then sited behind the main hall, or well to one side. Pagodas, whether of wood or masonry, may be circular, square or polygonal. The storeys, usually of an uneven number from three to fifteen, diminish in size from the lowest upward, and each storey has its own projecting roof. The variety of design, especially of the brick and stone category, is bewildering. While their inspiration and form are essentially Indian and outside the main Chinese architectural tradition, these pagodas constitute the most numerous class of early Buddhist monuments in China, and some are conspicuous features of the landscape.

Substantial remains of seventh, eighth and ninth century wooden architecture in the Chinese style have been preserved in Japan, but the earliest example discovered in China is the main hall of the Fo-kuang Ssŭ, a temple on Wu-t'ai Shan, the sacred mountain and famous place of Buddhist pilgrimage in Shansi Province. This sturdy relic of the mid-ninth century, together with the Japanese examples, give us a faint idea of what must have been, from literary and circumstantial evidence, the most glorious epoch of Chinese architecture, the T'ang Dynasty (AD. 618–907). There was another burst of activity under the Sung Dynasty (960–1279). Remains, even of this period, are few; however, they and the literary sources indicate that Sung buildings were less overwhelming in size and extravagance than those of the T'ang, but that there was a tendency to build higher, to the employment of gold, silver

Pagoda of the Sung Yueh Temple (523), the oldest brick building in China

and jewels in decoration, and notably to a great extension of the use of roof-tiles with coloured glazes.

Another landmark of the Sung Dynasty was the presentation to the throne in 1100 of the first comprehensive treatise on architecture, the *Ying-tsao fa shih*, or 'Method of Architecture', by Li Chieh. This work was printed in about 1103, and again in 1145, but no copy of either impression is known to exist. A handsome but not entirely satisfactory reprint from a manuscript copy was published in China in 1925.

The third emperor of the Ming Dynasty, generally known by his regnal title of Yung-lo (1403–23), transferred his seat of government from Nanking to Peking, which ever since, apart from one interval of twenty years, has remained the capital of China. It is here that the most famous buildings in China, such as those considered in the following pages, are now to be found. Yung-lo laid out the city much as we see it today, the earliest surviving example of town-planning on anything like such a monumental scale. While the plan and some of the imperial and official buildings of the fifteenth and sixteenth centuries remain, most of the latter have been destroyed by disastrous fires, and restored or rebuilt in the seventeenth or eighteenth centuries. The work was carried out with the customary reverence for tradition, without limitation of cost, and at a period when craftsmanship was at a level of unsurpassed excellence.

ALTAR OF HEAVEN

*The central shrine of the national
religion of imperial China and the
scene of an ancient and imposing ritual*

The cult of T'ien, or Heaven, has its origins in high antiquity, even if its practice does not go back to the dawn of Chinese civilization, as tradition says it does. In inscriptions of the early Chou Dynasty, from the eleventh century BC onward, the character equated with that now pronounced *t'ien* is seen to be composed of the pictogram for 'great' or 'great man', a figure with firmly planted legs and arms spread wide, with the addition of a disproportionately large head. The primary meaning was 'great spirit, or spirits'. Inscriptions regard the ancestors as residing in the sky, whence they are said to 'send down' blessings. It is but a short step to designate the residence of the ancestors by the ancestors' character. This usually had a plural or collective sense, 'the council, or conclave, of ancestors', thence by a gradual evolutionary process the impersonal power above. But in some early Chou Dynasty inscriptions the meaning of T'ien must, it seems, be spirits, rather than an impersonal Heaven. So *T'ien Tzŭ*, 'Son of Heaven', the emperor's title for many centuries past, may at first have meant 'son of the ancestral spirits'.

In inscriptions of the Shang Dynasty which preceded the Chou and covered the latter half of the second millennium, the name T'ien does not seem to have carried the meaning of a Supreme Power. The Shang people designated theirs by a character now pronounced *ti*. But when the Chou people conquered them and adopted the Shang culture, they identified their own T'ien with the Ti of the Shang. The two terms became nearly synonymous, though Ti usually carries a more personal meaning than T'ien. Ti, which we might translate 'Lord', was also a royal and imperial title, so that when it was necessary to specify the Deity, the name Shang Ti, 'The Lord on High', was used. This is the term for God used by Protestant Christians at the present day.

Although the character for T'ien has an anthropomorphic origin, it was not the practice of the ancient Chinese to make their Supreme God in the image of man; that is, to represent

The causeway leading to the Temple of Heaven

him by an idol in human form. Certainly no images were seen in the ritual at the Altar of Heaven, which appears to have remained the same in essentials for many centuries until the end of the last dynasty. The emperor himself was the high priest of the cult, and none but he might offer worship and sacrifice to Heaven, whose representative on earth he was. The traditional place of sacrifice was the T'ien T'an, the Altar of Heaven, a great circular dais of earth or masonry, in the open air to the south and outside the walls of the capital city, wherever that might be. For this reason it was often called Chiao T'an, the Suburban Altar. When the original one was built here in 1420, the Outer City had not been walled, so that it was in fact in the suburbs. The English name 'altar' which is always used for this structure is somewhat misleading: the French name, *le Tertre du Ciel*, is more appropriate.

It stands in a great walled park, about three and a half miles in circumference, within which the precinct is enclosed by another wall. It is usually entered from the west, past the House of Abstinence, a beautiful villa surrounded by a moat, with bridges, balustrades and staircases of white marble leading to the various halls and rooms. It was here that the emperor passed the night fasting in preparation for one of the great

View from the Altar northward

View from the Altar southward

rituals on the following day. Another gate is passed, and the Altar with all its associated buildings bursts upon the sight. It is planned as three circular concentric terraces of dazzling white marble elaborately carved, diminishing in width and rising in height towards the centre. The whole is 200 feet in diameter, and is surrounded first by a circular wall, and then by a square one. Each wall is pierced at the four cardinal points by triple arch-ways of white marble, and every wall and every building in sight is roofed with glazed tiles of ultramarine.

On the spacious pavement between the inner and outer walls stands a great furnace in which the sacrificial foods were burnt, and braziers for burnt offerings of silk. Three flights of marble steps lead to the centre of the top terrace, where so many emperors have stood and knelt in supplication, and looked northward over a sea of blue roofs, white arches and deep rose-coloured walls. To left and right are a hall for musicians, stores for utensils and sacrificial vessels, and a kitchen for the preparation of sacrificial foods and wine. Ahead, beyond the marble archways is another circular wall enclosing a beautiful little octagonal chapel, the Pavilion of the Sovereign Firmament. Here were laid up the votive tablets dedicated to Heaven, the elemental forces and the imperial ancestors, to be brought out and set up as objects of veneration and focal points in the ritual on the altar. Each was inscribed with a name, the one placed centrally and above the rest reading *Huang T'ien Shang Ti*, 'Sovereign Heaven, the Lord on High'.

General view of the Sacred Precinct, with the city of Peking in the distance

217

The Pavilion of the Sovereign Firmament in which
are enshrined the tablets of Heaven, of the
imperial ancestors and of the elemental forces

Beyond the pavilion stretches a broad paved causeway, several hundred yards long and spanned by three great blue-roofed gates, at the end of which stands the Chinese building best known of all to the outside world, the so-called Temple of Heaven. So-called, because it is not known as such to the Chinese, to whom it is the Ch'i Nien Tien, the Hall of Prayer for the Year. But by this or any other name it could not fail to move us to wonder and delight.

Leaving the Altar and walking northward, down the steps, through the archways to the pavilion of the tablets, out of the enclosure, and on to the causeway, one notices many interesting features; but one's attention will not wander far from the miracle that is never out of sight and grows clearer and loftier as one gate after another is passed. At last all are left behind at the entrance to a square with long single-storeyed, blue-roofed buildings to left and right. The great triple-roofed circular tower rises from, but rather seems to have just floated down upon, its cushion of white marble. It is 90 feet high, and its proportions are perfect, from whatever height or angle it is seen. To many old-fashioned Chinese it is Heaven in microcosm, and with almost any picture of it before one a description in words is a presumption. Surprising as it may seem, the Ch'i Nien Tien is a comparatively modern building. Its predecessor was struck by lightning and burnt down in 1889, and this was regarded as an evil omen, which subsequent events in China did much to confirm.

Services at the Altar and Temple of Heaven took place only three or four times a year, but were invariably magnificent spectacles. The principal sacrifice, the *Chiao T'ien*, Communion with Heaven, was held at the time of the winter solstice. At this season Peking is already in the grip of winter, but rain falls rarely except in July and August, and for most of the year the sun, or moon, shines in a cloudless sky. Essential elements of the service were a humble report by the emperor to the heavenly throne and an act of solemn dedication of himself and his people.

On the eve of the festival the emperor was borne in procession over the three miles from his palace in the Forbidden City to the sacred precinct, followed by a great company of the most honourable of his subjects. On arrival at the south gate he entered on foot and proceeded to the Pavilion of the Firmament, where he burnt incense and knelt before the tablets. He then inspected the preparations at the Altar, and retired to the House of Abstinence, where he spent the night in prayer and meditation. Two hours before dawn he was carried again to the south gate, and entered a tent of yellow silk set up inside the square outer wall. Here he was vested in his ceremonial robes, and at the summons of a herald he emerged and mounted to the second terrace of the Altar.

By now, in the dim light of great lanterns on tall poles and through clouds of incense rising from bronze censers on the terraces, the Altar presented a scene of extraordinary colour and animation. On an altar table at the far side of the top terrace

The Temple of Heaven

The main approach to the Temple of Heaven, with its carved marble dragon-pavement: an old photograph taken after the fall of the Empire, when the building was much neglected

and protected from the north by a screen, stood the Tablet of Heaven, some 2 feet high and 6 inches wide, inscribed with the sacred name in golden characters on a vermilion ground; to left and right on smaller tables the tablets of the imperial ancestors, and on other tables scores of dark blue porcelain vessels of antique shapes containing offerings of prepared delicacies in great variety – meat, fish, fruits and vegetables, rice and millet, soups and wines – and also offerings of jade and silk; on the second terrace, more tables supporting tablets of the sun and moon, the planets and constellations, and the spirits of rain, wind, clouds and thunder. On the lowest terrace stood the princes of the blood, ministers, members of the Board of Rites, and the servers who were to wait upon the emperor; on the pavement within the circle of the wall, a great company of musicians, dancers, chanters, and bearers of banners and standards; and beyond the wall, the rest of the congregation.

Three strokes on a drum were the signal for the service to begin, upon which the chanters and orchestra burst into the Hymn of Invocation, accompanied by the solemn posturing of the dancers. Similar music punctuated the long ritual, all details of which are prescribed in a venerable rubric. It consisted of three parts, and lasted until dawn. In the first the emperor offered incense before the Tablet of Heaven, and before each of the others in turn. In the second he offered jade and silk, receiving them in a basket from a server on his right and passing them after presentation to another on his left; he followed this with offerings of the foods and wines in their ritual vessels, similarly assisted by the servers. Last came the Ceremony of the Prayer. The prayer, which had been drafted by the appropriate ministers in consultation with the emperor, and inscribed on a tablet, was brought to an orator who read it aloud, while the emperor knelt before the Tablet of Heaven. Advancing to the centre of the Altar, he partook of the meat and wine himself, and then performed the ninefold prostration, in which he was accompanied by the whole congregation. Finally, while the emperor remained kneeling, the prayer tablet, the incense, the jade, the silk and the food were removed and consigned to the flames of the braziers, as the rays of the rising sun lit up the golden name on the Tablet of Heaven.

The principal service at the triple-roofed Hall of Prayer for the Year followed similar lines, but on a less extravagant scale. It took place early in the year, and while the prayer at the Altar had been of the nature of an annual report and a demonstration of harmony with the supernatural, this was a petition for national peace and prosperity.

Ritual of this kind has a very long tradition in China, and its careful performance was held by Confucius and his followers to be an essential element of just and stable government. It is notable that at least one Western country has recognized the value of a legally established national religion with a high moral content and with the sovereign as its Head.

S. H. HANSFORD

OPPOSITE: The perfectly proportioned Ch'i Nien Tien, Hall of Prayer for the Year or Temple of Heaven

FORBIDDEN CITY

*For five centuries the residence of
the Son of Heaven and the centre of
court life in the Chinese capital*

The city of Peking, capital of the Chinese People's Republic, stands on the site of an ancient settlement, first known to history as Chi. Through most of the first millennium BC it was the seat of the dukes of Yen, great feudatories of the Chou Dynasty; hence its literary and poetic name, Yen-ching. Since then it has always been a place of some importance, but never the capital of all China until the thirteenth century AD, when the great Mongol conqueror Khubilai Khan built his huge city of Khanbaligh on and adjacent to the site of modern Peking. For a few decades Khanbaligh was not only the capital of China but of a large part of the known world, the greatest land-empire of all time, stretching from the Baltic Sea to the Pacific. The architectural splendours of the city and the life of the Mongol court are vividly described in the writings of Marco Polo.

Most of the Mongol city was destroyed by fire at the fall of the dynasty, and the plan of the present city is essentially as laid out by Yung-lo in the fifteenth century. The walls enclose an area of about twenty-five square miles, and as one approaches it across the North China plain its appearance suggests that of a gigantic flat box of the kind used by milliners. The plan is that of two cities, a square superimposed on a rectangular parallelogram. The square is the Northern or Inner City, the parallelogram the Southern or Outer. Each is surrounded by lofty walls, pierced at regular intervals by splendid gates surmounted by guard-houses. Both are planned with remarkable symmetry, and the Inner City is traversed by great avenues and countless streets and lanes nearly all running due south to north or east to west. Most of the famous buildings and monuments are in this Inner City. Notable exceptions are the Altar of Heaven and the Altar of Agriculture, just within the south wall of the Outer City. In recent times there has been considerable building development beyond the walls.

The Inner City itself encloses a nest of walled areas, of which the largest is the Huang Ch'êng, or Imperial City. This occupies a central position, and is a rectangle measuring $1\frac{3}{4}$ miles from

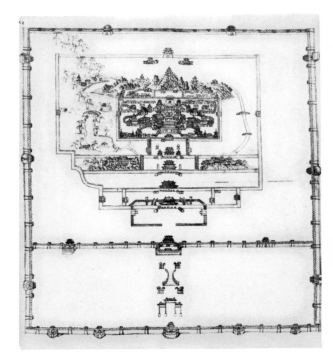

Chinese drawing of the Forbidden City, from an early nineteenth-century manuscript

View of the Forbidden City from the Ching Shan or 'Coal Hill'

Western wing of the Wu Mên or Gate of the Meridian

south to north and $1\frac{1}{2}$ from east to west. Most of its wall has in fact been demolished to ease the movement of traffic. The Imperial City contains many public buildings, former government offices, the Pei Ta University, the National Library, and the former imperial (now public) pleasure parks with their beautiful ornamental lakes. At the heart of all this lies the Tzŭ Chin Ch'êng, the Forbidden City, or Palace Quarter, yet another rectangle, only slightly less than a mile long from south to north and more than half a mile wide from east to west.

The English title carries an undertone of menace, and trespass in the imperial precinct would doubtless have been severely punished. But like royal residences elsewhere the Tzŭ Chin Ch'êng was closely guarded, so that unauthorized persons could only have gained admittance by force or by guile. The Chinese title suggests supreme power and authority, and the privacy appropriate to these. The emperor was deemed to rule, not only China but the whole world, by the mandate of Heaven, even if that mandate were not recognized by the more remote barbarians. The word *Tzŭ* in the context of the Chinese title means 'the Pole' around which all terrestrial affairs were believed to revolve in the manner of the heavenly bodies circling the Pole Star, its celestial counterpart. Since the establishment of the republic the Forbidden City has been regarded as a national monument, and most parts of it, including the famous Palace Museum, are open to all.

It is difficult to get an accurate impression of the size and scope of this extraordinary complex from anywhere on the ground, but the best view can be obtained from the summit of the little hill called Ching Shan, Prospect Hill (otherwise the 'Coal Hill'), just to the north of the Forbidden City. From here indeed the whole of Peking, the Inner and Outer Cities with their scores of landmarks cropping out through wooded courtyards, lies spread out, stretching away to the distant walls and gates, then to the great plain, and in the far distance the blue haze of the Western Hills. Immediately below stands the Shên Wu Mên, the Gate of Military Genius, the 'back gate' of the Forbidden City, and thence to left and right runs the wall and its lotus-filled moat to the graceful corner-towers. From them the wall continues to the corresponding towers at the southern end, enclosing a sea of glowing yellow tiles, the massive roofs of the great audience halls and the more modest ones of the old homes of princely families and court officials, surrounded by their courtyards and rock gardens filled with flowering shrubs.

From the Coal Hill a walk or drive of a mile and a half along the moat brings one to the south or 'front' gate, the T'ien An Mên, the Gate of Heavenly Peace. Here, in the enormous square outside the gate, are held the great parades and reviews on national anniversaries. The first of these reviews was that held by Yüan Shih-k'ai on his inauguration as First President of the Chinese Republic in 1912. Before the T'ien An Mên flows an ornamental canal spanned by five beautiful parallel bridges of white marble with elaborately carved parapets. These lead to

Corner tower and moat of the Forbidden City

Pavilion near the Shen Wu Mên or
Gate of Military Genius

Western end of the marble terrace of
the Hall of Supreme Harmony

five parallel carriage-ways tunnelled through the T'ien An Mên itself. The great imperial progresses comprised five cortèges moving forward side by side, with the emperor's chair carried in the midst, and the carriage-ways were devised accordingly.

The tunnels, each 70 to 80 feet long, lead to a spacious courtyard, across which the paved carriage-way continues in the shade of an avenue of great trees, towards a second gate, the Tuan Mên, similar to the first and pierced likewise by five tunnels. This is the entrance to another courtyard, shady but larger than the last, from the far side of which rises the main gate of the Forbidden City and the most splendid in all China, the Wu Mên, the Gate of the Meridian. The traffic and bustle of the street have now been left far behind, and as the visitor approaches this masterpiece the effect is overwhelming.

The central mass is somewhat larger than that of the first and second gates, and from its ends two wings extend southward at right angles, the whole gate forming three sides of a square. On the terrace above, behind a marble parapet, stands a long, double-roofed, rectangular building connected by corridors to two smaller ones at the north and south ends of each wing. Together they are known as the 'Five Phoenix Towers', formerly occupied by government offices and more recently by the National Historical Museum. From the square before the gate, the mighty structure seems to rise up and envelop everyone and everything within it, but on either wing are long ramps leading to the terrace above, and from here a breath-taking scene meets the eye.

From left to right across the next courtyard, in a wide curve shaped like a bow, flows the Chin Shui Ho, the Golden River, while beyond it and directly in front stands the T'ai Ho Mên, the Gate of Supreme Harmony. The glistening river, or canal to be precise, flows in a bed of white marble and between banks of the same material, from which rise carved marble balustrades. It is spanned by five marble bridges of elegant proportions and graceful form, said to be symbolic of the Five Virtues.

The T'ai Ho Mên is a complete contrast to the other gates. The much smaller building is nearly at ground level, being raised above it only by a double terrace of carved white marble. Beyond this point the emperor's progress was accompanied only by his immediate attendants and his sixteen bearers. The terrace is reached by two parallel flights of twenty-eight steps, between which is the carved and sloping 'dragon pavement'. The emperor's chair was carried over the pavement, the bearers supporting it on its long poles as they mounted the steps, with the attendants following in their wake. Passage through the gate is by three pairs of massive bronze-studded doors, the middle pair for use by the emperor and his bearers and the pairs to left and right by his attendants. The T'ai Ho Mên is one of the few buildings of the Forbidden City surviving from the Ming Dynasty. Before the gate squat two huge bronze lions on marble plinths.

OPPOSITE : Garden with extension
of the Golden River to the west of the T'ai Ho
Mên or Gate of Supreme Harmony

On descending from the Wu Mên, the visitor passes through it into the courtyard, crosses one of the bridges, ascends the marble steps of the T'ai Ho Mên, and walks between the vermilion columns supporting the roof and through the great doors. Some 150 yards away across a vast square, rises the great throne hall, the T'ai Ho Tien, or Hall of Supreme Harmony. This, with two smaller halls beyond it, the Chung Ho Tien and the Pao Ho Tien, stands on a triple terrace of marble with carved balustrades, and is reached by four parallel flights of steps with a longer 'dragon pavement' in the middle. The square looks even larger than it really is because of its emptiness and the fact that the surrounding buildings, apart from the throne hall, are comparatively low. But it has not always been empty. On occasions of high festivity, such as New Year's Day and the Imperial Birthday, or in celebration of a victorious campaign, it was here that the emperor received the congratulations of his loyal princes and officials. They assembled in their thousands, in ceremonial robes, their places indicated according to precedence by inscribed bronze markers fixed to the paving stones. When the emperor had taken his seat on the Dragon Throne, his presence

Bronze guardian lion in front of the T'ai Ho Mên

The Hall of Supreme Harmony

Third Audience Hall, Pao Ho Tien, near the Hall of Supreme Harmony

Second Audience Hall, Chung Ho Tien, behind the Hall of Supreme Harmony

The Throne Hall, or Hall of Supreme Harmony, on its triple terrace of marble

Bronze 'dragon-tortoise' on the upper terrace of the Hall of Supreme Harmony

Sun-dial on the eastern end of the
Hall of Supreme Harmony

was announced, and the whole company knelt as one man and performed the ninefold prostration.

Disposed on the terraces of the T'ai Ho Tien are eighteen great bronze incense burners symbolizing, it is said, the Eighteen Provinces, and recalling the Nine Tripods of Yü, the palladia of the ancient dynasties, which were supposed to pass from one sovereign to the next as his title to the mandate of Heaven. There is also a fine bronze figure of a crane, a monstrous bronze tortoise with the head of a dragon, and a great stone sundial. Tradition says that when the emperor received the candidate who had been placed first in the honours list at the triennial metropolitan examinations, the fortunate student might claim the privilege of mounting the dragon-tortoise and standing on its head.

Apart from these ceremonial quarters of the Forbidden City, there is, of course, much more to be explored, for which days or weeks of leisure would be needed – libraries, treasuries, armouries, temples, gardens, and, above all, the residential quarters formerly occupied by emperors and empresses, princes, dowagers, favoured concubines and great officers of the court. Each of these villas stands in a secluded courtyard, behind high red walls entered through massive doors from the 'streets' which separate them. It would be difficult to find one's way through this labyrinth but for the fact that each building has an 'auspicious' name, and that this name is inscribed in golden Chinese characters – and sometimes in Manchu as well – on a plaque fixed to the eaves. Thus a villa once occupied by the notorious Empress-Dowager Tz'ŭ Hsi is the Palace of Eternal Spring, while the Palace of Peaceful Old Age is the home to which the great Emperor Ch'ien-lung retired on his voluntary abdication in 1795 at the conclusion of a glorious reign of sixty years.

One may ask what are the features, apart from historical associations, that most deeply impress the visitor to the Forbidden City. Undoubtedly space, composition, majestic proportions and colour. Few of the buildings are of more than two storeys, and many of the largest are of only one. Roofs are the most conspicuous parts, accounting for more than half of the elevations. The appearance of excessive weight is relieved by their gentle curves and sometimes by the presence of little figures of guardian monsters breaking the skyline on ridges and gables. The reflection of light from the countless glazed tiles of imperial yellow and the vast stretches of white marble balustrades is dazzling, but mellowed at closer quarters by the warmth of the old red walls and the intricate polychrome painting of beams and brackets visible below the eaves.

The prevailing atmosphere is one of tranquillity and serenity. People, however numerous, are invariably quiet and orderly, and never seem to amount to a crowd. The Forbidden City, whose halls and palaces have been the scenes of so many historic events and dark intrigues, rests like a sleepy giant in honourable retirement, treasured and cared for by a people whose reverence for history and antiquity is proverbial.   S. H. HANSFORD

OPPOSITE: Doorways to the Second Audience
Hall, Chung Ho Tien, showing the intricate
painted designs of the beams and brackets

THE MING TOMBS

*The burial ground of thirteen emperors
and their consorts from the
fifteenth to the seventeenth century*

The imperial tombs of the Ming Dynasty (AD 1368–1644) stand in a wide valley thirty miles north-west of Peking, sheltered by mountains on the north, east and west. The floor of the valley measures approximately three miles from south to north, and two from east to west. The sites and aspects of tombs, and indeed of all buildings in old China were chosen with the advice of practitioners of *fêng-shui*, the pseudo-science of 'wind and water', which purported to ensure that the natural surroundings should provide maximum protection against evil influences, together with unobstructed access of benign ones. The valley was considered by these experts to be ideally placed for the great necropolis, which was established there by Yung-lo, the third Ming emperor and celebrated town-planner. His own tomb, the most imposing of them all, holds pride of place at the head of the valley, and all his dynastic successors, twelve in number, were buried in or near the foothills which fringe it. Peking people speak of them collectively as the Shih-san Ling, the Thirteen Tombs.

The entrance to the valley is marked by a splendid *p'ai-lou*, memorial arch, with five openings. This was erected in 1540, more than a century after the first burial. It is 90 feet long by 50 feet high, and consists entirely of white marble, apart from the six great rectangular plinths that support the columns. The plinths are of fine grey stone, contrasting effectively with the marble, and carved with mythical animals in high relief. Even the tiling is of marble, painted blue to simulate glazed pottery, while the whole structure imitates the traditional patterns and techniques of Chinese building in wood. Vestiges of green and red paint indicate that the architect's purpose was to produce the effect of a wooden monument. Here and elsewhere at the tombs it is evident that the Chinese were quite capable of large-scale building in stone, but regarded it only as a substitute for wood, to be used when exceptional durability was required.

Half a mile beyond the memorial arch stands the Ta Hung

Furnace for burnt offerings in front of the Ling-ên Tien or Hall of Sacrifice to the Emperor Yung-lo

OPPOSITE : The Soul Tower of Yung-lo, from the back of the Hall of Sacrifice. The tower encloses the emperor's tombstone, and beyond it is the great mound covering the 'underground palace'

233

The great memorial arch, *p'ai-lou*, which stands at the entrance to the valley of the tombs

Mên, Great Red Gate, which is really the entrance to the burial ground. It is a massive structure, pierced by three vaulted tunnels and roofed with yellow tiles, like the rest of the buildings from here onward. To left and right extend the remains of the red wall that formerly enclosed the whole valley. Here begins the Shên Tao, Spirit Way or Via Sacra, and of this we are warned by inscriptions on massive stone stelae at each side calling upon ministers and all other ranks to dismount.

The first monument of importance along the Spirit Way is the Pavilion of the Stele, which shelters a marble figure of a tortoise, 12 feet long, supporting on its back a 30-foot vertical slab, inscribed with a eulogy by the son and successor of Yung-lo. Next comes the famous avenue of gigantic stone figures, twenty-four animals and twelve humans. They are set up in pairs, facing inward – lions, camels, elephants, horses, and various mythological creatures, some standing, others sitting, followed by various civil and military officers. They vary considerably in size, but not in accordance with any natural scale. The standing elephants are 13 feet high, and the camels not much less. The domestic animals and the officers were there to provide the deceased with a retinue appropriate to his dignity,

234

The Hall of Sacrifice to the Emperor Yung-lo. It resembles the throne hall in an imperial palace, but the throne is replaced by a shrine containing the tablet of the sovereign inscribed with his posthumous title

An altar and altar vessels made of stone stand before the Soul Tower of Yung-lo

235

Life-sized stone elephant guarding the imperial Spirit Way

The Spirit Way in
the valley of the tombs

Stone camels alongside the Spirit Way

Stone statue of a military officer

237

The Sacrificial Chamber of the Wan-li Tomb, excavated in 1956, with marble thrones for the souls of the emperor and his two consorts, ritual vessels and porcelain oil-vats to provide 'everlasting lamps'

The Soul Tower of Wan-li enclosing his tombstone, from the entrance to the 'underground palace'

the lions and supernatural beasts to scare and repel enemies and evil spirits.

After passing several more honorific monuments and arches, vestiges of ornamental bridges and a kitchen for the preparation of sacrificial meats, we reach the tomb precinct itself. This, of course, is a walled enclosure, and apart from the actual place of burial it is planned very much as a small palace – a succession of gateways and courtyards leading to an imposing hall corresponding to an audience hall in an imperial residence. This, however, is a hall of sacrifice, the Lung-ên Tien, or Hall of Grace and Favour, in which the place of the throne is taken by a shrine containing the tablet of the sovereign inscribed with his posthumous title, Ch'êng Tsu, The All-Perfect Ancestor. Before it stands an altar-table supporting a massive incense-burner, flanked by two flower-vases and two candlesticks.

It is when the visitor passes around the shrine, and through a great door beyond, that he realizes he has left the home of the living. He is now in the last courtyard, and before him stands a high crenellated wall surmounted by the square Ming Lou, or Soul Tower. The wall encloses an enormous mound, half a mile in circumference, and covered with trees and shrubs. Below this, and contrived to be forever inaccessible, lie the 'underground palace' and its august tenant.

At the time of the interment the tomb was entered through a tunnel in the wall and one may still follow this for some 30 yards, but there it ends and one is obliged to turn to left or right, where ramps lead up to the top of the wall and the Soul Tower itself. The tower encloses and shields from the elements a tombstone which may be seen through the cavernous apertures in the four sides – a lofty marble stele, 5 feet wide by 3 feet thick, inscribed in enormous characters, deeply cut, 'The Tomb of the Accomplished Emperor, the All-Perfect Ancestor'.

One may ask why it was necessary to offer worship and sacrifice to the imperial ancestors both here and elsewhere, at the Altar of Heaven for example. The answer lies in the ancient Chinese belief that man is endowed with a dual soul, in effect two souls. The inferior and more material of the two was closely associated with the body in life, especially with the blood; at death it became a *kuei*, a ghost, hovering in and about the tomb with needs closely reflecting those of the living man. The superior, more ideal soul corresponded to the higher parts of the personality. It was capable of leaving the body, even during life, as in dreams and trances. At death this soul became a *shên*, spirit, dwelling on high with the *shen* of his ancestors, but constantly concerned with the affairs of the family. Both *shên* and *kuei* had to be served and cherished, if their favour was to be deserved and their displeasure avoided.

The remaining twelve tombs of the Shih-san Ling are planned similarly to the first, with all its principal features reproduced, but on a much more modest scale, with two notable exceptions. These are the tombs of Chia-ching (1522–66) and Wan-li (1573–1620), which are little inferior in size and magnificence to that of Yung-lo. During the earlier reigns of the Ch'ing Dynasty, which succeeded the Ming, the emperors were concerned to keep the tombs in repair, and to see that the sacrifices were maintained. For the latter purpose they ennobled a scion of the House of Ming, and charged him specifically with this duty. The reason was, doubtless, that if it were neglected, the outraged Ming ancestors might take some fearful revenge on the conquerors. As, however, the fortunes of Ch'ing declined, and especially in the demoralization of the final decades, all pretence of maintenance was abandoned, and many of the buildings fell into dilapidation, and some into ruin. In recent years the Peking Government, while expressing the strongest disapproval of the pride, extravagance and religious beliefs of the Ming emperors, have fully appreciated the importance of the tombs as national monuments, and have embarked on a large-scale programme of restoration, and on an important piece of archaeological excavation. Until 1956 our knowledge of the plan and construction of an 'underground palace' of the Ming Dynasty was dependent on literary evidence. In that year the government authorized the exploration of the great burial mound of the Wan-li tomb.

This emperor was only ten years old when he ascended the throne, and only twenty-one when he began to make plans for

General view of the tomb of the Emperor Wan-li.
In the centre is his Soul Tower, and beyond it
the burial mound above his 'underground palace'

239

'The Station of Cerimonies used at the funeralls of Great Persons' from *Atlas Chinensis* (1671) by Arnoldus Montanus

his own tomb. Such foresight was by no means unusual at the period. The work was put in hand, and completed in 1590 at a cost, it is reported, of eight million taels. Thirty years later, in 1620, the empress died, to be followed the same year by the emperor himself. His son and successor was the child of a concubine, who had died eight years previously. At the new accession she was promoted posthumously to the rank of empress-dowager, and her body was re-interred with the two others in the great tomb. This would have been regarded as an act of filial piety on the part of the prince.

Needless to say, in the case of a tomb specially constructed to resist access, the difficulties of excavation were immense, and six months were spent in penetrating to the vaulted entrance and the great gateway of the underground palace. Unlike the palaces of the living in China this one is built entirely of stone. The massive coping of the stone gateway is carved to imitate pottery tiling, complete with guardian animals on the ridges, while the massive double doors are of white marble. Each slab weighs six or seven tons, and is carved with rows of bosses to represent nail-heads. The doors are hung from a bronze cross-beam, 12 feet long, and were locked from the inside by a great 'self-acting stone' which fell into position at the closure. Owing, perhaps, to a subsidence the doors do not meet perfectly, and it was possible to pass a pole through the gap and push back the obstruction. Otherwise it would have been necessary to use explosives, resulting in disastrous damage.

The gateway led to an ante-chamber, 60 feet long by 16 wide, and thence through more marble doors to the Sacrificial Chamber, nearly twice as large, and with corridors leading to spacious side galleries on the left and right. At the far end of the Sacrificial Chamber stand three magnificent white marble thrones, the emperor's carved with dragons, flanked by those of the empresses, somewhat smaller, and carved with dragons and phoenixes. Before each are the usual altar vessels and great vats of blue-and-white porcelain. These had been filled with oil and carried floating wicks, to provide 'everlasting lamps'. Behind the emperor's throne is the last pair of great stone doors, giving access to the Burial Chamber, the largest of all and set at right angles to the main axis of the tomb. It is 60 feet long by 30 feet wide. On a long platform facing the entrance stood three catafalques supporting the red-lacquered coffins, their colours brilliant and fresh as when new. When opened they revealed the bodies – or rather the bones and dust to which they had mouldered – richly robed, crowned and bejewelled, while all around lay a great treasure of gold, jade, silk and porcelain.

Remains of Chinese architecture of all ages, except the most recent, being very scarce, the Ming Tombs provide an unequalled display of palatial building covering a period of more than two centuries in an unbroken tradition. There is every expectation that they will be preserved from further decay under their present administration, and continue to excite our wonder and admiration.   S. H. HANSFORD

OPPOSITE: Pavilion at the Ming Tombs

JAPAN

Introduction by John Figgess

From earliest times the architecture of Japan developed almost entirely in wood – naturally enough, perhaps, in a country covered with forests to the extent of nearly half its area – and, up to the end of the nineteenth century, buildings of stone or brick were almost unknown. It is remarkable therefore, considering the perishable nature of the building material and the destructive typhoons, earthquakes and fires to which Japan has always been subject, to say nothing of the ravages of civil war, that any of the great architecture of the remote past has survived. That it has is partly due to frequent restoration throughout the centuries and partly, no doubt, to the fact that despite the frequency of natural disasters, the climate of Japan, hot and humid during the summer months but cool and dry during the autumn and winter, is kind to wooden fabric.

While the ancient inhabitants of Japan in the fourth and fifth centuries possessed a primitive architecture of their own with elements traceable to both north-east and south-east Asia, the Japanese owe much to China in modifying and influencing their ideas. Here, as in so many other spheres, religion has played a leading part. It was in the erection of shrines for the early Shintô religion that the native Japanese architecture first found purposeful expression, and it was the powerful impact of Buddhism, newly introduced from the Asian mainland in the middle of the sixth century, that led to a fresh departure in the direction of the palace architecture of China, which, even prior to the period of radiant prosperity under the T'ang Dynasty (618–907), was already highly developed.

A general idea of ancient Japanese architecture before the introduction of Buddhism may be obtained from the Shintô shrines of the earliest types represented by the Grand Shrines of Izumo and Ise which, although they have been reconstructed on numerous occasions, still preserve their primitive forms. Notwithstanding the overwhelming impact of Chinese ideas on building in Japan from the early seventh century onwards, something of the spirit of this native architecture which is characterized by a remarkable simplicity, absence of ornament and lightness of construction, has been retained in Japanese architecture and especially in non-Buddhist and secular building throughout the ages. Moreover, it remains strongly in evidence even today in domestic architecture of the traditional kind. Nevertheless, the influence of the Buddhist religion on Japan can hardly be overestimated in any area and certainly not in the field of architecture which, impelled by Buddhism, has drawn repeated inspiration from China.

To outline these developments it is perhaps useful to follow the practice of art historians by distinguishing quite arbitrary but convenient periods. The first of these is the Asuka period (AD 538–645), so called because the court was established during those years in the near neighbourhood of a place of that name close to the modern city of Nara. This period saw the rise of Buddhism and Buddhist art and, as religious fervour grew, it was accompanied by a desire to acquire merit by creating images and having temples constructed to contain them. Early in the seventh century the influence of Chinese architecture became paramount. Many artists and craftsmen crossed over to Japan from Korea and China, attracted no doubt by the demand for their services created by the outburst of religious enthusiasm among the Japanese upper classes, and it is probably to them that a large part of the masterpieces created during the Asuka period must be ascribed. Even if Japanese workmen took part in the construction work at this time, they must have been wholly under foreign influence.

By remarkable good fortune certain splendid monuments preserving the architectural style of this period have survived, of which the most notable are the Main Hall and other buildings of contemporary or nearly contemporary date at the Hôryû-ji near Nara, a temple believed to have been founded in 607 by Prince Shôtoku, the outstanding personality of the time who was appointed regent to the Empress Suiko in 593. (The names of Buddhist temples in Japan all end in *ji*, *tera* or *dera*, which are variant readings

JAPAN

of the same Chinese character, e.g. Tôdai-ji, Asuka-dera. The term *in*, which has a meaning something like 'cloister' or 'priory', is used in a similar way, usually to denote a smaller temple within a larger one, e.g. the Tô-in of the Hôryû-ji, the Byôdô-in.) The Hôryû-ji was the greatest artistic achievement of the Asuka period. The buildings were all, of course, inspired by Chinese models or by Korean copies of Chinese originals, but they are not exact imitations; they show signs of adaptation to suit Japanese materials and tastes. In these buildings numerous statues, paintings and other treasures were enshrined and they were added to in later times.

In 710 the court moved to a new capital, Heijô (Nara), designed on a grand scale in emulation of the Chinese Sui Dynasty capital of Ch'ang-an, with the Imperial Palace at the centre of the northern outskirts and the streets laid out in a regular chess-board plan towards the south. The creation of the new capital naturally gave great impetus to architecture and the decorative arts, and although most of the buildings of that time have suffered destruction we know that they closely followed Chinese models.

During the Tempyô era (729–748), the name given to the reign of the Emperor Shômu, Japan for the first time attained a level of civilization comparable with that of China. The Emperor, a devout Buddhist, built the magnificent temple of Tôdai-ji or Eastern Great Temple, and ordered a huge bronze statue of Vairocana to be cast and installed there. The growth of the Tôdai-ji summarizes much of the social and political history of this time and it also provides a concise statement of Japanese artistic progress. It was founded in 738, but work was not begun in earnest until some years later; and though the Buddha Hall housing the colossal image of Vairocana was completed as a structure in about 751, more than a decade passed before

the temple was fully decorated within and without. Not much is left today of the original fabric of this ambitious project, but the restored remains and reconstructed portions give some idea of how fabulous the Tôdai-ji must have been in the time of its greatest glory.

Nara remained the capital of Japan until 784 when, for unexplained reasons, one of which was perhaps to escape from the dominance of the increasingly powerful Buddhist clergy, the court moved to Nagaoka a few miles away. This removal was only temporary however, for ten years later, in 794, an entirely new capital was established at Heiankyô, the modern Kyoto, ushering in the Heian period which was to last for nearly four centuries until 1185.

At the beginning of the Heian period and throughout the ninth century, Japanese civilization remained firmly under the influence of T'ang China, but with the decline of the T'ang empire and the abandonment in the year 894 of official intercourse with China, the culture of Japan began to change its character and to develop a more independent national spirit. The period of about three hundred years from the beginning of the tenth century, when contacts with the mainland were reduced to a mere trickle, saw the emergence under the enlightened patronage of the court and aristocracy of a truly national art differing markedly from the preceding century. With the year 894 as a demarcation line therefore, the Heian period is subdivided into the Early Heian period and the Late Heian or Fujiwara period. The last name derives from the predominant influence of the great Fujiwara family, which controlled most of the administrative positions in the government and dominated the court.

The Early Heian period was marked by the introduction from China of esoteric forms of Buddhism, incorporating mystic rites, magic and symbolism deriving from the Tantric Buddhism of India, which appealed to the Japanese of the time. This led to another wave of temple building promoted by the establishment in Japan of two sects of the new Esotericism, the Shingon and the Tendai, whose influence on Japanese art and architecture during the ninth century was profound and lasting.

The majority of the religious buildings of this time have, alas, suffered extinction, one of the few survivors being the very fine Five-storeyed pagoda of the mid-tenth century at the Daigo-ji, a temple of the Shingon sect associated with the Imperial family.

The aristocratic society of Kyoto at the beginning of the eleventh century seems to have been seized by a mood of pessimism, and gradually an easier path for salvation than the arduous metaphysics of the Shingon or the strict meditative practices of the Tendai sect was sought in Buddhism. There arose in the form of the *Jôdo* or Pure Land faith a simple and undemanding doctrine which held that salvation was open to all through the saving grace of the Amida Buddha (Amitabha) merely by faith and the frequent repetition of the name of Amida (*nembutsu*). The idea of building *Amida-dô*, or halls specifically dedicated to Amida,

Inner sanctuary of the Grand Shrine of Ise,
an example of pure Shintô architecture

The Five-storeyed Pagoda of the Daigo-ji,
a work of the mid-tenth century

things of Zen Buddhism which was to exercise a subtle influence on all aspects of Japanese intellectual life in the succeeding centuries.

Zen Buddhism is of course impossible to define in words, and a description of its influence on the arts of Japan could hardly be compressed into a voluminous book devoted to the subject. But it can be loosely stated that its practice favoured a mood of utmost simplicity, discouraged ostentation and led away from all artificiality towards an astringent appreciation of things in their unadorned natural state. Hence beauty came to be seen in a stone, in the gnarled root of a tree, in weathered wood or even in the surface of cleanly raked sand. This spirit enters very strongly into the tea ceremony, which essentially is a gathering – conducted according to a prescribed etiquette and in simple, quiet surroundings – of friends who have aesthetic tastes in common. In a small room, bare of all but a few essentials, a special kind of green tea is prepared and drunk in accordance with a strict set of rules, and the guests discuss quietly some subjects of mutual interest.

Such meetings, especially under the early influence of Zen ideas of restraint and simplicity, provided the atmosphere for a calm withdrawal from worldly cares and a serene enjoyment of beauty. During the fifteenth and sixteenth centuries, a turbulent time in Japanese history, members of the nobility and other wealthy men of taste constructed in the grounds of their mansions or country villas special buildings for the tea ceremony, called *chashitsu*. These teahouses, though often surprisingly costly, were of simple construction, the exterior usually resembling a rural cottage, with the aim of creating a feeling of rustic simplicity. One of the most celebrated of these early teahouses which served as a model for all later *chashitsu* is a small structure called Tôgudô in the grounds of the Ginkaku-ji or Silver Pavilion, a building of simple elegance in a charming garden which was built on the outskirts of Kyoto in 1489 as a country villa for the shogun Ashikaga Yoshimasa. In the arrangement of the living quarters of the Tôgudô are to be found the main features of the design of the Japanese house in subsequent periods, including sliding doors and screens and the alcove or *tokonoma*.

Numerous examples of teahouse-style buildings of the sixteenth and seventeenth centuries still exist, but the finest monument to the heights attained by Japanese architecture and gardens in this formalized tradition is surely the Katsura Imperial Villa in the south-west outskirts of Kyoto. The villa, which was built by an Imperial prince in the first half of the seventeenth century, belongs basically to the brand of Japanese architectural tradition that goes back to the aristocratic culture surrounding the Imperial Court of ancient times, but it also embodies something of the plebeian elements of the traditional Japanese farmhouse; in both the main buildings and the outbuildings designed for the tea ceremony may be seen that severe simplicity and functional clarity which modern architects strive for.

was first conceived by the Tendai sect and the practice became fashionable as the new *Jôdo* faith increased in popularity. The nobility, who had looked to esoteric Buddhism principally as a means of deliverance from the evil influences which they felt threatened them in this world, were irresistibly attracted by the promises of the *Jôdo* faith which offered salvation of the soul in the world of the hereafter. The *Amida-dô* was intended to represent in tangible form an earthly vision of the Pure Land or paradise of Amida, where all blessed souls would be received after death. Compared with the austere mood of the Buddhist art and architecture of the ninth century, these later works associated with the worship of Amida demonstrate a certain gentleness and mildness of aspect which is generally interpreted as a manifestation of the native Japanese spirit which showed itself increasingly in the artistic works produced from about this time. The Phoenix Hall of the Byôdô-in, built in 1053, epitomizes the art and architecture of this period.

The Heian period was followed by a century and a half of military rule under the leadership of the Minamoto *Bakufu* or military government. This time is known as the Kamakura period because the small town of that name on the Pacific seaboard was selected for their headquarters by the victorious Minamoto clan leaders, who chose to establish themselves there well away from the Imperial Court which remained in Kyoto as the nominal centre of power.

There were renewed contacts with China during the Kamakura period leading to the importation among other

THE HORYU-JI

An early Buddhist temple which contains some of the oldest wooden buildings in the world and houses many masterpieces of Japanese art

The Hôryû-ji is the most ancient of surviving Buddhist temples in Japan. It was founded in AD 607 and can boast several buildings in which the architectural style of the early seventh century is preserved. Among these, the magnificent Kondô or Main Hall, dating from about AD 623 may fairly claim to be the oldest wooden building in the world. The importance of the Hôryû-ji from the viewpoint of cultural history lies in its continuity. Not only does it reflect the pure beauty of the lost Chinese and Korean architectural styles of the fifth and sixth centuries, but it is a veritable treasure house of Buddhist art covering all the important epochs of Japanese history from the Asuka period (552–645) onwards.

The precise age of the present Hôryû-ji has been a subject of controversy among Japanese scholars for the past fifty years, but it is now generally accepted that although the temple was almost completely destroyed in a disastrous fire which swept through the precincts in AD 670, the building which is now the Kondô survived, and when, towards the end of the seventh century, reconstruction began it provided a model of architectural style which was consistently followed in the other buildings of the re-designed temple.

The general plan of the Hôryû-ji today consists of the western precinct (Sai-in) and the eastern precinct (Tôin). The principle buildings of the Sai-in are the Main Hall to which we have already referred, the Chûmon (inner front gateway), the Five-storeyed Pagoda, the Lecture Hall, the Sutra Repository (Kyôzô) and the Bell Tower. The Main Hall and the Five-storeyed Pagoda are arranged side by side on an east–west axis, a feature unique to temples laid out during the Asuka period. (Temples of later periods usually have the main hall and the pagoda disposed on a south–north axis.)

The entrance to the temple compounds is through the Nandai-mon, literally meaning the south main gateway. This is a handsome gate of later construction, built in 1439. To enter the central block of the western precinct, one passes through the

A celestial musician, carved in wood, from the canopy in the inner sanctuary of the Kondô or Main Hall

OPPOSITE: The Kairo (corridor) surrounding the western precinct of the Hôryû-ji

Aerial view of the Sai-in or western precinct

The Chû-mon or Inner Front Gateway of the western precinct, built in the early eighth century

The Lecture Hall, built about AD 990

Chû-mon gate. This is a two-storeyed building from either side of which extends the corridor (Kairô) to enclose the central block of the western precinct. It is an imposing gate in which the upper storey is perceptibly smaller than the lower and it has an unusual plan of four bays frontage and three bays in depth. Two huge wooden statues of temple guardians which are installed in the east and west bays of the gateway are recorded as having been carved in the year 711. After passing through the gate the magnificent Five-storeyed Pagoda comes into full view. It is three bays square in plan and over 105 feet in height. The appearance is of an unsurpassed elegance, achieved by the device of tapering the dimensions of the roof sizes of each storey, the ratio of the roof sizes from the bottom to the top storey being 10:9:8:7:6. The deep overhang of the roofs enhances the impression of elegance. Inside the pagoda a central pillar is bedded on a deeply buried foundation stone and passes through the whole structure.

On the ground floor of the pagoda are housed four groups of clay statuettes arranged to form a tableau. They are evidently the same as those recorded in the inventory of the Hôryû-ji as having been placed in the pagoda in the year 711, that is, contemporary with the carving of the two guardians standing in the Chû-mon Gate. The tableau on the east side represents a scene described in the sutra *Yuima-kyô* with the Buddhist saints Yuima and Monju in the upper part and fourteen figures of Bodhisattvas and male and female attendants. The tableau on the south side is probably meant to represent the Land of Maitreya, the Buddhist Messiah, but the figures here, with the exception of the central figure of Maitreya, have been much repaired. The west side represents the division of the Buddha's ashes among the disciples; here the tableau depicts Sakyamuni's coffin and a pagoda-shaped reliquary with twenty-nine figures of courtiers, monks and lay men and women all in different poses. The north side represents the Nirvana of Buddha with Buddha lying surrounded by heavenly beings, the ten great disciples, the eight supernatural guardians, monks, nuns and persons of various ages as well as birds and animals. Of these, thirty-two are registered as National Treasures.

Standing to the east of the pagoda is the Main Hall or Kondô, marked by its vigour and conciseness of expression as one of the great architectural masterpieces of the world. It is a two-storeyed building with a plan of five bays by four, the lower storey being surrounded by lean-tos on four sides for ceremonial use. The stout supporting columns have perceptible entasis. The roof, particularly beautiful with its elegantly curved eaves, is hipped and gabled in the manner termed *irimoya* in Japan. The bracket capitals to be seen within the building are of the ordinary assembled type, but those exposed on the outside are sculptured from solid blocks of wood and project outwards to present a profile in the form of trailing clouds. The interior consists of a rectangular chamber with walls of wood and stucco and a coffered ceiling.

OPPOSITE: The approach to the western precinct, showing the Five-storeyed Pagoda soaring above the enclosed outer corridor

The Kondô or Main Hall, dating from about AD 623. This may fairly claim to be the oldest wooden building in the world

OPPOSITE: One of the doors of the Yumedono or Hall of Dreams in the eastern precinct

A carved dragon
on one of the exterior pillars
of the Kondô

The famous Shaka Triad in the Kondô,
a bronze work of the early seventh century.
The central figure is about 3 feet high

Bronze statue of Yakushi
Nyorai, the Buddha of Healing, in
the Kondô (about 2 feet high)

The Yumedono or Hall of Dreams in the eastern precinct, built prior to AD 761 on the former site of Prince Shôtoku's Ikaruga Palace

Tenth-century wooden statue of Yakushi Nyorai, the Buddha of Healing, in the Lecture Hall. The figure is nearly 5½ feet high

Formerly the walls of the interior were decorated with beautifully painted frescoes depicting the 'Pure Land' or paradise of Amida Buddha, but these, alas, were all but completely destroyed in 1949 by a most unfortunate fire caused by the carelessness of workmen who were making copies of the wall paintings. Fortunately, damage to the building itself at that time was slight and it has been skilfully repaired; but it is sad to see that the ancient murals, which for sheer beauty were comparable with those at Ajanta, are now replaced by plain white walls.

Housed in the Main Hall are a number of magnificent bronze statues including the famous Shaka (Sakyamuni) Triad, the Yakushi (Bhaisajya-guru), the Buddha of Healing and Amida (Amitabha). An inscription engraved on the halo of the Shaka Triad states that it was made by the sculptor Tori in the thirty-first year of the reign of the Empress Suiko (623) for the peaceful rest of the Prince Shôtoku. Tori was one of the few Buddhist sculptors active in this period whose name has come down to us. He seems to have been a descendant of a naturalized immigrant from the mainland and his background is reflected in the sculptural style of his works. This style was not of his own creation. It derived from the severe, virile Chinese style of Northern Wei which survives in the stone Buddhist images of the Yun-kang and Lung-men caves.

The statue of Yakushi standing on the right-hand side of the Shaka Triad falls into the same stylistic category. The halo of this statue bears an inscription on the back to the effect that the Emperor Yômei made a vow in 586 to produce a statue of Yakushi Nyorai, the Buddha of Healing, but, since he passed away prior to the realization of the project, his sister the Empress Suiko and his son the Crown Prince Shôtoku fulfilled his desire. The inscription goes on to say that the statue was finished in the fifteenth year of the Empress Suiko's reign and the temple (i.e. the Hôryû-ji) was built to house it. There is some difficulty in reconciling the inscribed date with the sculptural style of this work which seems if anything rather more advanced than that of the Shaka Triad. This difficulty has encouraged a certain scepticism about the reliability of the inscription and the suggestion has been advanced that the present statue was made after the fire of 670 which destroyed the original Hôryû-ji; however, this view is not accepted by most Japanese scholars.

The three buildings we have considered so far all belong in style and manner of construction to the Asuka period. The next building in the western precinct, the Lecture Hall (Kôdô), is a replacement of later date. The building which formerly stood on this site was burned down in the year 925 and this one was brought in from Kyoto and reconstructed in its place, which accounts for the markedly different architectural style as compared with the other buildings in the compound. The Lecture Hall is distinguished by its simplicity of line and beautiful proportions. It houses a number of fine wooden statues of a date contemporary with the building, among them another version of Yakushi Nyorai, the Buddha of Healing, with Nikkô Bosatsu (Suryaprabhasa) on the right and Gakkô Bosatsu (Candraprabha) on the left.

To the right of the Lecture Hall is the Kyôzô or Sutra Repository, a small but elegant building dating from the middle of the eighth century, which houses the Tripitaka, the complete set of the Buddhist scriptures, and a statue of the Prince Shôtoku, the founder of the Hôryû-ji. On the other side of the Lecture Hall stands the Shôrô or Bell Tower which was built about a century later than the Sutra Repository and shows the stylistic features of the Early Heian period. The differences between the two buildings are seen most clearly in the shaping of the pillars and the construction of the eaves.

Situated within the western precinct and on the way to the Tôdai-mon or East Main Gate is a modern ferro-concrete building called the Daihôzô-den or Gallery of Temple Treasures. It is fire- and earthquake-proof and is equipped with the latest devices for maintaining a constant humidity. In this gallery are kept many of the great works of art and historical materials belonging to the Hôryû-ji which have been handed down over the course of the centuries.

Here we illustrate only two of them, both statues of Kannon Bosatsu, the Bodhisattva of mercy and compassion. The beautiful 'Kudara Kannon', which was named after the Korean kingdom of Paekche (called Kudara in Japanese) from which it is supposed to have come, is a large standing figure carved in wood with a very much elongated body and graceful lines. The carving, especially of the hands and the flowing scarves, is of great sensitivity. The Kannon stands on a lotus pedestal and the beautiful halo behind the head is in the shape of a lotus flower. There are traces of red, blue, and green colouring on the statue which must originally have been brightly painted. A surprisingly good reproduction of this famous statue, made about fifty years ago by a remarkable Japanese sculptor, is to be found in the Department of Oriental Antiquities in the British Museum. The other statue illustrated here, the 'Yumetagae Kannon', is a standing figure of bronze cast in the round. It is an eighth-century work, clearly showing in its rhythmic posture and full-cheeked face the influence of the sculptural style of T'ang China. A popular belief held that through prayers addressed to this statue an ominous dream could be changed into an auspicious one, hence the name Yumetagae (dream-changing) Kannon.

The most important of the buildings in the eastern precinct is the famous Yumedono or Hall of Dreams which, dating from the eighth century, is the oldest octagonal building in Japan. Although of small size it is very beautiful in design and stands on a double stone terrace with four flights of steps leading up to entrances facing east, west, north and south. The tiled, gracefully curved roof is surmounted by an elaborate ornament consisting of a lotus flower, a sacred vase, a canopy and a sacred jewel symbolizing the Buddhist Law.

The Kuze (or Guze) Kannon of the Yumedono, believed to date from AD 739. Carved in camphor wood and gilded, it is nearly 7 feet high

BELOW: The 'Kudara Kannon', a seventh-century statue measuring nearly 7 feet in height and carved from a single block of camphor wood

The eighth-century Yumetagae (Dream-changing) Kannon, about 3 feet high and made of bronze cast in the round

THE HORYU-JI

In the inner sanctum of the Yumedono is another rare and beautiful statue of Kannon known as Kuze (or Guze) Kannon, meaning 'Kannon the Saviour'. It has always been treated as a particularly sacred image and is kept piously hidden away in its shrine. Consequently it has survived in a perfect state of preservation with the original gilding intact. It is of carved wood and measures about 5 feet high from the lotus pedestal to the tip of the great jewel-shaped halo. In style it belongs to the school of the sculptor Tori who made the famous Shaka Triad in the Main Hall and it is believed to date from the seventh century. The crown, of bronze openwork, has beautiful honeysuckle patterns and is ornamented with pendant beads.

The other eighth-century building in the eastern precinct is the Dempôdô, or Preaching Hall, its purpose being similar to that of the Lecture Hall in the western precinct. It is of especial interest historically, because it was not built as a temple building but was originally a residence of the Lady Tachibana (Tachibana-no-Konakachi, a court lady in the service of the Emperor Shômu, who died in 759) by whom it was presented to the temple in 739. It therefore provides an idea of what domestic architecture of the early eighth century was like. It is of rather plain construction with a gabled roof and small doors and windows. About twenty fine examples of Buddhist wood sculpture of the Nara and Heian periods are displayed in the interior.

The remaining buildings of the eastern precinct are of much later date. They include the E-den (Hall of Paintings), a long single-storeyed building erected in 1219, the Shôrô (Bell Tower) of slightly later date and the Raidô (Hall of Worship).

This then is the Hôryû-ji as it is to be seen today after nearly fourteen centuries of existence marked by periods of extreme activity and other periods of extreme neglect. It is miraculous that it should have survived with the majority of its treasures when so much of Far Eastern art and architecture that was contemporary with it has been lost. But now that its unique importance as a veritable museum of early Buddhist art is recognized and it has acquired the full protection of the Japanese Government through the enactment of the Law for the Protection of Cultural Properties, there is every hope that the careful measures taken for its continued preservation will ensure its survival for posterity.

JOHN FIGGESS

'The Nirvana of Buddha', a tableau in clay sculpture on the north side of the ground floor of the Five-storeyed Pagoda

THE TODAI-JI

*A great temple of the eighth century whose buildings
and treasures represent a Japanese reflection of
the golden age of the T'ang dynasty of China*

The eighth century in Japan was a time of extensive importation and assimilation of the civilization and art of T'ang China. Under Chinese influence, the promotion of Buddhism as the national religion was accentuated and Buddhist temples were built on an unprecedented scale and in great numbers. In 710, the court moved to a new capital called Heijô (the modern Nara) which, to the Japanese of the time, must have seemed unbelievably splendid. It was modelled on the T'ang capital of Ch ang-an with the Imperial palace in the centre of the northern outskirts, and the streets laid out in a regular chess-board pattern towards the south. Many great temples moved with the court to the new location and the power of the Buddhist Church grew steadily greater, particularly in the second quarter of the century during the reign of the Emperor Shômu, who is known as the most devoutly religious of all the Emperors of Japan.

In the earlier part of Shômu's reign no special acts of piety are recorded but his religious inclinations were apparently stimulated by a terrible epidemic of smallpox which ravaged the country for two years between 735 and 737 and carried off many persons of high estate. According to an edict of 737 every province in Japan was to be provided with an image of the Buddha 16 feet in height and a copy of one of the sutras (Prajnâpâramitâ), and further edicts issued in 741 ordered that in every province monasteries and convents (Kokubun-ji) should be established and pagodas built. The monasteries were to be under the general supervision of the great Nara temple of Tôdai-ji, the Eastern Great Monastery, which was founded in 738 and which, through the patronage of the court, grew within a brief space of time to be the wealthiest and most influential of all religious foundations in Japan.

The Emperor, prompted it is thought by his close adviser, a priest of the Kegon sect of Buddhism named Rôben, also conceived the project of erecting a colossal image of the Buddha Rushana (Vairocana), the central figure of the Kegon sutra, as a measure of persuasion to the Gods and the Buddhas to grant

Portrait sculpture from the early eleventh century of the priest Rôben, founder of the Tôdai-ji

OPPOSITE: Interior of the Daibutsu-den or Great Buddha Hall
of the Tôdai-ji, showing the bracketing system

Segment from the twelfth-century scroll painting
Shigisan Engi E-maki, illustrating a story about
a nun who visited the Great Buddha of the
Tôdai-ji to seek help in finding her brother

The Great Buddha of the Tôdai-ji. It is more than
53 feet high, and although much restored it stands
as a memorial to the greatest accomplishment in
the long history of Japanese bronze casting

relief to the sovereign and his people. For various reasons, including no doubt the need to raise funds and prepare the vast amount of materials that would be needed, the project was deferred for some years, but in 745 work was begun in the precincts of the Tôdai-ji and at length after many disappointments a giant bronze seated image 53 feet high was roughly finished in 749. It was an enormous undertaking which consumed nearly all the copper resources of the country, and it is known from literary sources that something like 370,000 technicians and more than half a million other workers were employed on the project. It was taken as a special sign of divine approval that early in 749 gold deposits were discovered in the province of Mutsu, and a quantity of the metal was sent to Nara to aid in gilding the image.

The great Buddha Hall built especially to house this colossus was over 275 feet in frontage and 165 feet in depth, being eleven bays by seven, far greater than any building existing at the time even in China. The remainder of the temple complex was also laid out on a huge scale to match the Buddha Hall and comprised two seven-storeyed pagodas (each more than three times the height of that at the Hôryû-ji), magnificent gates, halls of worship and study, as well as numerous other buildings for the use of the monks. The total area allotted to the Tôdai-ji in fact equalled that taken by the Imperial palace and was four times as spacious as that of the next largest Nara temple, the Kôfuku-ji.

The construction of the Tôdai-ji following on the monumental task of casting the great Buddha was the symbol of a new national policy by which Buddhism was virtually adopted as the state religion. The tremendous enterprise took several decades to complete and called for the united resources of the

OPPOSITE: The Great Buddha Hall

nation. However, it must have given the Japanese of the time great satisfaction, for when in 752 the so-called 'eye-opening ceremony' for the Buddha took place there was an elaborate celebration attended by notables from all over the Buddhist world and, according to records of the time, thousands of priests were present at the ceremony, many of them having journeyed from China and Korea, and even from as far away as India.

Unfortunately, very little remains of all this glory today. The Tôdai-ji suffered more than its share of destruction from the elements and from civil war during the succeeding centuries. The Great Buddha Hall, protected perhaps by its size, survived the typhoons that twice blew down the magnificent south gate and the fires caused by lightning that destroyed both the tall pagodas. But it was twice deliberately burned by a marauding army, once in the late twelfth century and again in the mid-sixteenth when the country, torn by civil war, was in a state of near anarchy. Then the brutally damaged Buddha sat in the open for over a century.

When rehabilitation of the Tôdai-ji was at length undertaken towards the end of the seventeenth century, the official resources were apparently insufficient to attempt a complete restoration of the temple and reconstruction was limited to the Great Buddha Hall and the front half of the courtyard. The hall which we now see is the one erected then. It is shorter by nearly 100 feet (four bays) than the original and its construction has little in common with the architectural style of the eighth century, but in spite of all the changes, enough remains of the grandeur of the T'ang design to make it uniquely impressive and it is still the largest wooden building under one roof in the world.

An illustration in the third of a set of Japanese scroll paintings known as *Shigisan Engi E-maki* owned by the Chôgosonshi-ji, a temple in Nara, shows the Great Buddha and the hall as they looked to the artist in the twelfth century (page 258). The story as recounted in this scroll concerns a nun from the provinces who journeyed to Nara to seek her brother, a priest. In Nara she went to the Tôdai-ji to entreat the help of the Great Buddha. She spent the night in front of the statue and had a dream in which the Great Buddha told her to go towards a mountain which had a purple cloud over its summit where she would find what she sought. Awaking, she did as she was bid and in a joyful meeting was reunited with her brother. The illustration shows the Great Buddha of Nara with the nun in several different positions in front of it – entering the building, sitting before the statue, falling asleep there and worshipping in gratitude for her revelation as the story goes.

The statue of the Great Buddha which, like the building that housed it, suffered terrible damage from the ravages of natural and man-made disasters, has been skilfully repaired and looks down with an expression of calm indifference upon the thousands of visitors who come daily to gaze in awe or astonishment

The Nandai-mon or Great South Gate, built in the so-called *Tenjiku-yô* or Indian style in the late twelfth century

The Nigatsu-dô or Hall of the Second Month; a worshipper stands in an attitude of prayer before the principal image

opposite: The eaves of the Great Buddha Hall

The bell and lantern
of the Tôdai-ji

The Great Bell in the Shôrô. This is the largest of all the temple bells of Japan and is recorded as having been cast in AD 752

The Shôrô or Bell Tower, built in the thirteenth century

Octagonal bronze lantern which stands before the entrance to the Great Buddha Hall. It is an eighth-century work and originally was gilded

LEFT: One of the panels of the bronze lantern showing a Bodhisattva playing a musical instrument. The rendering of the figure is strongly influenced by the style of the Chinese T'ang dynasty

263

Shikkongô Shin (Thunderbolt Bearer) from the Sangatsudô of the Tôdai-ji. Nearly 6 feet high, this splendid example of eighth-century clay statuary is rarely taken from its shrine and is in a remarkably fine state of preservation

One of the colossal Kongô Rikishi (Guardian Kings), carved in AD 1203, which guard the passageway through the Great South Gate

at this stupendous human achievement. Although the pure glory of the original statue is to be seen only in a few engraved petals which form the lotus throne, the part from the right shoulder to the chest, the greater part of the knees and both sleeves of the robe are original, and though considerably repaired, provide ample testimony to the majestic quality of the eighth-century bronze casting. Indeed, the techniques required for the casting and gilding of this statue are hardly imaginable today, and, notwithstanding the repairs, the work still remains the grandest accomplishment in the long history of Japanese bronze casting.

A smaller but in its way no less important example of the bronze caster's technique is the beautiful octagonal lantern standing immediately in front of the Great Buddha Hall which dates from about the same time as the original building and has miraculously survived almost intact. A striking feature about it is the great size of the light chamber, the eight faces of which are decorated with openwork floral scrolls on a ground of diamond-shaped patterns. Each alternate face consists of a pair of doors opening outwards decorated with Chinese lions. The other four faces of the octagon are each ornamented with a Bodhisattva playing a musical instrument. The Bodhisattva on the south-east face is a fairly recent replacement but the others are original and display the rich beauty of the Chinese T'ang period influence on Japanese sculpture in bronze.

On the east side of the main courtyard stand a number of buildings belonging to the Tôdai-ji. They are all replacements or reconstructions of a later date than the original temple, but several of them are nevertheless very interesting. The first such building to be encountered after leaving the courtyard by the Chû-mon (main gate) is the Bell Tower, an attractive structure dating from the thirteenth century which houses the great bell of Tôdai-ji, the largest of all the temple bells of Japan. It is reliably recorded as having been cast in 752 and it is still in use. The beautifully modelled dragon headstock is of impressive proportions to match the bell itself.

The next building of note is the Sangatsudô (hall of the third month) otherwise known as the Hokkedô. The back part of this building on the north side is of eighth-century construction, but the entire front is an addition of the thirteenth century. The two parts are in surprising harmony, though the structural differences are soon apparent on close examination. This is traditionally considered to be the lecture hall of the priest Rôben who died in 773 and who is given a large share of the credit for the construction of the Tôdai-ji in the decades succeeding 740. A wonderfully life-like portrait sculpture of Rôben carved in wood during the first half of the eleventh century and painted in colours is in the possession of the Tôdai-ji and is sometimes shown. The Sangatsudô is a treasure house of Nara period sculpture. The principal image housed there is a magnificent statue of Fukûkensaku Kannon (Amoghapaśa), standing more than 20 feet high, executed in hollow dry lacquer, a technique much favoured in the Nara period. Besides this great master-piece there are several other eighth-century statues in the same medium, and two really remarkable examples of statues modelled in clay, a technique which was imported from China but which has survived only in examples to be seen in Japan. These two are the Nikkô Butsu (Suryaprabha) and the comple-mentary Gakkô Butsu (Candraprabha).

All these statues are superb sculptural works and are regis-tered National Treasures, but perhaps the most distinguished of the surviving masterpieces of clay sculpture of the Nara period is another statue in the Sangatsudô, the Shikkongô Shin (Vaj-rapani). This irascible figure, standing legs astride clad in armour, with the muscles of the neck tensed, the eyes and mouth wide open, and with a large *kongô-sho* (divine thunderbolt) brandished in the right hand, is in the cast of heroic realism which appealed to the sculptors of this period. Its vitality seems to come from inside; the illusion of life which was a prime aim of the Japanese sculptors of the Nara period is nowhere better captured. The shrine in which the statue is kept was made for it in the thirteenth century. Since it has been piously concealed in the shrine and taken out only on very rare occasions it has remained in a remarkably fine state of preservation, retaining the original decorative patterns of flowers and arabesques in their rich colours and gold.

The Nigatsudô (Hall of the Second Month) on rising ground in the north-east corner of the Tôdai-ji precinct, is a building of the early eighteenth century, constructed as a replacement for the original which was burned down in 1667. It is built on a platform and the outer corridor commands a view of the entire Tôdai-ji complex. Here also there is a so-called 'hidden image' which is seldom, if ever, exposed to public view.

The last building of importance in this grand temple is the Nandai-mon or Great South Gate through which we finally leave the precincts of the Tôdai-ji. This dates from the end of the twelfth century when the main buildings of the Tôdai-ji, which had been burned to the ground in the great civil war of 1180, were reconstructed in what is known as the *Tenjiku-yô* or Indian style, an architectural style imported from southern China. Nearly all these twelfth-century buildings have been destroyed or subsequently reconstructed in other styles, however, and only the Nandai-mon survives as a pure example of the *Tenjiku-yô*. It is marked by a grand scale, solid construction and an impressive boldness. Two giant *Niô* or temple guardians carved in wood stand one on each side of the passageway through the gate. These dramatic and powerful figures of menacing appearance each measuring 26 feet in height, were made, according to the temple records, in 1203 by two of the most famous sculptors of the Kamakura period, Unkei and Kaikei by name, with the help of two other carvers and sixteen assistants. The statues are full of vigorous movement, and their magnificent proportions and awe-inspiring demeanour, fully reflect the heroic spirit of the original Tôdai-ji.   JOHN FIGGESS

Tamon Ten, one of four guardian demi-gods from a set in the Kaidan-in. This eighth-century statue is sculptured in clay and painted in bright colours and gold leaf

THE BYODO-IN

*One of the most beautiful of all architectural
monuments in Japan, the Phoenix Hall epitomizes the
art of the aristocratic Fujiwara culture*

The Byôdô-in of Uji is a monastery located on an ancient high-way roughly halfway between Kyoto and Nara at a point where a bridge spans the turbulent Uji River. The existing modern steel and concrete bridge is the newest of several successors of the original bridge which, according to an inscription on an ancient memorial stone preserved in Uji, was built by a Budd-hist priest named Dôtô in AD 646. The place was famous for its scenic beauty from very early times, and in the ninth century some of the aristocratic families of Kyoto built villas in the neighbourhood. In the year 998 one such villa and the land surrounding it passed into the hands of Fujiwara-no-Michinaga, the distinguished scholar and statesman of the Early Heian period, and here in 1052 when he entered religion, Michinaga's son, the Regent Fujiwara-no-Yorimichi, converted the villa into a monastery which he named the Byôdô-in and built on the site a group of sacred edifices dedicated to the worship of the Buddha Amida (Amitabha).

Amida worship was by no means a new concept in Japan of the Heian period but it appears to have received a fresh impulse at the beginning of the eleventh century through the activities of a learned priest named Genshin (afterwards known as Eshin) who wrote a celebrated work *Ojôyôshû* or 'Essentials of Salva-tion', which taught that believers in the saving power of Amida could attain salvation merely by frequent utterance of the name of the Buddha through the formula 'Namu Amida Butsu'. This doctrine, which was known as Pure Land teaching, 'Pure Land' being the appellation of Amida's paradise, appealed to the

An *apsara* (celestial musician) from the
wall behind the Amida Buddha in the Phoenix Hall

The statue of Amida Buddha by the great sculptor Jôchô (*d* 1057).
It is constructed by means of the 'assembled wood blocks'
system devised by Jôchô and heavily gilded all over

267

The Bell Tower, showing the balk of timber suspended on ropes which is swung against the side of the bell to sound it

The Great Bell of the Phoenix Hall. Cast in bronze with fluent decorative patterns, this is regarded as one of the most beautiful temple bells in Japan

aristocratic society of the capital no less than to the poor and wretched throughout the country perhaps because a spirit of pessimism was abroad and people had been frightened by gloomy prophecies about *Mappô*, the End of the Buddhist Law which, it was said, would come about in 1052, ushering in a period of eclipse of all hope of escape from Karma, the interminable cycle of death and re-birth. It is of some significance that the time chosen by Yorimichi to set his hand to the construction of the Byôdô-in should have been none other than this very year of 1052. However, it must be added parenthetically that sixteen years later, in 1068, he staged a performance of music at the Byôdô-in for the Emperor, which suggests that many of the court and aristocracy continued to take pleasure in their faith despite having entered the gloomy epoch of *Mappô*.

The Byôdô-in was only one of many elaborate and lavishly decorated temples erected during the eleventh century under the stimulus of these religious ideas, but now it is unique, and only in the Phoenix Hall which was built to house its Amida image can we see today something of the splendour and magnificence of Fujiwara-period architecture at the height of its glory. The lovely building stands, mirrored in its lotus lake, 'a structure', in the words of Sir George Sansom, 'with such an airy grace that it seems to be rising to escape from earthly sorrows'. It is the sole survivor of the several sacred buildings erected in the temple precincts by Yorimichi, between about 1052 and 1055, the others having perished through fire, mostly in the civil wars of the early fourteenth century.

In the spring of 1053, a great celebration was held at the Byôdô-in, attended by many distinguished persons from the court and nobility, to mark the completion of this Amida Hall; and contemporary descriptions stress the building's likeness to the glories of the 'Pure Land' or paradise of Amida which it was undoubtedly meant to represent. Of some interest in this respect is a popular children's song, recorded in a document of the twelfth century, which goes:

Gokuraku ibukashikuba Uji-no otera wo uyamae
If you doubt that there is a Paradise,
Stand in worship before the bright temple at Uji.

Although not large, the building is exquisite in concept and construction. It consists of a central hall with two 'wing' corridors, and a short 'tail' corridor suggesting, it is said, a giant phoenix with outstretched wings.

The central hall is three bays (about 30 feet) in width and two bays (20 feet) in depth and has decorative roofs (*mokoshi*) surmounted by a double roof of the type known as *irimoya* in Japanese. The design is absolutely symmetrical, thus creating a harmonious sense of balance despite the variety of lines, especially in the intersecting roofs, while in general style with its exact symmetry, its magnificent ornamentation and the flaming vermilion colouring of its exterior set off by panels of white, it is closer to Chinese palace architecture of the T'ang

OPPOSITE: The Phoenix Hall, from across the lotus lake

General view of the beautifully
proportioned Phoenix Hall

Dynasty than to the traditionally simple style of Japanese
building. However, the delicacy of the construction, the small
scale and, above all, the way in which the building fits into its
setting are wholly Japanese.

The two bronze phoenixes perched upon the gable ends also
show strong Chinese influence, though it is to be doubted
whether they are contemporary with the building since the
modelling seems too strong and precise to be associated with the
Fujiwara period; the original building, it is thought, was
decorated with a single gilded phoenix mounted probably in
the middle of the roof.

The interior of the Amida Hall was elaborately decorated
with lacquer, mother-of-pearl inlay and metal-work, while the
walls and the interior surfaces of the doors were adorned with
painted scenes representing 'the nine grades of *raigô*'. The term
raigô (coming to welcome) refers to the belief that at the death
of a believer, the Buddha Amida with his attendants Kannon
(Avalokiteśvara) and Seishi (Mahâsthâmaprâpta), followed by
numerous other Bodhisattvas playing heavenly music, would
come down to earth to receive the soul of the departed and
grant him rebirth on a lotus flower in the lake of Paradise. The
kinds of rebirth are classified in nine grades according to the
degrees of faith held by believers during their earthly life, and
the *raigô* takes nine corresponding forms. While the greater part
of this decorative painting has disappeared, the richness and
technical excellence of the fragments which remain convey a
wonderfully clear idea of Fujiwara taste.

The ostensible purpose of all this lavish expenditure of money
and effort was, of course to provide a sumptuous worship hall
appropriate to house a large image of Amitabha, the 'Buddha
of infinite grace' and Lord of the Pure Land which had been
carved especially to the orders of Yorimichi by the famous
sculptor Jôchô. Jôchô, who died in 1057 at the age of eighty-
four, achieved distinction as the chief sculptor responsible for

OPPOSITE: Detail of the Phoenix Hall, showing a
bracket capital and the roof construction

271

The roof, showing one of the two decorative
phoenixes made of cast bronze

The Phoenix Hall
of the Byôdô-in

272

Detail of the eaves of the central block

The north wing

273

the production of statues for the Hôjô-ji, a temple on a grand scale founded earlier in the century by Fujiwara-no-Michinaga, Yorimichi's illustrious father. He devised a method of assembling statues from separately carved wood blocks instead of hewing them out of a single block, as had been the general practice in the past, and thus made possible a system of corporate labour by which less cumbersome statues of almost any size could be made more quickly and easily than previously. He was responsible for many statues made for temples associated with the Fujiwara family and the Imperial Court and was ultimately rewarded with the ecclesiastical rank of Hôgen (Eye of the Law), the first professional sculptor to be so honoured.

The Amida statue in the Phoenix Hall, which is of lacquered wood covered with gold leaf, is considered to be the finest of all his works; it is in fact the only surviving statue which can be attributed to him beyond all reasonable doubt. The image is said to have been praised by his contemporaries as 'flawless as the full moon', and certainly it is distinguished by its perfect proportions and graceful pose though it must be said that the serene face lacks the intense spiritual expression which was a feature of many of the great sculptural works of earlier periods. The artist has, however, skilfully interpreted the desires of his aristocratic patrons by fashioning for them an image of the tender Saviour of their imagination, a radiant being whose eyes are directed downwards in mercy towards the suppliants.

Mounted on the interior walls of the Amida Hall near the

Upper walls and roof of the Phoenix Hall, showing some of the *apsaras* behind the image of Amida

Detail of the halo of the Amida statue

ceiling are fifty-two wooden images of celestial beings in diverse attitudes, some on clouds, others dancing, yet others playing musical instruments or in an attitude of prayer. These animated and charming figures are virtually carved in the round, but with suppressed treatment of the third dimension, a subtle effect which is very pleasing. They are thought to have been carved by Jôchô and the group of sculptors who worked with him on the Amida statue. They were originally painted in gay colours and decorated with thread-like strips of gold leaf but nearly all this decoration has worn off and for the most part the grain of the wood is now exposed and only the barest traces of the former colouring remains.

Enough has been said in this short account of the Byôdô-in and its Phoenix Hall to give perhaps an idea of the elegance and grace which prevailed in architecture and the arts during the Fujiwara period side by side with an almost unbelievable degree of lavishness and extravagance. It is difficult to recapture the spirit of religious exaltation which inspired the construction of such luxurious buildings and the costly objects with which they were furnished, but one should perhaps remember that the Fujiwara family at this time were powerful and rich almost beyond modern comprehension. They were at the same time intensely religious and beset by fears and superstitions, so the building of lavish temples afforded an outlet at once for the display of their power and wealth and for the exercise of piety to relieve their fears.　　　　　　　JOHN FIGGESS

Door hinge from the Phoenix Hall

The Shoin group, from across the pond

KATSURA IMPERIAL VILLA

*Deceptively simple buildings set in a
beautiful garden designed by a seventeenth-century
nobleman of exquisite taste*

The Katsura Imperial Villa, called in Japanese, Katsura *Rikyû*
or Detached Palace, is on a site about five acres in area lying
along the west bank of the Katsura River on the south-west side
of Kyoto. Before the construction of the present villa and its
garden, the site on which it stands was occupied by a succession
of country houses commencing with one built at about the end
of the ninth century, when the place first became famous among
the aristocracy of Kyoto for flower- and moon-viewing. A
palace built at Katsura during the Heian period by a member
of the powerful Fujiwara family, Fujiwara-no-Takamichi, is
mentioned in contemporary poems and some of the happenings
there are thought to have inspired a number of incidents in the
Tale of Genji, set in the tenth century, the greatest of all Heian-
period novels, which has become famous throughout the
English-speaking world through the translation of Arthur
Waley.

Early in the seventeenth century – when Japan was under the
domination of the Tokugawa shogunate, and the Imperial
Family, though suffered to continue to exist, had been virtually
shorn of power – the property at Katsura came into the possession of the Imperial Prince Toshihito, and it was he who embarked upon the building of the present Katsura *Rikyû* as a
country retreat, mainly, according to his letters and diaries, for
moon-viewing, the appreciation of flowers, the enjoyment of
cool summer evenings and the exhibition of various skills and
pastimes.

The palace is known to have been constructed in three
separate stages, the first of which was begun in 1620 and completed in 1625. The second stage, from 1642 to 1647, was carried
out under Prince Toshitada, the successor of Prince Toshihito
who died in 1629, and the third stage of the construction was
carried out when Prince Toshitada was a man of ripe years, in
preparation for a visit by the Emperor Go Mizuno. The visit
took place in 1658, so it is assumed that the alterations and
additions were completed by then. So much for the historical

Detail of the cock and drum painting by Eikei Kanô
on the sliding doors in the Irori-no-ma or Room
with Hearth in the Old Shoin

277

The Onrin-dô, a small Zen temple in the garden

background; now we turn to look at the buildings as they are to be seen today in their idyllic garden setting.

The front entrance to the palace, known as the Onari Gate, stands about 55 yards in front of the Miyuki Gate, a recent replacement of one which was built in 1658 to receive the Emperor Go Mizuno. Paths paved with small bluish-black stones from the Kamo River lead from the Miyuki Gate to the Central Gate and here, for the first time, one catches a glimpse of the garden with its extensive pond, straight-line composition and cut stones, harmonizing with each other and with the architecture. Passing through the Central Gate one comes to a group of stepping-stones that lead diagonally across a mossy

OPPOSITE: A corner of the Shoin group of buildings

Amanohashidate island and the Shôkin-tei teahouse

The Shôkin-tei teahouse

garden to a stone stairway which serves as the front entrance to the central palace building or *shoin*. This building is composed of three sections known as the Old Shoin, the Middle Shoin and the New Shoin, each of the three sections being set at such an angle relative to the others as to afford the maximum frontage for moon-viewing in autumn, to provide coolness in summer and to receive the warm rays of the sun in winter.

On the eastern side of the Old Shoin is a broad verandah with a separate entrance at the north facing a detached teahouse known as the Gepparô (Moon-Wave Pavilion), and on the same side is the Tsukimidai (Moon-viewing Platform), which is in effect an extension of the verandah. From this vantage point one has an uninterrupted view of the main garden. Perhaps the best place for viewing the Shoin group as a whole is from Shinzen island, one of five different sized islands in the pond. From here, the vertical and horizontal lines of dark unpainted wood, varied by rectangular areas of opaque white plaster walls and translucent white paper-covered *shoji* crowned by the elegant thatched roofs with their severe straight lines, create a poem of geometric design. The austere beauty of the exterior of the Shoin group is repeated in the interior. The rooms have the same simplicity, with the plain *tatami* matting on the floor and the movable partitions which slide aside to reveal the adjoining rooms or an enchanting view on to the garden.

Such decoration as there is is subtle and restrained; a painting of a cock and drum by Kanô Eikei, an artist patronized by the Imperial Family, covers two cedar doors in the Irori-no-ma or Room with Hearth in the Old Shoin, while the sliding screens in the central rooms of the Middle Shoin are decorated with Chinese-style landscape *suiboku* (Indian ink) paintings by three brothers of the Kano family.

The building and the garden are planned in such a way as to present the beholder with a great diversity of views both inside and outside on the short tour from the Old Shoin through the

OPPOSITE: Interior of the Shôkin-tei teahouse or Pine-Lute Pavilion. In the foreground are a stone hearth and sink used in the preparation of the tea and the ceremonial washing of the tea bowls

281

Shelf and recess (*tokonoma*) in the first room of the Middle Shoin

Interior of the Irori-no-ma or Room with Hearth,
showing the sliding doors decorated by Eikei Kanô

Middle Shoin to the New Shoin. On the south side of the New
Shoin is a garden of charming simplicity consisting of little more
than a lawn. From here one passes again through the Central
Gate and out to a path that meanders around the outer edge of
the pond past an infinite variety of miniature landscapes, all
carefully planned to create a precise effect when viewed from a
particular angle. The very rocks in the garden have life. At
times they hint of deep ravines, at times they symbolize mountain peaks, at times they delineate the gentle flow of a river,
but always they seem in harmony with their surroundings.

The first feature encountered in pursuing the path round the
garden is a small rise known as Maple Mountain leading to a
teahouse called the Shôkin-tei or Pine-Lute Pavilion, a name
probably inspired by a passage in the *Tale of Genji* which speaks
of a certain moonlight night when the sound of lutes made
perfect harmony with the sighing of the wind in the pine trees.
The area in front of the Shôkin-tei is known as the Beach Garden. From here there is a fine view of a promontory on the
opposite side of the pond which is supposed to be a replica in
miniature of a well-known spit of sand at Amanohashidate,
traditionally one of the three most famous scenic places in
Japan (the other two are Matsushima and Miyajima).

Continuing along the path westwards from the Shôkin-tei one
crosses a small depression called Hotaru-dani or Valley of Fire-
flies to pass over a stone bridge to one of the five small islands.

OVERLEAF: Interior of the New Palace,
showing the Emperor's writing desk

OPPOSITE: Shelves on two walls of the Jôdan-no-ma
of the New Palace. They are made of precious woods, and
are regarded as among the finest sets of shelves in Japan

283

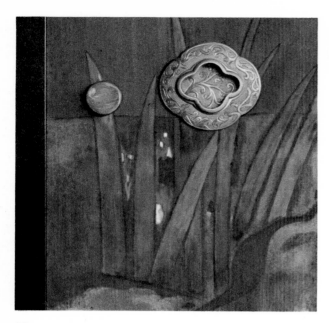

Finger catch in a sliding door of the
Music Room in the Middle Shoin

At the highest point on this island stands a small teahouse named Shoka-tei or Pavilion for the Enjoyment of Flowers. This teahouse, which has a boldly open west side, commands especially beautiful views of the cherry blossoms in spring, azaleas in early summer and flaming maple leaves in autumn. On fine clear days one can catch a glimpse from here of distant hazy mountains. From the Shoka-tei one descends and crosses a packed-earth bridge to return to the restful lawn south of the New Palace. On the southern bank is a rectangular pier for garden boats paved with square-cut stones, and on the opposite side of the pond, enclosed by the straight lines of the boat landing, stands the Shoiken or House of Happy Thoughts, a simple rustic structure and the largest of the out-buildings in the garden.

The essence of the Katsura Imperial Villa is functional clarity and simplicity, the very qualities which modern architects strive for, though not always with the same degree of success as was achieved by the builders of Katsura more than three hundred years ago. Though its owner was an Imperial prince, there is here no ostentation, no lavish display of the decorative skills with which Japan was plentifully endowed at the time and which have their most gaudy expression, for example, in the flamboyant buildings of the Tôshogû Mausoleum at Nikko, constructed at the very same time. In the Katsura Villa, with utmost simplicity and restraint, a truly satisfying artistic creation has been evolved in which a sense of freedom and harmony resides. In the Shoin group in particular, one senses a free flow of the outer space of nature with the inner space of the building, a marvellous feeling of release from the irksome confines of bricks and mortar and solid walls. This freedom of expression combined with austerity in decoration, which is a tradition in Japanese domestic architecture at its best, has its roots in Zen Buddhism and the tea ceremony, and it can be inferred that in this respect the Katsura Villa reflects the tastes of its founder, Prince Toshihito.

From the not inconsiderable amount of documentary material about the Prince which has come down to us it is evident that he was an unusually cultivated man even for his rank and times. He seems to have been versed in literature of the Heian period and was something of a poet in his own right. From his diaries and from musical scores of his that have been preserved it is also known that he played the *koto*, the Japanese harp, well. He was, besides, an accomplished practitioner of the cult of tea and took a special interest in architecture and gardens. Though both the buildings and their settings have admittedly suffered some changes in appearance since the Katsura Palace was completed in the middle of the seventeenth century, it is certainly to Prince Toshihito and his equally cultivated son Prince Toshitada therefore that we owe the freedom and originality to be found in this masterpiece of Japanese architecture and landscape gardening which in recent years has become an inspiration to modern architects the world over.   JOHN FIGGESS

Tatami floors and door slides in the Shoin group

ACKNOWLEDGMENTS

All photographs are by Ian Graham with the exception of those identified below. The publishers would like to thank the following institutions and photographers for their kindness in making these pictures available (numbers refer to pages):

Aerofilms and Aero Pictorial Ltd: 20, 27 top, 35
Benrido Company Ltd, Tokyo: 248 top, centre and bottom, 251 bottom centre and bottom right, 252 top, 253 top, bottom left and right, 258 top, 264 top and bottom, 265, 266, 267
Britain-China Friendship Association: 213, 217 bottom, 225, 234, 235 top, 239
British Museum (by courtesy of the Trustees): 43 right
British Museum (Photo J. R. Freeman): 14, 17, 19, 46, 53 bottom, 56, 59, 70 left, 92 top and bottom, 103 bottom, 131, 146 bottom, 151 bottom, 154, 165 right, 176, 179 top, 183 top, 201, 210, 223, 240
Camera Press Ltd: 196, 197 top
J. Allen Cash: 216, 217 top, 218, 219, 224 top and bottom, 226 top, 227 top, 228, 229 top and bottom, 230, 235 bottom, 236, 237 top, 241
Department of Archaeology, Baghdad, Iraq (Photo Ian Graham): 31
Werner Forman: 58, 61, 66, 222, 226 bottom, 227 bottom, 229 centre, 231
Derek Hill: 64 top, 67
India Office Library (by courtesy of H M Secretary of State for Commonwealth Relations): 68, 74 bottom, 77, 103 top, 111, 114 bottom, 121, 125 left and top right, 132 bottom, 179 bottom, 197 bottom, 198 bottom
Institute of Archaeology, Peking: 238 top
Manshichi Sakamoto, Tokyo: 244, 245, 254–55, 261 top
Lady Alexandra Metcalfe: 212, 221, 232, 237 bottom, 238 bottom
Dr Augustin Palát: 233
Paul Popper Ltd: 214, 215, 220
Josephine Powell: 60, 62, 63, 64 left and bottom right
Royal Geographical Society: 65
D. L. Snellgrove: 169 top and bottom, 175 top and bottom
Taikichi Irie (by courtesy of the Mainichi Newspaper): 257
Victoria and Albert Museum: 70 right, 242